Understanding Media Semiotics

Understanding Media Semiotics

Marcel Danesi

Director of the Program in Semiotics and
Communication Theory, University of Toronto

A member of the Hodder Headline Group
LONDON

Co-published in the United States of America by
Oxford University Press Inc., New York

First published in Great Britain in 2002 by
Arnold, a member of the Hodder Headline Group,
338 Euston Road, London NW1 3BH

http://www.arnoldpublishers.com

Co-published in the United States of America by
Oxford University Press Inc.,
198 Madison Avenue, New York, NY10016

British Library Cataloguing in Publication Data
A catalogue record for this book is available from the British Library

Library of Congress Cataloging-in-Publication Data
A catalog record for this book is available from the Library of Congress

ISBN 0 340 808837 (hb)
ISBN 0 340 808845 (pb)

1 2 3 4 5 6 7 8 9 10

Production Editor: Jasmine Brown
Production Controller: Martin Kerans
Cover Design: Terry Griffiths

Typeset in 11/13pt Minion by Phoenix Photosetting, Chatham, Kent
Printed and bound in Great Britain by MPG Books Ltd, Bodmin, Cornwall

What do you think about this book? Or any other Arnold title?
Please send your comments to feedback.arnold@hodder.co.uk

Contents

Introduction

Commercial jazz, soap opera, pulp fiction, comic strips, the movies set the images, mannerisms, standards, and aims of the urban masses. In one way or another, everyone is equal before these cultural machines; like technology itself, the mass media are nearly universal in their incidence and appeal. They are a kind of common denominator, a kind of scheme for pre-scheduled, mass emotions.

C. Wright Mills (1916–62)

In a 1997 James Bond movie entitled *Tomorrow Never Dies*, the evil villain, unlike the villains of previous Bond movies, seeks control over the world, not by means of brute force, but by gaining control of all mass communications media. The movie recites the exploits of Elliott Carver, a 'Bill-Gates-look-alike' scoundrel who, at the beginning of the movie, is on the verge of taking over the minds of common people, by determining what they will see and hear. Needless to say, the forces of good, spearheaded by the dauntless hero James Bond, end up 'saving the world' from the ruthless domination of a deranged and maniacal media mogul.

The transparent message of that movie, and of many others similar to it in theme that have come out since 1997, is that we live in a world that is being threatened more and more by those who hold the levers of 'media power', i.e. by those who control television networks, movie production studios, and computer media. But the fear of media moguls is not something that is felt exclusively by cineastes. Indeed, many are the volumes published in the last decade decrying the serious dangers that the media pose to all facets of contemporary society. Most of these scathingly criticize the individuals and groups who control media institutions. Many others seek to give a rational interpretation of the social conditions that have developed from the global spread of media culture. However, very few have attempted to understand the 'meaning structures' that the media have helped to spread into the system of everyday modern life. The purpose of this book is to do exactly that – to take a close look at those structures within the conceptual framework of the science called *semiotics*. The particular view taken here is that these structures seem so 'natural' and 'meaningful' to us because, as the late Canadian communications guru Marshall McLuhan (1911–80) aptly observed, the media that we make are unconscious extensions of our inbuilt sensory and cognitive processes.

Goal of the present volume

The academic study of the media traces its roots to America in the 1930s. It was not until the late 1950s, however, that semiotics ventured into this domain of investigation. That was the decade in which the French semiotician Roland Barthes (1915–80) showed, for the first time, the importance of studying media in terms of how they generate meanings. Semiotic method, as Barthes argued in his 1957 masterpiece *Mythologies*, is fundamental because, unlike other approaches to media, it focuses almost exclusively on hidden meanings. Incredibly, very few treatments of 'media semiotics' *à la* Barthes have come forward since the late 1950s. A large part of the reason for this is the fact that semiotics has never really found a niche in the academic landscape and, therefore, that very few 'full-time' professional practitioners of semiotics exist. Moreover, for some reason, in the decades following Barthes' work, semiotics quickly gained the unseemly reputation of a field that was too technical, laden with jargon, and highly abstruse. This book has been written, in large part, to show that just the opposite is true. Semiotics consists of a handful of basic notions that can be easily applied to the study of any kind of human meaning system.

This text is thus intended as an introduction to media semiotics. I have tailored it for students taking beginning courses in such fields as general semiotics, psychology, linguistics, mythology, education, literary studies, sociology, cultural anthropology, culture studies, communication studies, and media analysis, so that they can have a practical manual at their disposal to help them investigate and understand media from the particular standpoint of semiotic theory. To facilitate its reading, I have avoided making constant references to the relevant literature. The works that have informed the various commentaries, descriptions, and analyses that I offer in this book are listed at the back. Occasionally, I will put forward a critical assessment of a certain type of media product. But criticism is not the primary goal of this text. There are thousands of books on the market that critique media from all kinds of ideological angles. Some of these are included in the bibliography at the back of this book. My primary goal here is simply to demonstrate how semiotics can be applied to the study of media – no more, no less.

Semiotic method is characterized by two main investigative procedures:

1 *Historical inquiry* Meaning systems must first be examined historically. The reason for this is fairly obvious – to gain any true understanding of what something means, it is necessary to unravel how it came into existence

in the first place. Thus, in every chapter, the discussion will constantly be informed by historical matters related to the origin and evolution of a particular medium, as well as to the products and genres it has generated over time.

2 *Interpretation*   Semiotic inquiry aims to unravel the nature of the relation $X = Y$. The X is something that exists materially. It could be a word, a novel, a TV programme, or some other human artifact. The Y is what the artifact means in all its dimensions (personal, social, historical). Figuring out what the meanings of Y are constitutes the sum and substance of semiotic method. This procedure is generally referred to as 'interpretation'.

To keep the proportions of this volume within the limits of a practical introduction, I have had to limit my choice of topics and the degree to which I would be able to treat each one. Nevertheless, I have tried to cast as wide a net as possible, so as to gather within two covers the main themes, notions, and techniques that can be assembled to show how semiotic inquiry can be a truly effective form of media analysis.

Needless to say, what I have written about, and how I have gone about writing it, are bound to reflect my own background and preferences. Having issued this caveat, I wish to assure the reader that I have made every attempt possible to emphasize method of analysis, rather than my personal views. It is my sincere hope, therefore, that the reader will find my exposition of method usable in various ways. To this end, I have used a simple style and have made absolutely no assumptions about any prior technical knowledge on the part of the reader. A convenient glossary of technical terms is also included at the end. To get different, complementary, or supplementary views of the various topics I have treated, the reader is advised to consult the relevant works listed at the back of this book.

The opening chapter gives an overview of the various types of media and their historical development. It also provides an initial explication of semiotic axioms and notions. The second chapter introduces the main concepts and techniques of semiotic method that can be used to conduct a systematic examination of media representations and products. Then, in the third to eighth chapters, print, audio, film, television, computer, and advertising media and genres respectively are discussed from the viewpoint of semiotic inquiry. Since I live and teach in Canada, I have based most of the illustrations and examples for discussion and analysis in these chapters on the North American situation. However, whenever possible I have brought forth examples of genres with which I am familiar from other countries. The final chapter constitutes my own reflections on the relation between the media and contemporary culture, and especially on the impacts that the media are purported to have on the contemporary human psyche.

Acknowledgments

I thank Victoria College of the University of Toronto for having allowed me the privilege of teaching and coordinating its Program in Semiotics and Communication Theory over many years. In that regard, I would especially like to mention Dr Roseanne Runte, Dr Eva Kushner, and Dr Paul Gooch, the presidents under whom I have worked, as well as Dr Alexandra Johnston, Dr William Callahan, Dr Brian Merrilees, and Dr David Cook, the Principals of the College with whom I have had the pleasure of coordinating the Program. I am also thankful to Lynn Welsh, Julie Berger, Susan MacDonald, and Joe Lumley for their constant help and support over the years. Another debt of gratitude goes to the many students I have taught over three decades. Their insights and enthusiasm have made my job simply wonderful! They are the impetus for this book.

1 The mediated world

The bosses of our mass media, press, radio, film and television, succeed in their aim of taking our minds off disaster. Thus, the distraction they offer demands the antidote of maximum concentration on disaster.

Ernst Fischer (1899–1972)

In his often-emotional lectures, Marshall McLuhan (1911–80) would be wont to warn his students at the University of Toronto in the 1960s and 1970s that the media to which they were exposed on a daily basis constituted a blessing and a curse at the same time. While they do indeed make information more available and accessible to larger and larger groups of people, he argued, the media also engender a general feeling of alienation and 'disembodiment' in people. Since then, it has become obvious to virtually everyone that McLuhan's caveat was well-founded. Our modern *mediated* world is indeed a two-edged sword. The 'disembodiment' or 'de-personalization' that McLuhan warned about just a few decades ago has, seemingly, become widespread, at the same time that more and more people gain access to information that was once the privilege of the few.

How did this come about? Do the media moguls of the world truly control the minds and souls of common people (as intimated by the James Bond movie mentioned in the introduction to this book), brainwashing them into submission day in, day out with the resources of the 'distraction factory', as the cultural critic Goodwin (1992) calls the global media entertainment industry? Are the new 'robber barons' the CEOs of media empires such as the Disney Corporation, General Electric, and Time Warner, who now own and distribute most of what people see and hear? Clearly, these are important social questions. But they can hardly be answered in a simplistic way. The distraction factory was not built overnight. It is a product of cultural and historical forces. So, the logical point of departure on the road to answering such questions is to cast an initial glance at some of those forces. That is the first of the two main objectives of this opening chapter. The second one is to delineate some of the basic semiotic notions that will guide us on our journey through our mediated world in subsequent chapters.

What is a medium?

Before the advent of alphabets, people communicated and passed on their knowledge through the spoken word. But even in early 'oral cultures', tools had been invented for recording and preserving ideas in 'durable' physical forms. The forms were invariably pictographic – a *pictograph* is a picture representing an idea. So intuitive and functional is pictography that it comes as little surprise to find that it has not disappeared from our own world, even though most of our written communication is based on the alphabet. The figures designating 'male' and 'female' on washrooms and lavatories and the 'no smoking' signs found in public buildings, to mention but two common examples, are modern-day pictographs.

Pictography is a perfect example of what a *medium* (from Latin *medius* 'middle or between') is – a means of recording ideas on some surface (a cave wall, a piece of wood, papyrus) with appropriate technology (a carving tool, pigment, a stylus). More generally, a *medium* can be defined as the physical means by which some system of 'signs' (pictographs, *alphabet* characters, etc.) for recording ideas can be actualized.

Pictography did not alter the basic oral nature of daily communication, nor did it alter the oral mode of transmitting knowledge of early societies. That occurred after the invention of alphabetic writing around 1000 BC – an event that brought about the first true radical change in the world's social structure. The philosopher Thomas Kuhn (1922–96) called such radical changes 'paradigm shifts' (1970). The move away from pictographic to alphabetic writing was, to use Kuhn's appropriate term, the first great paradigm shift of human history, since it constituted the initial step towards the establishment of a worldwide civilization. Simply put, alphabetic writing made *print* the first viable global medium for storing and exchanging ideas and knowledge.

The second step in the establishment of a worldwide civilization was taken in the fifteenth century after the development of movable type technology – an event that made it possible to print and duplicate books cheaply. McLuhan designated the type of social order that ensued from that technological event the *Gutenberg Galaxy*, after Johann Gutenberg (1400?–68), the German printer who invented movable type in Europe. The Gutenberg Galaxy did indeed, as McLuhan pointed out, establish printed books as the primary tools for recording and preserving information and knowledge. But it did more than that. It also established the book as the first true 'mass distraction' device of history. And, indeed, to this day we read books not only for educational or reference purposes, but also to while away our leisure hours.

The third step towards the founding of a worldwide civilization was taken at the start of the twentieth century, after advancements in electronic technology established sound recordings, cinema, radio, and (a little later) television as new media for communicating information and, above all else, for providing distraction to larger and larger masses of people. Since electronic *signals* can cross borders virtually unimpeded, McLuhan characterized the world that was being united by electronic media as the 'global village'. To paraphrase the perceptive Canadian scholar, that world can be designated as the *Electronic Galaxy*. Near the end of the twentieth century, the fourth step towards establishing a worldwide civilization was taken right after computers became widely available and the Internet emerged as a truly global medium. In line with the terminological style established by McLuhan, the current world can thus be called the *Digital Galaxy*.

Representation

The process of recording ideas, knowledge, or messages in some physical way is called *representation* in semiotic theory. This can be defined more precisely as the use of 'signs' (pictures, sounds, etc.) to relate, depict, portray, or reproduce something perceived, sensed, imagined, or felt in some physical form. It can be characterized as the process of constructing a form X to call attention to something that exists either materially or conceptually, Y, in some specific way, $X = Y$. Figuring out the meaning of $X = Y$ is not, however, a simple task. The intent of the form-maker, the historical and social contexts in which the form was made, the purpose for which it was made, and so on and so forth, are complex factors that enter into the picture. The purpose of semiotics is to study those very factors. In order to carry out this task systematically, it has established a distinct terminology. As will be discussed in more detail in the next chapter, in semiotics the actual physical form of a representation, X, is generally called the *signifier*; the meaning or meanings, Y, that it generates (obvious or not) is called the *signified*; and the kinds of meanings that can potentially be extracted from the representation ($X = Y$), in a specific cultural ambiance, is called *signification*.

As an example of what representation entails, consider the notion of 'sex'. This is something that exists in the world as a biological and emotional reality. In semiotics, sex is called a *referent*, because it is something to which we desire to *refer* in some way as it 'presents itself' to our consciousness through our senses, emotions, and intellect. Now, as a referent, it can be *represented* (literally 'presented again') in some physical form constructed on purpose. For example, in modern-day culture sex can be represented with such forms as: (1) a photograph of two people engaged in kissing romantically; (2) a poem describing the various physical and emotional aspects of sex; or (3) an erotic movie depicting the more physical aspects of sex. Each of these constitutes a specific kind of signifier – something that has a particular physical form. The meanings that each captures constitute its signifieds. Note that these are built into each signifier not only by its maker, but also by certain pre-existing notions relative to the culture in which the signifier was made. Representations of sex in, say, London are vastly different from representations of the same referent that tend to be made, for instance, in Calcutta or San Francisco. Moreover, the medium used to portray the referent also shapes the signified. Photographs can show fairly limited views of the referent, whereas movies can provide much more graphic detail of sexual activity. Finally, the ways in which people living in London, Calcutta, or San Francisco will derive meaning from the above representations will vary widely. This is because they have become accustomed in their specific cultures to different signification systems that underlie perceptions of sex.

The process of representing sex can be summarized diagrammatically as follows. To indicate the different kinds of signifiers and signifieds involved in the three different representations, numerical subscripts are used. This is not, however, a standard practice in semiotics; it is employed here simply for the sake of clarity (see Figure 1.1).

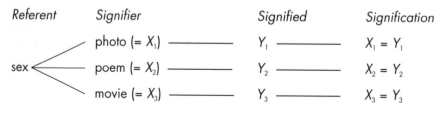

Figure 1.1

There is no way to pin down a signified or to predict what system of signification will be employed for figuring out precisely what a particular representation $(X = Y)$ will mean to specific people. The process of deriving meaning from some representation is not a completely open-ended process, however. It is constrained by social conventions, by communal experiences, and by many other *contextual* factors that put limits on the range of meanings that are possible in a given situation. A task of semiotic analysis is to figure out what that range is. That aspect of semiotic methodology is known as *interpretation*, as pointed out in the introduction.

Throughout this book little difference will be made between the medium used to construct a representation and the representation itself. So, for instance when a term such as *print medium* is used in this text, it can refer exclusively or jointly to: (1) the physical elements that are used to produce print signifiers (pictographs, alphabet characters), (2) the types of signifieds that these allow people to encode (words, texts, etc.), and (3) the physical materials used (paper, papyri, etc.) to make print representations.

Transmission

Representation is to be differentiated from *transmission*. The former refers, as we have just discussed, to the depiction of something in some specific way; the latter refers instead to the delivery, broadcasting, or communication of the message in some sensory-based way (see Table 1.1).

Table 1.1

Sensory Modality	Examples
Auditory–vocal	vocal speech, singing, whistling, crying
Visual	pictography, sign languages for the hearing-impaired, drawings
Tactile	Braille for visually-impaired or sightless people (in which varied arrangements of raised dots representing letters and numerals are identified by touch), alphabetic toy blocks used to impart familiarity with letter shapes through touch
Olfactory	perfumes and colognes, religious incense
Gustatory	chemical ingredients in food that attempt to reproduce certain natural tastes

At a purely biological level, a message can be received successfully (i.e. recognized as a message) by another species only if it possesses the same kind of sensory modality used to transmit it. Of these, the tactile faculty is the one that seems to cut across human and animal sensory systems. There is no doubt in my mind that my cat and I enter into a rudimentary form of tactile communication on a daily basis. Sharing the same living space, and being co-dependent on each other for affective exchanges, we do indeed transmit our feeling-states to each other by sending out body signals and especially by touching each other. However, even within the confines of this versatile communicative mode, there is no way for me to convey a broader range of tactile feeling-states to my cat that are implied by words such as 'embrace', 'guide', 'hold', 'kiss', 'tickle', etc. Clearly, interspecies communication is realizable, but only in a very restricted sense. It can occur in some modalities, partially or totally, to various degrees according to species. If the sensory systems of the two species are vastly different, however, then virtually no message transmission is possible.

Representations can also be transmitted through *technology*, i.e. through some artifact or invention. Early societies developed simple tools for transmitting messages, such as drums, fire and smoke signals, and lantern beacons, so that they could be seen or heard over short distances. Messages were also attached to the legs of carrier pigeons trained to navigate their way to a destination and back home. In later societies, so-called 'semaphore' systems of flags or flashing lights, for example, were employed to send messages over relatively short but difficult-to-cross distances, such as from hilltop to hilltop, or from one ship to another at sea.

A tool is an artifact that extends some sensory, physical, or intellectual capacity. An axe extends the power of the human hand to break wood; the wheel, of the human foot to cover great distances; and so on. For the sake of scientific accuracy, it should be mentioned that tool-making is itself an outgrowth of bipedalism – the capacity to walk with an erect posture on two legs. Fossils discovered in Africa provide evidence that hominids walked erect and had a bipedal stride even before the great increase in their brain size millions of years ago. Complete bipedalism freed the human hand, allowing it to become a supremely sensitive limb for precise manipulation and grasping. The erect posture gave rise to the subsequent evolution of the physiological apparatus for speech, since it brought about the lowering and positioning of the larynx for controlled breathing.

McLuhan (1964) claimed that the type of technology developed to record and transmit messages determines how people process and remember them. Human beings are endowed by Nature to decipher information with all the senses. Our *sense ratios*, as he called them, are equally calibrated at birth to receive information. However, in social settings, it is unlikely that all the senses will operate at the same ratio. One sense ratio or the other increases according to the modality employed to record and transmit a message. In an oral culture, the *auditory* sense ratio is the one that largely shapes information processing and message interpretation; in a print culture, on the other hand, the *visual* sense ratio is the crucial one. This raising or lowering of sense ratios is not, however, preclusive. Indeed, in our own culture, we can have various sense ratios activated in tandem. For example, if one were to hear the word 'cat' uttered by someone, the auditory sense ratio would be the operational one in processing the meaning of the word. If, however, one were to see the word written on a sheet of paper, then the visual sense ratio would be activated instead. A visual depiction of the cat accompanied by an utterance of the word would activate the auditory and visual sense ratios in tandem.

Types of media

Media can be divided into three basic categories:

- A *natural medium* is one by which ideas are transmitted in some biologically-based way (through the voice, facial expressions, hand gestures, etc.).
- An *artifactual medium* is one by which ideas are represented and transmitted by means of some artifact (books, paintings, sculptures, letters, etc.).
- A *mechanical medium* is one by which ideas are transmitted by means of mechanical inventions such as telephones, radios, television sets, computers, and so on.

Obviously there is much slippage between the artifactual and mechanical media. Indeed, the former subsumes the latter, since mechanical media are really particular kinds of artifactual media. The 'non-biological' media can be subdivided into three broad categories: *print*, *electronic*, and *digital*. Essentially, these differ in what has been called *enunciative mode*, i.e. in the way in which they encode their messages. Print media allow people to 'enunciate' verbal messages on stone, murals, papyrus, paper, and other print-retaining surfaces or materials. Electronic media allow people to enunciate them instead through the electronic channel by means of such devices as records, radio, and television. Records are objects that register sound, such as audiocassettes and compact discs (CDs). Radio is an audio system that allows for the sending and reception of radio signals (electromagnetic waves) on devices known as radios. Television is a visual system that allows for the sending of visual images, with accompanying sound, as electromagnetic waves that are reconverted into visual images by receiving devices known as television sets. Digital media are computer-based systems such as the *Internet* – a matrix of networks that connects computers around the world – and the *World Wide Web* – an information server on the Internet composed of interconnected sites and files, accessible with a program known as a browser.

Development of the mass media

One of the first civilizations to institutionalize pictographic writing as a means of recording ideas, keeping track of business transactions, and transmitting knowledge was the ancient Chinese one. According to some archeological estimates, Chinese pictography may date as far back as the fifteenth century BC. It was, more specifically, *logographic*, since it employed pictorial symbols to represent entire words (without reference to their pronunciation). Another fully-developed ancient pictographic system, called *cuneiform* because it consisted of wedge-shaped picture symbols, was the Sumerian–Babylonian one that was developed nearly 5000 years ago. The Sumerians recorded their representations on clay tablets, making cuneiform writing a very expensive and impracticable means of communication. For this reason it was developed, learned, and used primarily by rulers and clerics. From about 2700 to 2500 BC another type of pictographic writing, called *hieroglyphic,* was invented in Egypt. The Egyptians used papyrus (a type of early paper made from reeds) to record their writings. The hieroglyphic system eventually developed *phonographic* elements within it – phonographs are forms standing for parts of words, such as syllables or individual sounds.

A complete phonographic system for representing single sounds is called alphabetic. The first alphabetic system emerged in the Middle East, and was transported by the Phoenicians (a people from a territory on the eastern coast of the Mediterranean, located largely in modern-day Lebanon) to Greece. It contained symbols for consonant sounds only. When it reached Greece, symbols for vowel sounds were added to it, making the Greek system the first full-fledged alphabetic one. The advent of alphabetic writing brought about, as mentioned, a true paradigm shift, because it allowed societies to store and preserve knowledge in a more stable manner.

Paper and Printing

The first lightweight material used to record writing was, as mentioned, papyrus, made by the Egyptians from grasses called reeds. From as early as the second century BC, Europeans wrote on thin layers of tanned and scraped animal skins called parchment or vellum, with quill pens made from bird feathers. Parchment was not as light as papyrus; but it was more durable. It thus made it possible to store knowledge for longer periods of time. Many parchment manuscripts and books from the Middle Ages still exist today. But parchment was expensive, and thus literacy remained largely the privilege of the few.

Paper was invented in the second century AD by the Chinese, who developed it from silk fibres. It was the Arabs who took the Chinese technology to Europe in the eleventh century AD. Paper was lighter than parchment, and thus more portable. It was also relatively inexpensive. Paper technology was, in effect, the first technological event that made it possible to transform print into a mass medium.

Until the 1400s, all paper documents were written by hand. Copyists called scribes, many of whom were monks, made duplicates of manuscripts and books. By the fifteenth century, however, the need arose for an easier way to reproduce documents. In 1450, the German printer Johann Gutenberg perfected movable metal type technology, introducing the first mechanical device, the printing press, for printing and producing numerous copies of paper documents. The Gutenberg Galaxy had come, *ipso facto*, into being. The number of printing shops grew dramatically over the next century. Printers published books, newspapers, pamphlets, and many other kinds of paper documents. Because they were cheap, they became extremely popular.

As a result of the printing press, more books became available and more people became literate. With literacy came exposure to new ideas and independent thinking. And with independent thinking came many revolutions of a religious, political, social, and scientific nature. Moreover, since cheaply printed books could be sent all over the world, scientists, philosophers, artists, educators, historians, poets, and story writers read and translated each other's books. Ideas started crossing borders and vast spaces, uniting the world more and more. Standardized ways of doing things in the scientific and business domains emerged. In a phrase, the invention of the printing press was the technological event that paved the way to the establishment of a true global civilization.

In the twentieth century, printed documents became even more inexpensive and available en masse. Photocopying, for instance, made document duplication easier and more rapid. And in the mid-1980s, computer typesetting and printing became so efficient and economical that it largely replaced the typesetting technology that had been in place, virtually unchanged, since the fifteenth century. Sophisticated word-processing and graphics software are used today to set type and compose pages on the screen, just as they will look in the final print version. Page layouts are also transmitted digitally via fax machines, computer modems, telephone networks, and satellite systems to other locations for editing, redesign, and printing.

The spread of word-processing technology has led to the growth of so-called *desktop* publishing. Today, almost anyone can prepare books, newsletters, newspapers, or magazines on his or her computer, and then transmit the publication almost anywhere at the speed of light. Early advocates of business computers prophesied, in fact, the eventual coming of a 'paperless world'. But their predictions have proven so far to be wrong, or at least premature. The ease of copying, printing, and transmitting print documents made possible by digital technology has, ironically, led to more demand for paper, not less.

Telegraphy

The first electrical device for the transmission of written messages was the telegraph – a system that could send and receive electrical signals over long-distance wires. The first commercial telegraph systems were developed in Great Britain in the early nineteenth century. A little later, in 1844, the American inventor Samuel F.B. Morse (1791–1872) introduced a *code* that came to be adopted internationally. The code – known logically enough as the Morse Code – utilized 'on' and 'off' signals to represent individual letters of the alphabet. The telegrapher at one end of the line would tap on an electrical key, and the telegrapher at the other end would *decode* the tapping as it came in, write down the message, and send it to the recipient by messenger.

Telegraph cable was laid under the Atlantic Ocean in 1858, and regular transatlantic service began in 1866. It was the first interconnected global communications system. Telegraphy was gradually replaced by *telex* systems in the early twentieth century. These gradually eliminated the need to use a code such as the Morse Code. Users could type in a message, and the identical message would appear at the recipient's end, carried over telegraph and telephone lines to telex machines anywhere in the world. As early as the 1930s these lines were also used to transmit pictures, an event that introduced the so-called 'Wirephoto' service in international communications.

The telephone

In 1876, the Scottish-born American inventor Alexander Graham Bell (1847–1922) patented the first telephone, a device with the capacity to transmit sound over wires. Originally, Bell believed his invention would be used to transmit musical concerts, lectures, and sermons. But after founding his own company, he quickly discovered that the appeal of the phone lay much more in allowing ordinary people to talk to each other. So, in 1878 the Bell Telephone Company established the first telephone exchange – a switchboard connecting any member of a group of subscribers to any other member. By 1894, roughly 260,000 Bell telephones were in use in the United States, about one for every 250 people. By the 1960s the telephone was perceived in many parts of the world as an 'essential service'. Near the end of the twentieth century, the telephone played a critical role in ushering in the Digital Galaxy, providing subscribers with access to the Internet and the World Wide Web by means of devices called modems (modulator–demodulators). And, needless to say, the cellular (cell) phone has greatly enhanced the functionality and regularity of distance communication in our system of everyday communal life.

Radio

The earliest system for sending electrical signals through the air without wire (via electromagnetic waves) was at first called 'wireless', and a little later 'radiotelegraphy' (abbreviated to 'radio'). The background scientific principles for its development were those elaborated by the British physicist James Clerk Maxwell (1831–79). It was the Italian-born American electrical engineer Guglielmo Marconi (1874–1937), however, who applied them to the invention of the world's first true wireless radio device in 1895. His radio system could send and receive a signal at a distance of close to 3 km.

In 1901, Marconi developed an alternator device that could send signals much farther and with much less background noise. This led, about two decades later, to the commercial technology that established the radio as the first electronic mass medium. In the United States, the first regularly scheduled public radio broadcasts were made in 1920 from station KDKA in Pittsburgh, Pennsylvania. Other stations sprung up shortly thereafter across the country, and companies such as the Radio Corporation of America (RCA) and Westinghouse established radio networks for producing and sharing programming. By the mid-1920s radio had become, alongside film, a highly popular mass medium, shaping trends in music, drama, advertising, and verbal communication generally. Radio could reach many more people than print, not only because it could span great distances instantly, but also because its audiences did not necessarily have to be print literate. Programming could thus be designed with mass appeal. As a consequence, radio spawned 'pop culture' – a culture for all, not just the 'literati' and the 'cognoscenti'. Radio thus ushered in the Electronic Galaxy, a Galaxy in which an increasingly standard form of distraction became available to virtually everybody, as radio receivers became cheaper and thus highly affordable to the masses.

Television

The scientific principles underlying the technology leading to the invention of television were established by John Logie Baird (1888–1946), a British electrical engineer. A workable television camera was developed by the Russian-born American engineer Vladimir K. Zworykin (1889–1982) in 1923 and the American inventor Philo T. Farnsworth (1906–71) in 1927. The first television sets for mass utilization became available in England in 1936 and in the United States in 1938. After the Second World War, technical improvements and prosperity led to a growing demand for these sets. In the United States, six television stations were established at first, each one broadcasting for only a few hours each day. By 1948, 34 all-day stations were in operation in 21 major cities, and about one million television sets had been sold. By the end of the 1950s national television networks were established in most industrialized countries. TV had emerged, in effect, to replace radio as the primary source of mass distraction virtually across the world. As the twentieth century came to a close, TV entered the Digital Galaxy with the advent of *digital television* – television that is transmitted in a digital (computer-based) format.

With the widespread growth of cable television in the 1960s and then of *Direct-broadcast satellite* (DBS) services in the 1990s, many new channels and types of programming are now available to people across the globe. As a consequence, debates about TV's impact on children, world culture, politics, and community life have become common and widespread. On the one side, critics say that television feeds a constant stream of simplified ideas and sensationalistic images to unwitting viewers, that it negatively influences politics and voting patterns, that it destroys local cultures in favour of a bland 'Hollywood-oriented' distraction culture, and that it encourages passivity in people. On the other side, defenders say that television provides a great deal of high-quality educational and cultural programming, and that it is the major source of local, national and international news for many modern-day citizens who would otherwise remain uninformed. Whatever the truth, one thing is for certain – TV has turned out to be *the* technological invention that has consolidated McLuhan's global village, because it has made the same pattern and kind of distraction (the same TV sitcoms, adventure programmes, and variety shows) available across the globe.

Computers

The British mathematician and inventor, Charles Babbage (1792–1871), designed mechanical computing machines in the 1820s and 1830s on the basis of principles that anticipated the modern electronic computer. In the 1890s Babbage's ideas were applied to the building of calculating machines that could be operated automatically with punched cards. In the 1930s, electromechanical punched-card operating systems were developed. The International Business Machines Company (IBM) in the United States produced the first of these for widespread business usage. Incidentally, during the Second World War, the British Secret Service used IBM's design principles to build ten electronic computers, called *Colossus*, to help it crack the Germans' secret military codes. The first general-purpose computer in the United States, called the *Electronic Numerical Integrator and Computer* (ENIAC), was built shortly thereafter in 1946 at the University of Pennsylvania.

As computer technology improved steadily after the war, smaller and cheaper computers could be built for all kinds of purposes. By the 1970s, it even became economically feasible to manufacture a personal computer (PC) for mass consumption. The first PCs were mainly 'word processors'; i.e. they added computer-processing capacities to typewriters so as to make writing and changing printed text significantly easier and more sophisticated. In 1975, the first true microcomputer was introduced to the world. It had the power of many larger machines, but could fit onto a desktop. This was accomplished because of new miniaturization technologies that allowed manufacturers to compress the memory and processing power of thousands of circuits onto tiny chips of materials called semiconductors. The first word-processing software appeared shortly thereafter in 1978.

At the same time that computers were becoming faster, more-powerful, and smaller, networks were being developed for interconnecting them. In the 1960s, the Advanced Research Projects Agency (ARPA) of the US Department of Defense, along with researchers working on military projects at research centres and universities across the country, developed a network called the ARPANET for sharing data and mainframe computer-processing time over specially equipped telephone lines and satellite links. Used at first for military purposes, the ARPANET became the first functional major electronic-mail network right after the National Science Foundation connected universities and non-military research sites to it. ARPANET was renamed the Internet – a term conveying that it was designed as an 'interconnected' network serving many different functions, not just military ones.

Today, the Internet is the largest and most prevalent computer network in the world. Commercial online service providers – such as America Online, CompuServe, and the Microsoft Network – sell Internet access to individual computer users and companies. Smaller networks for specific utilization are also available. Called local area networks (LANs), these can be installed in a single building (or in several buildings) for the exclusive usage of a single organization. Wide area networks (WANs), on the other hand, are 'organization-specific' networks that can be used over a large geographical area. LANs and WANs require telephone lines, computer cables, and microwave and laser beams to carry digital information around a smaller area, such as a single university campus. In turn, they can interconnect users to the Internet. Today, most computer networks can carry any type of digital signal, including video images, sounds, graphics, animations, and text.

The PC has transformed business, education, and the distraction factory radically. People can use computers to design graphics and full-motion video, send electronic mail (*e-mail*), make airline or hotel reservations, search for all kinds of information, play games, listen to the radio, watch some television programmes, and even visit 'electronic rooms' to chat with other people over the World Wide Web. In the history of human communications, no other device has made it possible for so many people to interact with each other, irrespective of the distance between them.

Media convergence

In the Digital Galaxy, it is no longer correct to talk about 'competing' media. Advances in digital technology and in telecommunications networks have led to a *convergence* of all media into one overall mediated system of communications. This has led, in turn, to the emergence of new lifestyles and careers, to the creation of new institutions, and to radical paradigm shifts in all domains of social organization.

Convergence is manifest, first and foremost, in the digitization of all media technologies and in the integration of different media into computer networks:

- *Telephone*
  The first telecommunications medium to be digitized was the telephone in 1962, with the installation of high-speed lines in phone networks capable of carrying dozens of conversations simultaneously. Phone equipment of all kinds is now fully digitized. Moreover, the phone is the technological device that permits people to gain access to the Internet. A new high-speed phone technology, called *digital subscriber line* (DSL), is being currently installed across the globe. It has the capacity to transmit audio, video, and computer data over both conventional phone lines and satellite.

- *Print Media*
  The digitization of print media started in 1967. Today, most major newspapers are produced by means of digital technology and are available in *online* versions.

- *Film*
  The special effects created for the movie *Star Wars* in 1977 introduced digital technology into filmmaking. The first computer-generated movie, *Toy Story*, debuted in 1995. Such movies are now common. In the domain of home video technology, the *digital versatile disc* (DVD) is gradually supplanting the VHS tape.

- *Recordings*
  The digitally-produced compact disc (CD) started replacing vinyl records and audiocassette tapes in the mid-1980s, shortly after its introduction in 1982. The Internet has also become a source of music, not only for listening purposes, but also increasingly as a means for recording it – a process known as 'downloading'.

- *Television*
  Cable TV went digital in 1998, allowing broadcasters to increase their number of channel offerings. This technology was introduced primarily to meet competition from the direct-broadcast satellite (DBS) industry, which started producing digital multi-channel programming for reception by

home satellite dishes in 1995. TV broadcasting in general has also become digitized. So-called *high-definition television* (HDTV), which consists of transmitters and receivers using digital formats, became commercially available in 1998.

- *Radio*
  Digital audio broadcasting (DAB) is the corresponding technology in radio broadcasting to television's DBS system. Radio stations now use digital technology for creating their programmes.

Media convergence is a consequence of developments in computer technology. The computer is to the movement of ideas today, what the automobile was to the movement of people at the start of the twentieth century. If the 'roads' on the digital 'highway' continue to converge, we may well end up living in one global cyber-universe.

Overview

The above brief trek through the history of media holds a very important lesson – namely, that any major change in how information is represented and transmitted brings about a concomitant paradigm shift in cultural systems. Ancient cuneiform writing, impressed indelibly into clay tablets, allowed the Sumerians to develop a great civilization; papyrus and hieroglyphics transformed Egyptian society into an advanced culture; the alphabet spurred the ancient Greeks on to make extraordinary advances in science, technology, and the arts; the alphabet also made it possible for the Romans to develop an effective system of government; the printing press facilitated the dissemination of knowledge broadly and widely, paving the way for the European Renaissance, the Protestant Reformation, and the Enlightenment; radio, movies, and television brought about the rise of a global pop culture in the twentieth century; and the Internet and the World Wide Web ushered in McLuhan's 'global village' as the twentieth century came to a close.

Our historical journey has also made it obvious that two events in particular have transformed the course of human history. The first one was the invention of writing and the spread of literacy. Reading and writing activate linear thinking processes in the brain, because printed ideas are laid out one at a time and can thus be connected to each other sequentially and analysed logically in relation to each other. Orality, on the other hand, is not conducive to such precise thinking, because spoken ideas are transmitted through the emotional qualities of the human voice and are, thus, inextricable from the 'subject' who transmits them. Literacy engenders the sense that knowledge and information are disconnected from their human sources and thus that they have 'objectivity'; orality does not. This perception is bolstered by the fact that printed information can be easily categorized and preserved in some durable material form such as books. Simply put, without the advent and institutionalization of literacy, the spread of philosophy, science, jurisprudence, and the many other human intellectual activities that we now hold as critical to the progress of human civilization would simply not have been possible in the first place.

But orality has not, of course, disappeared from human life. The spoken word comes naturally; literacy does not. Through simple exposure to everyday dialogue, children develop the ability to speak with little or no effort and without any training or prompting whatsoever. Literacy, on the other hand, does not emerge through simple exposure to printed texts. It is learned through instruction, practice, and constant rehearsal. Schools were established, in fact, to impart literacy and print-based knowledge.

The second event that changed the course of history occurred in the twentieth century – millennia after the advent of alphabetic writing – with the emergence and diffusion of the electronic mass media. These not only facilitated distance communications, but they also brought about a global form of culture anchored in the 'distraction factory'. Known generally as pop culture, it constitutes a system of everyday life that is implanted in movies, television shows, detective novels, fast-food chains, musical styles, and the like, blurring the line between what is meaningful and what is merely entertainment. In turn, pop culture has generated two social phenomena of its own. One was called 'neomania' by Barthes (1957). Barthes defined it as a constant craving for new objects of consumption and new forms of entertainment inculcated into the modern psyche by media images, messages, and spectacles of all kinds. The other phenomenon can be called *juvenilization* – the widespread tendency of people to think of themselves as 'forever young' and attractive, both physically and socially, just like the actors and personalities they see every day on television, in ads, and in movies. Of course, juvenilization did not come about exclusively because of the media. Advances in medicine and in health-care delivery, and a diffusion of affluence in society at large, were primary factors in its emergence, given that they raised the average life expectancy considerably. Since it became possible to live longer, it also became possible to think of oneself as being 'young' for a longer period of time. But it is accurate to say that the media have spread and ensconced juvenilization into the social mindset through movies, television shows, and advertisements that constantly privilege images of youth. At no other time in history, consequently, have overall lifestyle trends been equated with trends in the youth culture. In the late 1990s, for instance, the fashion trends of hip-hop artists, Latin-American musicians, and 'girl power' groups not only infiltrated the world of adolescents, but also that of adults. Belly shirts, frosty lipstick, wobbly footwear, and blue nail polish became part of the 'cool female look', no matter what the age of the female. So, too, tattoos and earrings became intrinsic to the 'cool male look', regardless of the age of the male. Today, a parent could wear his or her 13-year-old's clothes without getting a second look and, vice versa, the 13-year-old could wear his or her parent's clothes without appearing in any way precocious.

Basic notions

The study of such phenomena as literacy, neomania, and juvenilization can take one of three main directions. One could, for example, focus on the social conditions that favoured the advent of a phenomenon. One could, also, investigate the interconnection between technological innovation and social phenomena. Finally, one could examine the ways in which a medium represents ideas and how these tend to become part of cultural phenomena. The latter direction is the one taken in this book. As such, it requires that certain theoretical distinctions be made from the very outset. One of these is the notion of *representation*, which was discussed and illustrated above. The others will be examined briefly below.

Needless to say, the other two approaches cannot be excluded from any serious analysis of the media. So, commentaries related to social conditions and technology will be interspersed throughout the discussion to follow in this and subsequent chapters. However, from the standpoint of semiotics, these are secondary to the main issue at hand – probing how representation reflects the system of everyday life.

Mediation

Signs never really tell the whole truth. They *mediate* reality for us, because they necessarily constitute convenient selections from the infinite realm of the knowable. For instance, by calling some creature 'rabbit', we have in effect singled out that creature as distinct from all other creatures. When we use the word 'rabbit', consequently, we highlight a chosen portion of the animal realm, in the same way that, by analogy, we highlight a chosen portion of an on-screen document on our computers. By doing this regularly, we eventually come to see that portion as having some necessary *raison d'être*, rather than constituting a convenient selection.

The representation of anything is, thus, a mediational process. Consider, for example, how different TV programmes have represented gender in different eras. The 1950s American TV sitcom called *I Love Lucy*, for instance, portrayed the female gender through the character of Lucille Ball as a strong-willed, independent female, in charge of her situation. On the other hand, the 1980s–1990s sitcom *Married ... with Children* depicted the same gender mockingly through the character of Betty as a boorish, sex-starved female who lived out her existence mindlessly day after dreary day. The two programmes thus mediated the meaning of 'female gender' through differences in character portrayal. Consider, moreover, how the death of Princess Diana was portrayed on British and American television as a great tragedy and a huge loss to humanity, despite the fact that the majority of people did not know her personally. The late princess affected people emotionally because of the 'TV-mediated' representations in those countries. But in other parts of the world, her death was portrayed in much less tragico-dramatic ways. And, in some countries, it was ignored.

In sum, the way something is represented, and the medium chosen to do so, can greatly influence how people perceive it. As the great twentieth century philosopher Ernst Cassirer (1944: 25) once remarked, humans live no longer only in a physical world, but also in a *symbolic* one. As their representational activities advance, their direct contact with physical reality recedes in proportion.

Messages

The terms *message* and *meaning* are often used interchangeably by people. But from a semiotic standpoint this is incorrect. To grasp the difference, consider a simple greeting such as 'Nice day, today!' It is, of course, a simple *message*, i.e. an oral transmission from one person to another. However, the *meaning* of that message can be literal, whereby the speaker is acknowledging the kind of day it is simply to make contact; on the other hand, it could be ironic, if uttered on a rainy and miserable day. More will be said about this distinction in the next chapter. Suffice it to say at this point that, as this example shows, the notion of 'message' is not coincident with that of 'meaning' – a message can have more than one meaning, and several messages can have the same meaning. In the mass media, as in art, it is often the case that many layers of meanings are built into the same message.

Semiotically-speaking, a message is a signifier; and its meanings are its signifieds. A message is something that is transmitted physically from one person or device to another. It can contain blocks of text as well as various types of information (such as to whom or what it is destined, what the nature of its content is, and so on). A message can be routed directly from *sender* to *receiver* through a physical link, or it can be passed, either in whole or in part, through intervening electronic, mechanical, or digital media.

The meaning that a message is designed to transmit can only be determined in reference to other meanings. Needless to say, this creates problems of interpretation and comprehension of various sorts. The dictionary definition of 'cat', for instance, as 'a small carnivorous mammal domesticated since early times as a catcher of rats and mice' is said to be the *meaning* of the word. But this is a problematic strategy because it employs the word 'mammal' to define 'cat', thus making the unwarranted assumption that 'mammal' somehow explains what a cat is. Looking up this term in the dictionary is also of little value because 'mammal' is defined as 'any of various warm-blooded vertebrate animals of the class Mammalia' – a definition that leads to yet another question: what is an animal? The dictionary defines an animal as an organism, which it defines in another listing as 'an individual form of life', which it defines further as 'the property that distinguishes living organisms'.

At that point, the dictionary has gone into a conceptual loop, since it has employed an already-used word, 'organism', in the definitional process. To avoid such looping problems, semioticians often employ the technique of binary *opposition* to flesh out what something means in relation to something else. This approach assumes that meaning is something that cannot be determined in the absolute, but only in relation to other signs: e.g. 'cat' vs. 'dog'; 'cat' vs. 'bird'; etc. From such oppositions we can see, one or two features at a time, what makes a 'cat' unique among animals. In effect, such oppositions cumulatively allow us to pinpoint what 'cat' means by virtue of how it is different from other animals.

Information

In psychology and communication science, the terms *information* and *meaning* are often used as substitutes for each other. But, again, semiotically speaking this is not correct. Information is data that can be received by humans or machines. The amount of information in a message can be 'measured' in terms of its probability – a ringing alarm signal carries 'more' information than one that is silent, because the latter is the 'expected state' of the alarm system and the former its 'alerting state'. The one who developed the mathematical aspects of information theory was the American telecommunications engineer Claude Shannon (1916–2001). He showed, essentially, that the information contained in a signal is inversely proportional to its probability. The more probable a signal, the less information 'load' it carries with it; the less likely, the more.

Information and meaning are, clearly, not the same thing. The former refers to the probability that a certain message will occur in a certain situation; the latter to the special kinds of nuances the message entails, or is intended to have, in the given situation. This applies to any message, from alarm signals to sophisticated statements. Take, for instance, a coin-tossing game in which it is decided that three heads in a row constitutes a win. If a certain player ends up consistently with the desired outcome, defeating all who challenge him or her, then we tend to interpret the outcome either *mythically* as the work of

Fortune, or else as clever and undetectable cheating on the part of the winning player.

Communication

Shannon devised his mathematical model of information in order to improve the efficiency of telecommunication systems. But shortly after it was formulated, psychologists started applying it en masse to the study of human communication. Known as the 'bull's-eye model', it essentially depicts information transfer between two humans as a mathematical process dependent on probability factors, i.e. on the degree to which a message is to be expected or not in a given situation. It is called the bull's-eye model because a *sender* is defined as someone aiming a *message* at a *receiver* as if he or she were in a bull's-eye target range (see Figure 1.2).

Figure 1.2   The bull's-eye model

Shannon also introduced several key terms into the general study of communication: *channel, noise, redundancy,* and *feedback.* The channel is the physical system carrying the transmitted signal. Vocally-produced sound waves, for instance, can be transmitted through air or through an electronic channel (e.g. radio). The term 'noise' refers to some interfering element (physical or psychological) in the channel that distorts or partially effaces a message. In radio and telephone transmissions, noise is equivalent to electronic static; in voice transmissions, it can vary from any interfering exterior sound (physical noise) to the speaker's lapses of memory (psychological noise). However, as Shannon demonstrated, communication systems have redundancy features built into them for counteracting noise. These allow for a message to be decoded even if noise is present. For instance, in verbal communication the high predictability of certain words in many utterances ('Roses are red, violets are …') and the patterned repetition of elements ('Yes, yes, I'll do it; yes, I will') are redundant features of language that greatly increase the likelihood that a verbal message will get decoded successfully. Finally, Shannon used the term 'feedback' to refer to the fact that senders have the capacity to monitor the messages they transmit and modify them to enhance their decodability. Feedback in human verbal communication includes, for instance, the physical reactions observable in receivers (facial expressions, bodily movements, etc.) that indicate the effect that a message is having as it is being communicated.

The bull's-eye model was expanded in the early 1980s by the American communication theorist Wilbur Schramm (1982). Schramm broke down the bull's-eye model into four major components:

1 a source (S) or originator of the communication
2 a message (M) and its information content
3 a channel through which the message is transmitted from one place to another
4 a receiver to whom the message is directed

Logically, it has come to be known as the source-message-channel-receiver model, or SMCR model for short. Schramm also retained the feedback and noise components of the original bull's-eye model. He defined the former as any mechanism between the source and the receiver that regulates the flow of the communication; and the latter as any distortion or errors that may be introduced during the communication exchange. Schramm completed his model with two other components: (1) the encoder, which converts the message into a form that can be transmitted through an appropriate channel; and (2) a decoder, which reverses the *encoding* process so that the message can be received successfully.

The SMCR has been used extensively in media studies, because of its simplicity and generalizability to all types of media. It can, for instance, be used to portray the physical components of TV broadcasting simply, yet revealingly, as shown in Figure 1.3.

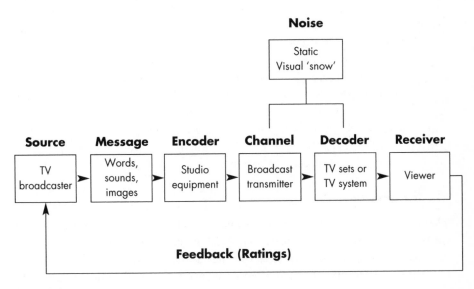

Figure 1.3

In the case of oral verbal communication, the source and receiver are also the encoder and decoder respectively. Encoding and decoding in this case involves knowledge of the language code used, as well as facial expression, gesture, and other non-verbal codes. The channel is the vocal apparatus that transmits the message through the medium of air. The message is adjusted according to the feedback behaviour observable in a receiver; noise in this case can be of both a physical and psychological nature.

In recent work, the notion of *delivery mode* has been added to the basic SMCR model. For example, the tone of voice with which the word 'Yes' is uttered will carry different meanings. If one delivers it with a normal tone of voice, it will be understood as a sign of affirmation ('Yes, you're right. I agree with what you just said.'). If, however, one delivers it with a raised tone ('Yes? You're kidding, no? I just can't believe it!'), it would be interpreted as conveying doubt or incredulity instead.

The audience

In media studies, the receiver in the SMCR model is commonly called the 'audience'. The audience is defined as the type of reader, spectator, listener, or viewer attracted by a certain media genre. In broadcasting theory, most audiences are divisible into 'segments' defined by specific sociological and lifestyle characteristics. The contemporary speciality radio stations and TV channels in particular have taken this aspect of broadcasting seriously into account by providing programming that is aimed at audiences with specific kinds of interests tied to age, gender, class, and other kinds of social variables. To describe this type of programming, the term *narrowcasting*, rather than broadcasting, is now used.

Typically, specific audiences relate to certain types of media genres, rather than to others. Some kinds of audiences perceive, say, a certain type of TV programme as representing real life and thus tend to interpret it in terms of personal life experiences; others may view the same programme more critically, in terms of the assumptions that it makes. For example, a non-religious viewer of a televangelism programme will tend to interpret it critically and sceptically, whereas an audience of 'faithful' viewers will perceive it as relevant directly to personal life experiences.

Media genres

The various types of books, movies, and TV programmes that are produced for mass consumption are called 'genres'. The term originated within literary criticism but was adopted by media studies in the 1960s.

Genres are identifiable by certain conventions, which audiences come to recognize through regular exposure. A soap opera, for instance, is a serial drama, involving stock characters and situations; a talk show involves an announcer who interviews people, such as authorities in a particular field or else common people with specific kinds of problems or issues that they wish to discuss publicly; and so on. Since each media genre attracts a particular kind of audience regularly, such programmes are produced by commercial stations and are, thus, often sponsored by specific advertisers. Indeed, the term soap opera comes from the fact that the genre was originally sponsored by soap companies, and was designed to appeal to homemakers who stayed at home to do house chores, such as washing dishes and clothes (which, of course, requires the use of soap products).

Semiotic method

The study of media genres from the semiotic perspective was initiated, as mentioned in the introduction to this book, by Roland Barthes in the 1950s. Barthes applied basic sign theory, introduced briefly above, to the analysis of all kinds of media spectacles and genres, showing how it can expose the implicit meanings built into them. Recall that a sign is defined as something physical (X) standing for something else (Y), material or conceptual, in some particular way $(X = Y)$. The sign can be a simple form such as a word, or a complex form such as a novel or radio programme. The latter is designated more specifically a *text* in semiotic theory. But a text is still a sign. That is why, for instance, we read and remember a novel as a singular form (X), not as an aggregate of its individual words, having a specific type of meaning or range of meanings (Y), that we derive from it on the basis of personal, social, and other kinds of experiences $(X = Y)$.

Barthes' goal was to expose pop culture as a huge distraction factory, aimed at uprooting the traditional forms of art and meaning-making. In so doing, he showed that it constitutes an overarching system of signs that recycles deeply-embedded meanings within Western culture, subverting them to commercial ends. These are called 'structures'. The primary goal of media semiotics is to catalogue and analyse these structures as they manifest themselves in media products.

In identifying and documenting media structures, the semiotician is guided by three basic questions:

1 *What* does a certain structure (text, genre, etc.) mean?
2 *How* does it represent what it means?
3 *Why* does it mean what it means?

Figure 1.4 is a simple example of how semioticians would go about the work of formulating answers to such questions.

Figure 1.4

In semiotic terminology, the figure is classified as a visual signifier, i.e. as a form, X, constructed with elements that can be seen (rather than heard, felt, smelt, etc.). The answer to the question of *what* it means, Y, is of course 'a bright idea'. As mentioned above, this is called the 'signified'. Now, the answer to *how* it represents this meaning ($X = Y$) is by means of a bright light bulb in a bubble (which is an analogue for the mind). Finally, looking for an answer as to *why* it means 'bright idea' is where the real work of semiotic analysis begins, since it involves delving into the origin and history of this specific visual sign – something that need not be done here. Suffice it to say that figuring out the *signification system* that underlies the $X = Y$ relation in this case involves knowing that: (1) light bulbs are sources of light; (2) light is a metaphorical vehicle for knowledge; and (3) balloons in comic books encircle words or thoughts which issue from the mouth or head of the character speaking.

There are two general kinds of *referents* that signs encode, *concrete* and *abstract*. A concrete referent, such as 'rabbit', is something that is physically demonstrable and thus perceptible by the senses; an abstract referent, such as the 'bright idea' concept designated by the light bulb figure above, is something that is formed in the mind and is thus not demonstrable as such. Now, as the semiotician Charles Morris (1938, 1946) suggested, the sign is a powerful mental tool precisely because its X part can evoke any type of referent, concrete or abstract, whether or not the referent is at hand for demonstration or for explication. This is known technically as *displacement*, and is defined as the ability of the human mind to conjure up the things to which signs refer even though these might not be physically present for the senses to perceive. The displacement property of signs has endowed the human species with the ability to think about the world beyond the stimulus–response realm to which most other species are constrained, and thus to reflect upon it at any time and in any situation whatsoever within 'mind-space'. Signs allow us, figuratively speaking, to carry the world around with us in our minds. But this is not the actual world; it is a mental world that has been brought into being by the selected *domains of reference* that signs have delineated.

As another concrete example of semiotic analysis, involving, however, more sophisticated reasoning than the 'bright idea' example above, consider a magazine ad for Airoldi men's watches that was common in Italian lifestyle magazines published in the early 1990s. To answer the question of *what* it means, we start by describing the signifier in terms of its constituent parts, in much the same way that a physicist or chemist would describe the physical properties of some substance or material. These are as follows:

- An Airoldi watch has apparently been 'stabbed' by a woman's hand holding a dagger.
- The woman's fingernails are painted with nail polish.
- She is wearing a man's ring on her thumb.
- A finger-less leather glove covers the woman's palm.
- A diamond-studded handcuff is discernible on her wrist.

In order to derive an overall meaning for the ad, it is best to consider first what each one of these suggests in cultural terms:

- The stabbing suggests some form of violence, perhaps of the 'prey hunting' variety.
- The woman's painted fingernails suggest sensuality.
- The man's ring is probably that of her lover; wearing it on the thumb suggests that it is one of the spoils of the 'hunt'.
- The finger-less leather glove is suggestive of sadomasochism.
- The diamond-studded handcuff reinforces the sadomasochism imagery, implying 'capture' and 'captivity'.

The 'female-as-huntress' image that this ad generates has a mythic etiology in Western culture. As the mythologist Joseph Campbell (1969: 59–60) aptly put it, the fear of women has been 'for the male no less an impressive imprinting force than the fears and mysteries of the world of nature itself'. The image of a fierce and sexually powerful female surfaces in all kinds of popular narratives – from ancient myths such as that of the Greek goddess

Diana to contemporary female movie characters seen in Hollywood films such as *Fatal Attraction* (1987). This image, therefore, seems to constitute the signification system evoked by the ad (at least to the present observer).

The action implied by the ad suggests that the female is stabbing the centre, or 'heart', of the watch. The watch is thus, by analogy, her male prey, who cannot escape from her violent act, since the handcuff on the woman's wrist will not allow the watch to 'slide' beyond it. The woman has, in effect, 'caught' her man. The act is final and decisive. The female-as-huntress theme, with its sadomasochistic connotations, is reinforced in print by the single word *sfidare*, which means 'to dare'. The ad 'dares' female consumers to hunt down and capture their lovers by buying them an Airoldi watch. By implication, this will neutralize their lovers' potential sexual interests in other women.

In order to establish the above interpretation of the ad as a plausible one, clearly, the context in which it has been fashioned is a key factor. The term context in semiotics refers to the real-world conditions – physical, psychological, historical, social, etc. – that ultimately determine how a sign is made and what it means. The interpretation that I fleshed out of the Airoldi ad was made possible by my own knowledge of the fact that it was directed towards a female audience, and by my knowledge of the mythic themes that were available to the ad-maker. In a phrase, contextual information provides the semiotician with a frame of reference that allows him or her to determine which meaning structures have been utilized in the construction of a specific signifier.

The Airoldi ad is an example of what the semiotician Umberto Eco (1979, 1990) calls an *open text* – a representation that elicits interpretations other than the one offered here. A *closed text*, on the other hand, is one that evokes a singular meaning, or a very limited range of meanings. A map, for instance, elicits a fairly straightforward interpretation of what it means. It is an example of a closed text. A poem by a symbolist poet, conversely, evokes different responses and different opinions on the part of readers. It is an example of an open text. The more interpretations a text evokes, the greater seems to be its psychological effectiveness.

Clearly, the semiotician must have knowledge of the culture in which a representation is created in order to put forward an interpretation of it. Rather than calling it 'culture' in this book, I will refer to it as *signifying order* so as to highlight the fact that it constitutes a network of meaning structures. Michel Foucault (1972) characterized this network as an 'interrelated fabric' in which the boundaries of meanings are never clear-cut. Every signifier is caught up in a system of references to other signifiers; it is a node within a network of distributed signifieds – the actual meanings used. As soon as one questions its unity, it loses its self-evidence; it indicates itself. To extract meaning from a text, therefore, one must have knowledge of this network and of the meanings that constitute it. For instance, in the Western signifying order, Biblical themes are interconnected with literary practices and with the style and content of everyday discourse, even though Western society now largely defines itself as secular (Frye 1981): e.g. the expression 'He fell into disgrace' has its roots in the story of Adam and Eve (note as well that the word 'disgrace' is composed with the word 'grace', which refers to a state of being protected or sanctified by the favour of God); similarly, the expression 'She has just started out on her life journey' is based on Biblical journey stories such as the one of Noah's Ark.

The network of interconnected meanings that constitute a signifying order is configured with domains known as 'codes'. These are 'organizational grids' within the network. As a concrete example of a code, take 1950s rock and roll music. This constitutes a specific type of *musical code* because it provides a system of musical structures that were developed over time from previous musical sources. From this system, an infinite variety of songs were composed that were easily recognizable as exemplars of the code. Differences in actual songs are attributable to stylistic difference, i.e. to the specific way in which a particular song has been composed. Thus, one can talk of an 'Elvis Presley style' or a 'Little Richard style', which are characteristic actualizations of the same musical code by particular artists. In addition, because of stylistic variation, codes are constantly changing. This is why we can talk of a '1960s rock code', a '1970s rock code', and so on. Nevertheless, all such codes retain the essential structures of the code(s) from which they have been derived. Only when the structures become radically transformed can one talk of a totally 'new musical code' as having emerged.

2 An outline of semiotic theory

A science that studies the life of signs within society is conceivable. It would be part of social psychology and consequently of general psychology; I shall call it semiology (from Greek semeion 'sign'). Semiology would show what constitutes signs, what laws govern them.

Ferdinand de Saussure (1857–1913)

Human intellectual and social life is based on the production, use, and exchange of signs. When we gesture, talk, write, read, watch a TV programme, listen to music, or look at a painting, we are engaged in sign-based behaviour. To study this behaviour, the nineteenth-century Swiss linguist Ferdinand de Saussure and the American philosopher Charles Peirce proposed an autonomous discipline. The former called it *semiology*; the latter 'semeiotics' (as had the seventeenth-century British philosopher John Locke before him). Today, Peirce's term – spelt 'semiotics' – is the preferred one, as is his definition of semiotics as a 'system of principles' for the study of sign-based behaviour. A clever, yet perceptive, definition of semiotics was put forward by the contemporary writer and semiotician Umberto Eco (1932–). Eco (1976: 12) defined it as 'the discipline studying everything which can be used in order to lie, because if something cannot be used to tell a lie, conversely it cannot be used to tell the truth; it cannot, in fact, be used to tell at all'. This is, despite its apparent facetiousness, a rather insightful definition, since it underlines the fact that we have the capacity to represent the world in any way we desire through signs, even in misleading and deceitful ways. This capacity for artifice allows us to conjure up non-existent referents, or to refer to things without any back-up empirical proof that what we are saying is true.

A large part of the increase in the popularity of semiotics in the late twentieth century was brought about by the popular fictional writings of Eco himself. The success of his best-selling novels (*The Name of the Rose, Foucault's*

Pendulum, The Island of the Day Before) has stimulated considerable curiosity vis-à-vis semiotics in recent years among the public at large. The efforts of Thomas A. Sebeok (1920–2001), who was a distinguished professor of semiotics at Indiana University, were also instrumental in showing the relevance of semiotics to large audiences. But, as mentioned in the introduction, it was Roland Barthes who first introduced semiotic method to a general public in the 1950s as a tool for gaining a discerning understanding of our mediated culture. The goal of this chapter is to describe the basic aspects of semiotic method, since these will inform and guide the remainder of our journey through our mediated culture in subsequent chapters.

Background and general notions

As a matter of historical fact, it was Hippocrates (460–377 BC), the founder of Western medical science, who coined the term 'semeiotics', defining it as a branch of medicine for the study of *symptoms* – a symptom being, in effect, a semeion: 'a mark or sign' that stands for something other than itself. The physician's primary task, Hippocrates claimed, was to unravel what symptoms indicate in bodily terms. The study of how 'things stand for other things' became the prerogative of philosophers around the time of Plato (*c*.428–*c*.347 BC), who suggested that signs were deceptive 'things' because they did not 'stand for' reality directly, but as idealized mental approximations of it. Plato's illustrious pupil Aristotle (384–322 BC) took it upon himself to investigate the 'stands for' ($X = Y$) phenomenon more closely, laying down a theory of the sign that has remained basic to this day. He defined the sign as consisting of three dimensions: (1) the physical part of the sign itself (e.g. the sounds that make up a word such as 'rabbit'); (2) the referent to which it calls attention (a certain category of animal), (3) its evocation of a meaning (what the referent entails psychologically and socially). As we saw in the previous chapter, nowadays (1) is called the 'signifier', (2) the 'signified', and (3) 'signification'.

The next major step forward in the study of signs was the one taken by St Augustine (AD 354–430), the philosopher and religious thinker who classified signs as *natural, conventional,* and *sacred*. A *natural sign* is one that is found, literally, in Nature. Bodily symptoms, the rustling of leaves, the colours of plants, etc. are all natural signs, as are the signals that animals emit in response to physical and emotional states. A *conventional sign*, on the other hand, is one that is made by humans. Words, gestures, and symbols are examples of conventional signs. In modern-day semiotic theory, these are classified as verbal and non-verbal – words and other linguistic structures (expressions, phrases, etc.) are examples of verbal signs; drawings and gestures are examples of non-verbal signs. As St Augustine emphasized, conventional signs serve a fundamental need – they allow humans to refer to and, thus, remember the world. Without them we would have to experience things anew each time we came across them or each time we imagined them. Signs make thinking and recognition fluid and routine. Finally, St Augustine defined *sacred signs* as those conveying messages from God. Miracles, for instance, are sacred signs that can only be understood through faith.

St Augustine's views lay largely forgotten until the eleventh century, when interest in the nature of human representation was rekindled by Arab scholars who translated the works of Plato, Aristotle, and other Greek thinkers. The result was the movement known as *Scholasticism*. Using classical Greek ideas as their intellectual framework, the Scholastics wanted to show that the truth of religious beliefs existed independently of the signs used to represent them. But within this movement there were some – the *nominalists* – who argued that 'truth' was a matter of subjective opinion and that signs captured, at best, only illusory and highly variable human versions of it. The French theologian Peter Abelard (1079–c.1142) proposed an interesting compromise to the debate, suggesting that the 'truth' that a sign purportedly captured existed in a particular object as an observable property of the object itself, and outside it as an ideal concept within the mind. The 'truth' of the matter, therefore, was somewhere in-between.

It was the British philosopher John Locke (1632–1704) who introduced the formal study of signs into philosophy in his *Essay Concerning Human Understanding* (1690), anticipating that it would allow philosophers to understand the interconnection between representation and knowledge. But the task he laid out remained virtually unnoticed until, as mentioned above, the ideas of the Swiss linguist Ferdinand de Saussure (1857–1913) and the American philosopher Charles S. Peirce (1839–1914) became the basis for circumscribing an autonomous field of inquiry.

Saussure suggested that the study of signs be divided into two branches – the *synchronic* and the *diachronic*. The former refers to the study of signs at a given point in time, normally the present, and the latter to the investigation of how signs change in form and meaning over time. As a simple case-in-point of what diachronic analysis entails, consider the word 'person'. In ancient Greece, the word 'persona' referred to a 'mask' worn by an actor on stage. Subsequently, it came to have the meaning of 'the character of the mask-wearer'. This meaning persists to this day in the theatre term *dramatis personae* 'cast of characters' (literally 'the persons of the drama'). Eventually, the word came to have its present meaning of 'living human being'. This diachronic analysis of 'person' explains, incidentally, why we continue to use 'theatrical' expressions such as 'to play a role in life', 'to interact', 'to act out feelings', 'to put on a proper face', and so on, in everyday discourse.

Saussure saw the sign as a 'binary phenomenon', namely a form that consisted of two interrelated parts – the signifier ('le signifiant' in French) and the signified ('le signifié'). The relation between the two is conceptual and determined by social convention. A word such as 'rabbit' evokes, Saussure claimed, a 'mental sound image' that is tied to an 'idealized' social picture of the animal in question.

At about the same time that Saussure was elaborating his version of sign theory, Charles Peirce was doing virtually the same thing. He defined the sign as consisting of a *representamen* (literally 'something that does the representing'), referring to some *object* (whatever the representamen calls attention to), eliciting a meaning, called the *interpretant* (whatever it means to someone in some context). The relation among the three dimensions is not a static one, but dynamic, whereby one suggests the other in a cyclical manner. Peirce also provided a typology of 66 species of signs, classifying them according to their function. For example, he defined a 'qualisign' as a sign that draws attention to, or singles out, some *quality* of its referent. In language, an adjective is a qualisign since it draws attention to the qualities (colour, shape, size, etc.) of referents. In non-verbal domains, qualisigns include the colours used by painters, the harmonies and tones used by composers, etc.

In the twentieth century, semiotic theory was developed by a host of semioticians, linguists, psychologists, and culture theorists. Among these, one can mention, in addition to Barthes, Sebeok, and Eco, scholars such as Roman Jakobson (1896–1982), Louis Hjelmslev (1899–1965), Jacques Lacan (1901–81), Charles Morris (1901–79), Claude Lévi-Strauss (1908–), A.J. Greimas (1917–92), Juri Lotman (1922–93), and Jacques Derrida (1930–). However, the basic Saussurean–Peircean paradigm, with its foundations in the writings of Aristotle, St Augustine, the medieval Scholastic philosophers, and John Locke has remained intact to this day.

In this book, Saussurean terminology will be used in the main, not because of any partisanship towards that particular version of sign theory, but because: (1) it is much more prevalent in the research literature related to media semiotics, and (2) it can be complemented by Peircean notions if the analytical situation should require it. I should say, however, that the paradigms of Saussure and Peirce are not isomorphic, nor so transparent that one can fill in the gaps to render them translatable. The 'cut and paste' approach adopted here is envisioned simply to help the reader grasp the essence of semiotic method in an unpartisan way. However, I should also say that it is not inconsistent with the general conduct of semiotic analysis today. Indeed, a perusal of the relevant literature shows a tendency within semiotics to amalgamate Saussurean and Peircean notions, especially when it comes to the analysis of cultural phenomena.

Signifying orders

It is truly amazing to ponder that, without any training whatsoever, infants intuitively grasp what signs are and what functions they serve. When they hear a string of sounds, such as those that constitute the word 'r-a-b-b-i-t', for instance, they perceive them not as random noises, but rather as standing for 'a long-eared, short-tailed, burrowing mammal with soft fur'. Just as remarkable is the fact that, well before the age of 2, children start using the sound sequence purposefully and intelligently to refer not only to real rabbits, but also to representations of rabbits, such as drawings of them in picture books. In effect, every child is 'programmed' by Nature, so to speak, to recognize and use signs and, in a short period of time, to acquire effortlessly the system of signs – called the 'signifying order' – of the culture in which he or she is being reared.

Signifying orders allow people to encode and store knowledge. But such orders always leave gaps, offering up only a portion of what is potentially knowable in the world. The great British writer of children's books Lewis Carroll (1832–98) invented his own language, which he called 'Jabberwocky', to show that the English language, as constituted, does not tell all there is to tell about reality. Jabberwocky words such as 'brillig', 'slithy', 'tove', and 'wabe' (from *Through the Looking Glass*, 1871: 126–9) were needed, Carroll argued cleverly, to refer to common things, concepts, or events that would otherwise go regularly unnoticed by speakers of English: 'brillig' = 'the time of broiling dinner'; 'slithy' = 'smooth and active'; 'tove' = 'a species of badger, with smooth white hair, long hind legs, and short horns'; 'wabe' = 'the side of a hill'. Carroll's argument also shows, on the other hand, that even though gaps exist in signifying orders, humans have the ability to fill them any time they wish. They do so not only by creating new signs, as Carroll did, but also by altering already-existing ones to meet new demands, by borrowing signs from other signifying orders, and by many other means.

Signifying orders are 'organizational templates' that make a manageable set of signs available for people to use and remember. Take, as an example, colour terminology. The light spectrum consists of a continuous gradation of hues from one end to the other. There are potentially 8 million gradations that the human eye is capable of distinguishing. If one were to put a finger at any point on the spectrum, there would be only a negligible difference in gradation in the hues immediately adjacent to the finger at either side. Yet, a speaker of English describing the spectrum will list the gradations as falling under the labels 'red', 'orange', 'yellow', 'green', 'blue', 'indigo', and 'violet'. This is because the speaker has been conditioned by the specific lexical categories the English language makes available to him or her for classifying the content of the spectrum. Without this restricted set of categories, he or she would have to refer to each perceived gradation in some way, thus needing millions of signs to do so!

Note, however, that there is nothing inherently 'natural' about the organizational scheme that English imposes on the spectrum. By contrast, speakers of Shona, an indigenous African language, divide it up into *cipswuka*, *citema*, *cicena*, and speakers of Bassa, a language of Liberia, divide it into *hui* and *ziza*. When an English speaker refers to something as 'blue', a Shona speaker might refer to it as either *cipswuka* or *citema*, and a Bassa speaker as *hui*. Bassa speakers would refer both to purple and to green objects as *hui*. But this does not stop them from seeing the difference in gradation encoded by the two English terms. Bassa speakers have many resources at their disposal to do so, as do speakers of all languages. In English, for example, the words 'crimson', 'scarlet', and 'vermilion' make it possible to refer to 'shades' or even 'types' of red, as do constructions such as 'bright red', 'dark red', and so on. Bassa speakers have similar resources at their disposal to differentiate between what we in English refer to as purple and green colours.

The object of media semiotics

As mentioned several times, it was the French semiotician Roland Barthes (1915–80) who drew attention in the 1950s to the value of studying media and pop culture with the theoretical tools of semiotics. After the publication of his pivotal book *Mythologies* in 1957, semiotic theory became widely used within the fields of critical analysis, a branch of cultural studies that examines the relationship between audiences and media genres, and functional analysis, a branch of sociology that studies media institutions and their effects on group behaviour. Scholars from both these fields were attracted particularly by Barthes' thesis that the meaning structures built into media products and genres were derived from the ancient myths, bestowing upon media events the same kind of significance that is traditionally reserved for religious rituals. They also tended to side with Barthes' trenchant critique of this ploy as a duplicitous and morally vacuous one that was ultimately subversive of true cultural evolution.

As early as the 1960s, another well-known French semiotician, Jean Baudrillard (1929–), continued from where Barthes left off. Like his compatriot, Baudrillard has scathingly attacked the entire consumerist pop culture industry as one large distraction-producing factory intent on lulling the masses into soporific stupor, so that they will acquire material objects habitually and for no other purpose than to possess them (Genosko 1999). However, it is my opinion that the critiques of Barthes and Baudrillard, as well-meaning as they were, may have unintentionally 'politicized' semiotics far too much, rendering it little more than a convenient tool of social critics.

Semiotics is, as we have seen, a discipline aiming to study sign-based behaviour, not a tool for carrying out critiques of political and social systems.

So, while the truly brilliant insights of these two semioticians will certainly be incorporated into the present treatment, their more acerbic critiques of Western society will be largely ignored, unless they can be seen to inform the discussion at hand. It was the political tone of Barthes' work, in my view, that may have given semiotics the 'bad name' it has acquired in recent years, as a field that is too esoteric and laden with political innuendo. Hopefully, this book will show that this is hardly the case.

The primary object of media semiotics is to study how the mass media create or recycle signs for their own ends. It does so, as we saw in the previous chapter, by asking: (1) what something means or represents, (2) how it exemplifies its meaning, and (3) why it has the meaning that it has.

As a simple case-in-point, consider the comic book figure of Superman, who was introduced in 1938 by *Action Comics*, and published separately a little later in *Superman Comic Books*. What or who does Superman represent? The answer is, of course, that he stands for 'a hero' in the tradition of mythic superhuman heroes, such as Prometheus and Hercules. As a heroic figure Superman has, of course, been updated and adapted culturally – he is an 'American' hero who stands for 'truth', 'justice', and 'the American way'. But like the ancient heroes, Superman is indestructible, morally upright, and devoted to saving humanity from itself. Moreover, like all mythic heroes, he has a 'tragic flaw' – exposure to 'kryptonite', a substance that is found on the planet where he was born, renders him devoid of his awesome powers.

Now, answering the question of why Superman (or any comic book action hero for that matter) appeals to modern-day audiences requires us to delve into the origin and history of the archetypal heroic figure. In mythology and legend, a hero is an individual, often of divine ancestry, who is endowed with great courage and strength, celebrated for his bold exploits, and sent by the gods to Earth to play a crucial role in human affairs. Heroes are character abstractions, in short, who embody lofty human ideals for all to admire – truth, honesty, justice, fairness, moral strength, and so on. Modern-day audiences feel this intuitively, as did the ancient ones who watched stage performances of Aeschylus' (525?–456 BC) *Prometheus Bound, Prometheus Unbound,* and *Prometheus the Fire-Bringer* in Greece. Rather than being sent by the gods from the afterworld to help humanity (something that would hardly be appropriate in a secular society), Superman came to Earth instead from a planet in another galaxy; he leads a 'double life', as promethean hero and as Clark Kent, a 'mild-mannered' reporter for a daily newspaper; he is adored by Lois Lane, a reporter for the same newspaper who suspects (from time to time) that Clark Kent may be Superman; and he wears a distinctive costume. This 'Superman code' was used from one issue to the next by the creators, making Superman extremely popular. The character continues, in fact, to be a favourite in our contemporary pop culture and has also appeared on radio and television, as well as in motion pictures.

The gist of the semiotic story of Superman, therefore, is that he is a 'recycled' or 'mediated' hero. The 'signification system' that undergirds the Superman figure can be summarized in Table 2.1.

Table 2.1

Mythic hero . . .	Superman . . .
sent by the gods to Earth	comes from another planet
helps humans run their affairs	helps 'good' people in trouble and defeats the 'bad guys'
has a tragic flaw	is rendered powerless and vulnerable by exposure to kryptonite, a substance that is found on his home planet
exemplifies virtue, honesty, and all the ideals that humanity looks up to, but which common people rarely embody	represents 'truth', 'justice', 'the American way', and all the virtues that modern-day people aspire to have, but often fail to manifest

As this concrete example shows, media representations are, more often than not, recycled signifiers, dressed up in contemporary garb to appeal to contemporary audiences. As Barthes correctly observed throughout his many writings on pop culture, this is precisely why media characters, such as movie cowboys and detectives, and spectacles, such as hyped-up wrestling matches, have enduring appeal. Like their ancestors, modern-day people need heroes subconsciously to 'make things right' in human affairs, at least in the world of fantasy.

Mediated meanings

The 'heroic figure' meaning associated with Superman is an example of a 'mediated meaning', i.e. of a signifier that has been recycled by the media. This meaning is, of course, not derivable directly by someone who has never been exposed to Superman, to action comic books, or to the notion of hero – which is, of course, very unlikely. Assuming that such an uninformed onlooker exists, then to that person Superman would appear to be a 'man in tights and red cape, who has the unusual ability to fly, and who possesses superior physical powers'. This 'literal' perception of Superman is known, technically, as *denotation*. As the psychologist C.K. Ogden and the philosopher and literary critic I.A. Richards argued in their classic 1923 work, titled appropriately *The Meaning of Meaning*, like the axioms of arithmetic or geometry, the notion of 'denotative meaning' is best left undefined. Essentially, it is the 'face value' linkage established between a sign and its referent. Ancient audiences probably believed that Prometheus was a real being and, thus, would have interpreted his stage character *denotatively*. Children, too, might tend to interpret Superman in this way today. But modern-day adult audiences would not; they would know that Superman represents an imaginary figure, not a real one. Incidentally, to use Peircean theory, it can be said that the difference in meaning between Prometheus and Superman occurs at the interpretant level of the sign. Recall from above that the interpretant encompasses the specific designations that a sign evokes for a person or group at a certain point in time (Peirce 1931–58, II: 228).

Denotative meaning is not something that can be pinned down exactly. It is a generalization. The comic book, television, and movie versions of the Superman figure are similar, yet different. The details vary from one medium to the other, but the general qualities associated with Superman remain intact. So long as he is indestructible, wears the same suit, has the ability to fly, etc. he will instantly be recognizable as Superman – no matter which particular actor portrays him in a movie, and no matter which particular artist draws him.

The interpretation of Superman as an 'imaginary heroic figure' is known instead as *connotation*. This can be defined as a meaning that has a particular 'cultural history behind it' – i.e. it can only be understood in terms of some signifying order. In connotative terms, everything about Superman has an historical dimension to it (see Table 2.2).

Connotation is the operative mode in the production and deciphering of creative texts such as poems, novels, musical compositions, and art works. And, of course, all mass media texts and genres are grounded in connotation, since they are designed to generate culturally-significant meanings. Indeed, the whole mediated world in which we live can be characterized as one huge connotative signifying order. Unless one watches the weather channel simply to find out what the weather will be that day, there is very little on TV that is designed to impart straightforward, denotative meaning. And even weather forecasts are hardly ever completely denotative events. TV announcers often line their forecast with connotative remarks such as 'Mother Nature has not been very good to us this winter,' 'Where has the sun gone to?' and the like.

Table 2.2

Denotative features	Connotative interpretations
He has unusual physical powers (he can fly; he can see through substances; he cannot be harmed by human weapons; etc.).	He acquired these powers by virtue of the fact that he is not of this world.
He helps good people in trouble and defeats the villains.	Heroes have been sent from another world to help humans run their affairs. They embody human virtues.
He is rendered powerless and vulnerable by exposure to kryptonite.	Heroes have a tragic flaw, which is an acknowledgement of the belief that all things of this world (including good things) are ultimately imperfect.
He wears an unusual costume.	Clothing sets heroes apart from common folk. This is also why military personnel and clerics, for instance, wear different types of clothing. Clothing sets leaders apart from those who depend on them.

Connotation is powerful because it evokes feelings and perceptions about things. As the American philosopher Susanne Langer (1948) argued, artistic forms are effective because we 'feel' that they have much to say to us, far beyond what they at first appear to convey. Media messages are powerful too because we react to them in terms of feeling. Superman is emotionally appealing to many people, especially children, because he is a figure imbued with mythic connotation. His actions in stories literally 'make sense' to us because they are consistent with what heroic figures are wont to do.

To show that connotation evokes emotions and perceptions, the psychologists Osgood, Suci, and Tannenbaum developed a technique which they called the *semantic differential* in 1957. It consists of posing a series of questions to subjects about a specific concept – 'Is it good or bad? weak or strong?' etc. – as seven-point scales, with the opposing adjectives at each end. The answers are then analysed statistically in order to sift out any general pattern from them (see Table 2.3).

Table 2.3

Evaluate the concept of *American President* in terms of the following seven-point scales:

modern								traditional
	1	2	3	4	5	6	7	
young								old
	1	2	3	4	5	6	7	
attractive								bland-looking
	1	2	3	4	5	6	7	
practical								idealistic
	1	2	3	4	5	6	7	
friendly								stern
	1	2	3	4	5	6	7	

An informant who feels that the President should be modern would place a mark towards the modern end of the modern–traditional scale; one who feels that the President should not be too young or old would place a mark near the middle of the young–old scale; someone who feels that the President should be bland-looking would place a mark towards the bland end of the attractive–bland-looking scale; and so on. If a large number of people were to be asked to rate the term 'President' in this way, then an ideal profile of the presidency could be drawn in terms of the statistically-significant variations in the connotations that the term evokes. Interestingly, research utilizing the semantic differential has shown that the emotional connotations that concepts evoke are not purely random, but tend instead to cluster around culture-specific norms: e.g. the word 'noise' turns out to be a highly emotional concept for the Japanese, who rate it consistently at the ends of the scales presented to them; whereas it is a fairly neutral concept for Americans, who place it in the mid range of the scales.

A technique also used in semiotics to flesh out the connotative meanings built into signs is that of *opposition*. Take, as a simple example, the connotative differences that are associated with the white–dark dichotomy in Western culture. The colour 'white' connotes 'cleanliness', 'purity', 'innocence', etc., while its antonymic counterpart 'dark' connotes 'uncleanness', 'impurity', 'corruption', etc. This dichotomy is used with such regularity by the mass media that it goes generally unnoticed. From early cowboy movies, in which the heroes wore white hats and the villains black ones, to contemporary advertisements, such as the Airoldi one discussed in the previous chapter, in which such items as 'dark leather gloves' evoke impressions of sadomasochism, the set of opposing connotations associated with the white–dark dichotomy is being constantly recycled by the media's distraction factory.

On the other hand, this same dichotomy could be utilized for the reverse purpose: i.e. to link the connotations associated with darkness to heroes so that they can be perceived as mysterious and dauntless, fighting Evil on its own terms. This is why the *Zorro* character of cinema fame wears black, as did several Hollywood Western characters of the past (such as Lash Larue).

Incidentally, oppositions are called *paradigmatic* – a technical term which indicates, essentially, that signs bear meaning in relation to other signs. We recognize the qualities that Superman possesses as being distinctive and meaningful because they contrast blatantly with those possessed by the 'villains' or 'opponents' he encounters during his many escapades (see Table 2.4).

Table 2.4

Superman . . .	His opponent . . .
is actively friendly and conscientious.	is actively hostile and unscrupulous.
is benign.	is malicious.
is selfless and considerate.	is self-serving.
embodies Goodness.	embodies Evil.
is honest, frank, and open.	is cunning, insincere, and deceitful.
is brave.	is a coward.

Note, moreover that the above 'paradigmatic features' are not preclusive of each other. Rather, they allow us to form a composite mental portrait of Superman:

Superman = physically powerful, honest, selfless, considerate, brave, etc.

Technically, such compositions are said to be *syntagmatic*. This refers to the fact that signs are put together in some consistent way. As a linguistic example of syntagmatic structure, take the words 'pin', 'bin', 'fun', 'run', 'duck', and 'luck'. These are legitimate signifiers because the combination of sounds with which they are made is consistent with English syllable structure. On the other hand, 'mpin', 'mbin', 'mfun', 'mrun', 'mduck', 'mluck' would not qualify as legitimate verbal signifiers in English because they violate its syllable structure.

In essence, something is a legitimate sign if it has a discernible (repeatable and predictable) form and is constructed in a definable (patterned) way. Signs are like pieces of a jigsaw puzzle. These have features on their 'faces' that keep them distinct from each other, as well as differently-shaped 'edges' that make it possible to join them together in specific ways to complete the overall picture.

Types of signs

Various classifications of signs have been elaborated since Aristotle and St Augustine. Of these, the most comprehensive is the taxonomy developed by Charles Peirce. Of the 66 species he identified, there are three – *icons*, *indexes* and *symbols* – that reveal themselves to be highly useful for the investigation of cultural phenomena, such as media products.

An *icon* is a sign that resembles its referent in some way. Portraits of people are visual icons showing the actual faces of people from the perspective of the artist. Onomatopoeic words such as 'drip', 'plop', 'bang', 'screech' are vocal icons designed to replicate the sounds that certain things, actions, or movements are perceived to make. Perfumes are olfactory icons simulating natural scents. Chemical food additives are gustatory icons approximating the tastes of natural foods. A block with a letter of the alphabet carved into it is a tactile icon that can be figured out by touch. Superman also has well-defined 'hero-iconic' qualities: i.e. he has been devised to look like past heroic figures. And indeed like Prometheus, Hercules, Achilles, and Samson, he is muscular, tall, and attractive.

An *index* is a sign that stands for, or points out, something in relation to something else. Indexes do not resemble their referents, as icons do; they identify them or indicate where they are. The most typical manifestation of human indexicality is the pointing *index* finger, which people the world over use instinctively to point out and locate things, people, and events. Many words, too, manifest an implicit form of indexicality: e.g. words such as 'here', 'there', 'up', and 'down' refer to the relative location of things when speaking about them. Indexicality is also a feature of identity-construction. A name, for example, identifies a separate individual and, usually, his or her national origin. This is why Superman, not being of this world, but having to live in it, takes on an alter ego with a human name, Clark Kent. The latter identifies him moreover as a member of American society rather than, say, of French society.

A *symbol* is a sign that stands for something in an arbitrary convention-based way. Words in general are symbolic signs, as are many hand gestures. But any signifier – object, sound, figure, colour, musical sound, etc. – can have symbolic meaning. A V-sign made with the index and middle fingers can stand symbolically for the concept 'peace'; the colour white, as we saw above, can stand for 'purity' and 'innocence'; and the list could go on and on. The thing to note is that symbolic meanings are all established by social convention, and thus cannot be figured out directly. Here is a list of a few colour connotations used to symbolize an array of referents in Western representational practices:

- *white* = purity, innocence, virtuous, chastity, goodness, decency, etc.
- *black* = evil, impurity, guilt, vice, sinfulness, indecency, immorality, etc.
- *red* = blood, passion, sexuality, fertility, fecundity, anger, sensuality, etc.
- *green* = hope, insecurity, naiveté, candour, trust, life, existence, etc.
- *yellow* = liveliness, sunshine, happiness, tranquillity, peacefulness, etc.
- *blue* = hope, sky, paradise, tranquillity, calmness, mysticism, mystery, etc.
- *brown* = earthiness, naturalness, primordiality, constancy, etc.
- *grey* = dullness, mistiness, obscurity, mystery, nebulousness, etc.

The colours of the costume Superman wears are also suggestive of symbolism. His red cape suggests 'noble blood' and his blue tights the 'hope' he brings to humanity. Of course, the red and blue combination is also indicative of 'American patriotism' – these are, after all, colours of the American flag. Superman himself is a symbol. As discussed several times above, he represents the embodiment of all the heroic virtues that human beings aspire to possess but, being weak, fail to possess – honesty, valour, etc.

The overall figure of Superman has thus been assembled with iconic, indexical, and symbolic features or meanings (see Table 2.5).

Table 2.5

Iconicity	Indexicality	Symbolism
He resembles in physical appearance heroes of the past: he is tall, handsome, muscular, etc.	He takes on a human name, Clark Kent, so that he can fashion an alter ego and thus fit in with American society.	He symbolizes the embodiment of virtues such as honesty, valour, considerateness, etc.

Codes

How Superman acts, how he behaves, how he looks, and what he does are all predictable aspects of the 'Superman story', no matter who tells it or in what medium it is told. These aspects constitute a 'Superman code' – a set of basic 'ingredients' or 'directions' for making representations of Superman in comic book, television, or movie form. Some of these include the following, as we have seen several times above:

- Superman lives a double life as hero and as reporter Clark Kent.
- He is adored by Lois Lane. As Superman he ignores her advances. However, as Clark Kent he shows amorous interest in her.
- As Clark Kent he dresses like a typical American male reporter. He changes into his Superman costume (away from the public eye) only when the situation calls for heroic intervention.
- Superman never shows favouritism. He is always straightforward and honest.
- Given his tragic flaw, Superman may become momentarily overpowered by some villain who comes into possession of kryptonite.
- He has all the qualities and virtues of heroes.

Codes are 'organizational systems or grids' for the recurring elements that go into the constitution of anything that humans make, including signs, rituals, spectacles, behaviours, and representations of all kinds. They can be highly formal as, for example, the code of arithmetic in which all the structures (numerals) and rules (addition, subtraction, etc.) are firmly established. Or they can be highly flexible as, for example, the code for greeting people, which varies according to who the participants in the greeting ritual are.

A code can be compared to a recipe. This consists of information (a set of directions for preparing something to eat or drink) that must be converted into another form (the actual food or drink item) by someone. Note that the end result will vary according to the user of the recipe. But all results are still recognizable as having been made from the same recipe. Generally speaking, for some particular representational need there is an optimum code or set of codes that can be deployed. For example, the composer of a work of operatic art will need to deploy at least three code-making sources in the construction of his or her text – the musical code, the verbal code, and the theatre code (all in place at the time of the composition).

Needless to say, knowledge of codes is culture-specific. Carl Jung (1875–1961), the great Swiss psychoanalyst, was fond of recounting how codes had the power to affect even what one sees. During a visit to an island tribal culture that had never been exposed to illustrated *magazines*, he found that the people of that culture were unable to recognize the photographs in the magazines as visual representations of human beings. To his amazement, he discovered that they perceived them, rather, as smudges on a surface. Jung understood perfectly well, however, that their erroneous interpretation of the photographs was not due to defects of intelligence or eyesight; on the contrary, the tribal members were clear-sighted and highly intelligent. Jung perceptively understood that their primary assumptions were different from his own and from those of individuals living in Western culture, because they had acquired a different signifying order that blocked them from perceiving the pictures as visual signs.

A common strategy of the mass media is to build 'coded meanings' into representations – i.e. to fashion something on the basis of some hidden code or codes. Take, as an example, the name 'Acura' given to a Japanese automobile first built in the 1990s. This name has been fashioned, clearly, to be culturally ambiguous – it is imitative of both the structure of some Japanese words (such as *tempura*) and of most Italian words, which end typically in a vowel. This inbuilt ambiguity generates a system of connotations that are based on two sets of perceptions: (1) the popular view that Japanese technology and manufacturing is *accurate* and advanced; and (2) the common view of Italian as a language of 'love', 'poetry', and 'song', and of Italians generally as 'artistic', 'romantic', and 'friendly'. These are the 'coded meanings' that are built into the name 'Acura'. Like a recipe, they provide 'hidden directions' for interpreting the name at a connotative level (see Table 2.6).

Table 2.6   Acura

Coded 'Japanese' meanings	Coded 'Italian' meanings
accuracy	melody
precision	beauty
reliability	artistry
technology	poetry

Texts

The 'Superman code' can be used in various ways to generate a 'Superman story'. The actual story is called a text. Conversations, letters, speeches, poems, television programmes, paintings, scientific theories, and musical compositions are other examples of texts. A text constitutes a specific 'weaving together' of elements from a code (or codes) in order to express something. A *novel*, for instance, is a verbal text constructed with a set of codes, including the language code, the narrative code, and many other codes and subcodes. Note, however, that the novel is interpreted not in terms of its constituent parts, but rather holistically as a single sign. This is why when we ask someone what a novel means, he or she does not refer to the novel's actual words used in the sequence in which they occur, but rather to the overall meaning that he or she has extracted from it: e.g. 'The novel *Crime and Punishment* paints a grim portrait of the human condition'.

A text is, in effect, a *composite signifier*. The stories that are written about Superman's adventures are composite signifiers, which recount his exploits in a specific way according to the 'Superman code'. So, in any specific comic book story we can expect to find that Superman will be involved against some villain; that he may flirt at some point with Lois Lane as Clark Kent; that he will come across a crisis that he must resolve with his extraordinary powers; and so on.

The meaning of a text is conditioned by the context. The context is the situation – physical, psychological, and social – in which a text is constructed or to which it refers. If read in its comic book format, a Superman text will be interpreted as an adventure story. However, if a satirist such as the American cineaste Woody Allen were to portray Superman in a movie, then the movie text would hardly be construed as an adventure, but rather as a satire or parody of the Superman figure, of its media representations, or of some other aspect related to the 'Superman code'.

As another example of how context conditions the meaning of something, consider a discarded Superman comic book. If one were to come across this item on a sidewalk on a city street, one would interpret it as 'rubbish'. But if the same person saw the comic book displayed in a frame in an art gallery, then he or she would be inclined to interpret its meaning in a vastly different way. Clearly, the object's physical context of occurrence and social context of reference – its location on a sidewalk vs. its display in an art gallery – will determine how one will interpret it.

The semiotician and linguist Roman Jakobson (1896–1982) argued persuasively that context should be considered a basic component of any model of communication, along with the notions of *addresser, message, addressee, contact,* and *code.* Using Superman as a case-in-point, these terms can be defined as follows:

- The *addresser* is the creator of a particular Superman episode.
- The *message* is what a specific episode is designed to convey.
- The *addressee* is the audience, i.e. the intended receiver of the Superman episode.
- The *context* is what permits an audience to recognize that the episode is authentic. If it is found in an adventure comic book, then it will be interpreted as a genuine 'Superman story'. If the episode is found in a Woody Allen movie, then it will be interpreted instead as a 'parody of the Superman story'.
- The mode of *contact* is the method by which the addresser and addressee are linked. In media terms, it is equivalent to the 'medium'. A Superman episode can be delivered in comic-book, TV, radio, or movie form.
- The *code,* as we saw above, is the system of recurrent story elements that

allow audiences to decipher a Superman text as an adventure story extolling heroism.

Jakobson suggested, moreover, that each communicative act (e.g. each Superman episode) serves or entails a specific function. A specific Superman episode can: (1) reveal the writer's particular slant, (2) produce a different effect on its audiences (than previous episodes), (3) refer to specific aspects of the Superman story, (4) produce a highly aesthetic effect on audiences, (5) maintain interest in the Superman story by simply exposing the audience to a predictable version of it, or (6) make a reflective commentary on the Superman story itself. These functions were labelled respectively *emotive, conative, referential, poetic, phatic,* and *metalingual* by Jakobson.

Contextual analysis involves, in sum, determining who says what to whom; where and when it is said; how and why it is said; what effects it produces; and what codes are involved in the creation and production of a text.

Narrative

What makes comic books, TV programmes, movies, best-selling novels, and other media products highly popular and entertaining is the fact that they generally tell stories, not unlike those that were told orally in villages before the advent of print and electronic technologies. There is no culture without its stories; and there almost is no human being alive who does not understand what a story is. Indeed, people think of their very lives as stories and proceed to recount them as such. This is why autobiographical stories impart sense and meaning to people's lives, functioning as 'narrative signs' standing for some kind of purposeful existence.

Features

Narratives may be fact-based, as are the stories in newspapers, or fictional, as are those in a novel, a comic strip, a film, etc. Needless to say, it is often difficult to determine the boundary line between narrative fact and fiction. Indeed, even in the recounting of life stories, fiction is often intermingled with fact in order to give the stories more coherence. Psychologists call this the *Othello effect.* It is a kind of lying in order to emphasize the truth.

Narratives are texts (composite signifiers) that are distinguished by several features. The *plot* is basically what the narrative is all about – it is the 'narrative signified', encompassing the sequence of events to which the narrative draws attention. *Character* is a representation of the people who are the perpetrators and/or participants in the plot. The *setting* is the location where, and the time when, the plot takes place. The teller of the story is referred to as the *narrator,* who can be a character of the narrative, the author of the narrative, or some other person. Each type of narrator provides a different *perspective* to the story.

Myth

As Barthes argued, the themes of humanity's earliest stories, known as myths, continue to permeate and inform pop culture's story-telling efforts. As in the myths of Prometheus, Hercules, and other ancient heroes, Superman's exploits revolve around a universal mythic theme – the struggle of Good versus Evil. This is what makes Superman, or any action hero for that matter, so intuitively appealing to modern audiences.

Implicit mythic narrativity is a common ploy of *advertising*. Consider, as a case-in-point, a *Russell & Bromley* ad that was found typically in lifestyle magazines in the early 1990s. Several features of the ad instantly caught the eye. First, the ad featured a young, attractive woman, who was attired almost entirely in white, except for the points of her shoes and the colour of her hair, both of which were dark. The white colour of the woman's dress matched several other features in the ad scene – the lace curtains and walls behind her, the steps on which she sat, her purse, and the colour of the lettering at the bottom of the ad. Also highly conspicuous was the vulvic configuration of her legs, of the folds made by her skirt, and of the outline formed by her arms and legs. Finally, the dark toes of her shoes could be seen to point mysteriously to an invisible place at the end of the staircase, beyond the visual portion of the ad scene itself.

When viewed together, the features suggest an 'implicit narrative' lying suspended within the ad text. Here is one possible interpretation of the ad. Whiteness connotes the woman's sexual innocence, and darkness a foreboding and impending transgression of her purity. In effect, the white and dark contrasts in the ad suggest a struggle within the woman between innocence and sexuality. This 'subtext' is reinforced by the nature of the product itself. Shoes indicate a journey. Does the downward pointing of her shoes indicate a journey to the 'underworld', to the 'dark regions' of sexual experience? Supporting this interpretive hypothesis are several iconic cues:

1 As mentioned, the folds of the woman's skirt and the configuration of her legs and arms suggest vulvic symbolism.
2 The texture of the lace dress, together with the 'feel' conveyed by the leather shoes and handbag, impart a fetishistic texture to the whole scene.
3 The young woman's legs are partly spread open (in a V-shape) and her knees are exposed, both of which invite the viewer to gaze upon her in a sexual way. This is an obvious voyeuristic 'turn-on', as the expression goes.

4 Her posture and facial expression are also highly suggestive of sexual readiness and desire.

The steps of the staircase are made of concrete, but they have conspicuous cracks in them. This reinforces the suggestion that the 'underworld' is opening up to engulf the woman. Symbolically, the doorway can be interpreted as a portal, leading from one state (innocence) to another (sexuality). The woman has just crossed the threshold of the portal, ready to be engulfed by the sexual underworld. The woman is apparently suspended, on the staircase, between the two states, as is the viewer. The tension that this causes – like the tension produced before sexual orgasm – is powerfully ambivalent, creating excitement. The underworld is inviting, but dangerous. In sum, the *Russell & Bromley* ad would appear to be a modern-day advertiser's version of a mythic 'coming-of-age' theme portrayed by a descent into the underworld.

Barthes (1957) argued that such implicit narratives are embedded regularly in the texts that our mediated culture produces for mass consumption. This is why people rarely challenge the authority of ads, commercials, and other 'mediated products'. They seem intuitively to have intrinsic validity. And the reason for this, Barthes argued, was that they continued the oldest and most meaningful tradition of all – the telling of basic mythic stories about human actions and motivations.

The word 'myth' derives from the Greek *mythos*: 'word', 'speech', 'tale of the gods'. It can be defined as a narrative in which the characters are gods, heroes, and mystical beings, in which the plot is about the origin of things or about metaphysical events in human life, and in which the setting is a metaphysical world juxtaposed against the real world. In the beginning stages of human cultures, myths functioned as genuine 'narrative theories' of the world. This is why all cultures have created them to explain their origins. The Zuñi Indians of America, for instance, claim to have emerged from a mystical hole in the earth, thus establishing their kinship with the land. Myths function as a 'metaphysical knowledge system' for explaining human origins and actions. And this system is the one we instinctively resort to even today for imparting knowledge of the world initially to children. But even in contemporary adult life, the mythic personification of natural events continues to be an instinctual strategy for making sense of things. Climatologists, for example, refer to the warming of the ocean surface off the western coast of South America that occurs every 4 to 12 years, when upwelling of cold, nutrient-rich water does not occur, as a person, *El Niño*, 'the little one' in Spanish. This makes the climatological condition much more understandable in human terms. Although people do not think of *El Niño* as a person, they nonetheless find it convenient to blame it for certain weather repercussions. This is how original myths worked cognitively – the difference being that the personified conditions of the past were actually believed to be real gods or mythical beings.

The use of mythic themes and elements in media representations has become so widespread that it is hardly noticed any longer, despite Barthes' cogent warnings in the late 1950s. Implicit myths about the struggle for Good, of the need for heroes to lead us forward, and so on and so forth, constitute the narrative underpinnings of TV programmes, blockbuster movies, advertisements and commercials, and virtually anything that gets 'media air time'.

Metaphor

As we saw above, the figure of Superman symbolizes 'mythic heroism'. Superman is, in effect, a *metaphor* of idealized human virtues, representing them in a concrete way through his personality, through his actions, etc. Metaphors pervade media representations. It can be claimed that the very nature of such representations is metaphorical, since they symbolize psychological or social themes concretely through character portrayals (in comic books, on TV programmes, etc.) and situations that are familiar and understandable. The TV character Buffy the Vampire Slayer, for instance, is a metaphor of feminine prowess, Homer Simpson of boorish fatherhood, and so on. Interpretation too is essentially metaphorical, since it is based on making associations and analogies that are designed to bring out concretely what something means or entails.

Metaphor as a sign

In a compelling 1978 book, *Illness as Metaphor*, the writer Susan Sontag argued rather persuasively that, although illnesses are not metaphors, people are invariably predisposed to think of specific illnesses in metaphorical ways. Using the example of cancer, Sontag pointed out that in the not-too-distant past the very word 'cancer' was said to have killed some patients who would not have necessarily succumbed to the malignancy from which they suffered: 'As long as a particular disease is treated as an evil, invincible predator, not just a disease, most people with cancer will indeed be demoralized by learning what disease they have' (Sontag 1978: 7). Sontag's point that people suffer more from conceptualizing metaphorically about their disease than from the disease itself is, indeed, a well-taken and instructive one.

It was Aristotle who coined the term 'metaphor' – itself a metaphor (*meta* 'beyond' plus *pherein* 'to carry'). Understanding abstract things generally involves metaphorical reasoning, Aristotle contended. However, he also affirmed that, as knowledge-productive as it was, the most common function of metaphor was to spruce up literal ways of speaking. Strangely, this is the view that became the dominant one in Western society at large. But since 1977, when a seminal study (Pollio *et al.* 1977) showed that speakers of English uttered, on average, 3000 novel verbal metaphors and 7000 idioms per week, it has become clear that metaphor can hardly be considered an option to literal language. It would seem, on the contrary, to constitute the core of everyday discourse.

Defining metaphor semiotically poses an interesting dilemma. In the metaphorical sentence 'The professor is a snake', for instance, there are two referents, not one, that are linked to each other through concrete association:

- There is the primary referent, professor, called the *topic* of the metaphor.
- Then there is another referent, snake, which is known as the *vehicle* of the metaphor.
- The correlation of the two referents creates a new meaning, called the *ground*, which is not however the simple sum of the meanings of the two referents.

Note, moreover, that it is not the denotative meaning of the vehicle that is transferred to the topic, but rather the connotative ones that it evokes. So, in the above metaphor it is not the meaning of 'snake' as an actual reptile that is implied, but rather the characteristics that such a reptile is perceived to symbolize – 'slyness', 'danger', 'slipperiness', etc. It is this complex of connotations that constitute the ground of the metaphor. Metaphor is, in effect, a complex signifier that stands for an abstract signified by associating it with something concrete.

Metaphor reveals a basic tendency of the human mind to think of certain referents in terms of others. The question now becomes: is there any psychological motivation for this? In the case of 'The professor is a snake', the probable reason for correlating two seemingly unrelated referents is the deeply-ingrained perception within us that humans and animals are interconnected in the natural scheme of things. In other words, we create metaphors if we feel that referents are related or interconnected in some way.

Conceptual metaphors

In their groundbreaking 1980 book, *Metaphors We Live By*, the linguist George Lakoff and the philosopher Mark Johnson showed meticulously how metaphorical reasoning is the cornerstone of everyday thought and discourse, not just a device of poets and orators. The main claim made by the two scholars is that most abstract concepts have a metaphorical origin. To distinguish 'metaphorically-constructed' concepts from other types, Lakoff and Johnson introduced the term *conceptual metaphors*. For example, the above expression 'The professor is a snake' is really a token of a conceptual metaphor, i.e. of something more general that has the underlying form [people are animals]. The same formula can, in fact, be seen to underlie any other construction in which animal vehicles are used to describe human beings:

- John is a *gorilla*.
- Mary is a *puppy*.
- My friend is a *pig*.
- Greedy people are *insects*.
  etc.

Each specific metaphor ('John is a gorilla', 'Mary is a puppy', etc.) is not, therefore, an isolated example of poetic fancy. Rather, it is a manifestation of the general metaphorical idea [people are animals]. Such an idea is what Lakoff and Johnson call a conceptual metaphor:

$$
\begin{array}{ccc}
people & are & animals \\
\downarrow & & \downarrow \\
\text{John} & & \text{a gorilla} \\
\text{Mary} & & \text{a puppy} \\
\text{My friend} & & \text{a pig} \\
\text{Greedy people} & & \text{insects} \\
\text{etc.} & & \text{etc.} \\
\uparrow & & \uparrow \\
specific\ topics & & specific\ vehicles
\end{array}
$$

Each of the two parts of the conceptual metaphor is called a 'domain': (1) 'people' is the target domain because it is the abstract topic itself (the 'target' of the conceptual metaphor); and (2) 'animals' is the source domain because it is the class of vehicles that can be used to create specific metaphors (the 'source' of the metaphorical concept). Lakoff and Johnson then assert that cultural groupthink is largely based on linkages that are established over time among conceptual metaphors. They call such linkages 'idealized cognitive models'. Consider, as a case-in-point, several conceptual metaphors that are commonly deployed in English-speaking cultures to deliver the topic of 'ideas':

[Ideas are geometrical figures]

- Those ideas are *circular*.
- I don't see the *point* of your idea.
- Her ideas are *central* to the discussion.
- Their ideas are *diametrically* opposite.

[Ideas are things that are to be seen in the light]

- I was *illuminated* by that speaker.
- Your idea is very *clear*.
- Her example *shed light* on several matters.
- That lecture was *enlightening*.

[Ideas are buildings]

- Hers is a *well-constructed* theory.
- Your idea is on *solid ground*.
- My theory needs more *support*.
- Their theory *collapsed* under criticism.
- She put together the *framework* of a very interesting theory.

[Ideas are plants]

- Her ideas have finally come to *fruition*.
- That's a *budding* new theory.
- Saussure's ideas have contemporary *offshoots*.
- Euler's idea of networks has become a *branch* of mathematics.

[Ideas are commodities]

- That man certainly knows how to *package* his ideas.
- Her idea just won't *sell*.
- There's no *market* for that idea.
- That's a *worthless* idea.

The constant juxtaposition of such conceptual formulas in common discourse produces, cumulatively, an idealized cognitive model of ideas that has the associative conceptual structure depicted in Figure 2.1.

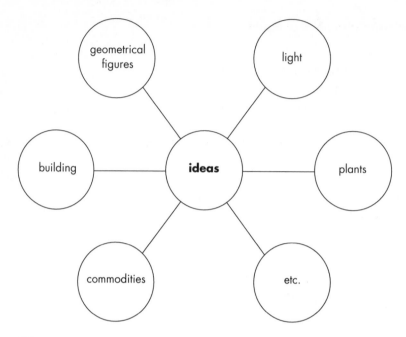

Figure 2.1

In the area of media studies, conceptual metaphor theory, as it is now called, has started producing many interesting insights. For instance, the narrative content of such 1950s TV sitcoms as *The Adventures of Ozzie and Harriet* and *Father Knows Best* was structured, in effect, by a metaphorical model of the family as a patriarchal institution. This is why the father was portrayed as 'all-knowing', as someone 'in charge' of the household, as a reliable 'provider', and so on. Those were the source domains on which the sitcoms were grounded conceptually. On the other hand, the narrative content of the 1950s sitcom *Honeymooners* and of the 1980s–1990s sitcom *Married with Children* was structured on a contrasting metaphorical model of the family. In those programmes, the father was portrayed as a 'selfish boor', as a 'moronic adolescent', as a 'lazy provider', and so on. Those were, in effect, the source domains on which the sitcoms were grounded.

Before Lakoff and Johnson's trend-setting work, the study of metaphor fell within the field of *rhetoric*, where it was viewed as one of various *tropes* – i.e. figures of speech. But since the early 1980s the practice has been to use the term metaphor to refer to the study of all figurative language and to consider the other tropes as particular kinds of metaphor. But there are two types that are regularly considered separately from metaphor – metonymy and irony. *Metonymy* involves the use of an entity to refer to another that is related to it. Unlike metaphor, it consists in the use of a part of a domain to represent the whole domain: e.g. in 'The White House spoke out today on the issue' one part of American Government is employed to stand for the whole of it. In parallelism with the notion of *conceptual metaphor*, the idea of conceptual metonym can be suggested. Particularly fruitful in our culture is the conceptual metonym [the face stands for the person], which manifests itself not only in discourse ('He's just another pretty face', 'Let us speak face to face', What face are you putting on today?' etc.), but also in non-verbal domains of representation – it is the reason why portraits, in painting and photography, focus on the face. *Irony* is a representational strategy that satirizes or parodies something so that it can be understood indirectly or reflectively. Most TV sitcoms are fashioned ironically, since they typically present common situations in satirical, parodic, or sarcastic ways.

3 Print media

Tis pleasant, sure, to see one's name in print. A book's a book, although there's nothing in't.

Lord Byron (1788–1824)

'A book is a part of life, a manifestation of life, just as much as a tree or a horse or a star. It obeys its own rhythms, its own laws, whether it be a novel, a play, or a diary. The deep, hidden rhythm of life is always there – that of the pulse, the heart beat.' With these eloquent words, the American author Henry Miller (1891–1980) expressed what virtually everybody feels intuitively when they read a book. It also makes clear why books seem to have such an impact on people. Without books, human life as we know it today would indeed be inconceivable. The vast repository of written words contained in books, which has preserved human ideas throughout the ages, and to which we can have access if we know the appropriate language codes, constitutes the 'print memory system' of human civilization. If somehow all the books in the world were to be destroyed overnight, human civilization would be in serious danger. Writers, scientists, educators, lawmakers, and many others throughout the world would have to start all over literally 'rewriting' knowledge in print form.

But 'knowledge-storage' is not all that print allows humans to do. Since the late medieval period, *fictional* books have provided entertainment and enlightenment for masses of people across the world. Even in the Digital Galaxy, the great fictional works of history continue to hold the fascination of all kinds of audiences. As crass as they might appear to be, contemporary 'bestsellers' are among the most popular items produced by the pop culture distraction factory. In this eclectic era of 'anything goes', paper-based books continue to thrive, even as they are being transferred, more and more, to the digital medium.

Print is the target of interest of this stop on our journey through the world of mass media. The goal here is not, however, to unravel the *specific* meanings of a book such as *Crime and Punishment* or a newspaper such as *The Times*.

Such would be the goal of literary criticism and journalism studies respectively. Rather, the objective here is to focus on the *types* of meanings that print artefacts encode and the 'semiotic effects' they produce in contemporary cultures. Needless to say, in order to conduct a semiotic analysis of print, it is necessary to take into account the history and development of each type of print artefact and genre throughout the discussion.

The development of print media

Many culture historians argue, and with good cause, that print technology and print literacy are essential conditions of advanced civilizations. But it must not be forgotten that, long before the advent of the printing press, *orality* served many of the same cognitive and social functions of *literacy*, as we saw in the opening chapter. Moreover, even oral cultures utilized pictographic writing to give expression to, and record, ideas. Incidentally, the earliest that have been discovered to date are over 30 000 years old.

Essentially, ancient oral cultures preserved their cultural histories and traditions through the oral communication and transmission of stories, songs, and wise sayings – as do modern-day tribal groups. By retelling a tale learned from one another, people passed on what they knew and considered to be of lasting value to subsequent generations. Although each time a story was told it changed according to the storyteller, the essential 'knowledge system' of such cultures survived nonetheless, as ideas, values, and essential skills were passed on in much the same way as they are today by parents to pre-literate children – by word of mouth. Moreover, even though children's stories are now also written down, the same story varies according to author and according to when it is told. The tale of *Cinderella*, for example, is told and retold in various versions, as are tales about fairies, legendary heroes, and mythical animal characters. It all depends on *who* tells them and *where* and *when* he or she tells them.

Oral traditions

The underlying narrative structure of the earliest oral stories was fundamentally mythological. Mythic narration is universal, and may thus be said to mirror the structure of human cognition. This would explain why essentially the same stories told to children in early cultures are told to children today, albeit in different versions and in different media (such as illustrated storybooks, cartoons, and animated movies). The first oral myths were 'theories of the world'. Known as *cosmogonic*, these had the function of explaining how the world came into being and what role humans were assigned by the gods in the cosmological scheme of things. To explain the origin of life, for instance, some myths portrayed the creation of the world as proceeding from nothing; others depicted it instead as emerging from some metaphysical realm. To explain death and the end of the world, the early cultures also told *eschatological* myths. These usually predicted the destruction of the world by a divine being who would send human beings either to a paradisiacal existence or to one of eternal torment, depending on the ways in which they had lived their lives. The theme of an apocalyptic final battle of the gods was a common one as well in eschatological traditions. To counteract the apocalypse, many cultures also told myths of *birth and rebirth*, which informed people either about how life could be renewed or else about the coming of an ideal society or of a saviour.

The implicit idea embedded in all myths is that there is life beyond death. This is perhaps why the early storytellers were considered to have the gift of prophecy, receiving the substance of their stories from supernatural beings directly. As a consequence, they were thought to possess magical powers that allowed them to cure diseases and to influence the course of events in the world. Early ritualistic practices were invariably organized and supervised by storytellers.

The early mythological and religious accounts of human origins and destiny continue to be a part of the signification systems of modern-day secular societies, even if people living in such societies are no longer aware of their presence. The Canadian literary critic Northrop Frye (1912–91) argued, in his book *The Great Code* (1981), that the themes of the early myths are latent in the artistic practices and in the everyday discourse patterns of even those societies that define themselves as largely secular. Frye showed how the Bible is the implicit 'code' sustaining and informing Western literature, art, and social institutions. Anyone who has never been exposed to this code, Frye suggested, will simply not understand the Western world. The stories of Adam and Eve, of the Tower of Babel, of Paradise lost and regained, of the Flood and Noah's Ark, and many others have supplied not only the themes for the great artistic and literary works of Western civilization, but also the symbols shaping the daily thought and discourse patterns of Western peoples, even if most have never read the Bible. Similarly, the anthropologist Claude Lévi-Strauss (1908–) argued that mythic ideas continue to exercise an unconscious control over humanity because they have become, in effect, embedded in the parts of speech. Lévi-Strauss (1978) maintained, for instance, that certain clusters of relationships in myth match the systematic order of words in sentences. The earliest 'subjects' of myths were divine beings who acted physically and 'verbally' upon human and terrestrial 'objects'. From this *subject–verb–object* structure of myth, the first sentences emerged. That very structure was subsequently extended to encompass non-metaphysical referents. As radical as this mythic explanation of syntax may seem, it certainly would explain why language appears to have an intuitive natural connection with the things to which it refers.

The Austrian psychoanalyst Sigmund Freud (1856–1939) also saw the mythic stories as 'theories of mind', claiming essentially that they were invented to give expression to unconscious desires and impulses. For example, he interpreted the myth of Oedipus as giving narrative expression to the unconscious sexual desire in a child for the parent of the opposite sex, usually accompanied by hostility to the parent of the same sex. In Greek *mythology*, Oedipus was abandoned at birth. He unwittingly killed his father and then unknowingly married his mother. The Swiss psychoanalyst Carl Jung (1875–1961) saw myth as an unconscious form of language giving expression to universal ideas, which he called *archetypes*. These ideas constitute the 'collective unconscious' of humanity and continue to manifest themselves in modern-day symbols, fictional characters, and the like. The 'trickster' archetype, for example, is found in stories we tell children, in character roles such as jokers and comedians, and so on. We relate intuitively to this archetype, without requiring any explanation of what a trickster is, because it is buried deeply in our collective unconscious.

Whether or not Frye, Lévi-Strauss, Freud, or Jung are right, one thing is for certain – the ideas expressed in the early myths have hardly disappeared from modern cultures. From them we have inherited, for instance, the names of the days of the week and months of the year: e.g. Tuesday is named after the Germanic war god Tir, Wednesday the chief god Wotan, Thursday Thor, Friday the goddess of beauty Frigga, Saturday the god Saturn, January the Roman god Janus. Our planets bear a similar pattern of mythic nomenclature: Mars is named after the Roman god of war, Venus after the Greek goddess of beauty, and so on. We continue to read horoscopes, implore the gods to help us, cry out against Fortune, and perpetuate numerological superstitions, such as avoiding the labelling of the thirteenth floor of a high-rise building with the number '13'. And, as Barthes pointed out, mythic themes are being constantly recycled by the mass media. Stories of heroes and villains, of legendary exploits and trials permeate media representations, from Disney's *Snow White* to contemporary wrestling spectacles. As the American mythologist Joseph Campbell (1904–87) aptly observed, the first myths explained the world in ways that continue to be intuitively understandable by everyone, no matter how literate or technologically sophisticated a person may be.

Written traditions

Writing originates in pictography. The earliest pictographic systems were used, in part, to represent mythic stories, characters, and symbols.

Pictographs are visual signs that stand for entire concepts; they are, in semiotic terms, visual signifiers representing signifieds directly (iconically). The earliest pictographs so far discovered come from the Neolithic era in western Asia. They are elemental shapes on clay tokens that were probably used as image-making casts (Schmandt-Besserat 1978).

One of the first pictographic systems to be employed regularly for a variety of practical social functions was the ancient Sumerian system around 3500 BC. It was a highly versatile system because it contained pictorial signs for abstract notions – 'to sleep', for example, was represented by a picture of a person in a supine position. It was thus used for such purposes as recording agricultural transactions, chronicling astronomical observations, educating children, writing laws, and preserving knowledge. Pictographs that stand for abstractions are called, more precisely, *ideographs*. The Sumerian ideographs were called 'cuneiform', which means 'wedge-shaped'. Their shape made it easier to inscribe them on clay tablets with a stylus. To facilitate the speed of writing even more, the Sumerians eventually streamlined their cuneiform signs into abstract characters standing for various sounds of words, rather than for the words themselves. The cuneiform system was subsequently adapted by the Assyro-Babylonian language, known as Akkadian, which became the language of mass communication in the ancient Middle East.

By about 3000 BC the Egyptians also started using a pictographic system, known as 'hieroglyphic', for many social functions – to record hymns and prayers, to register the names and titles of individuals and deities, (hieroglyphic derives from Greek *hieros*: 'holy' and *glyphein*: 'to carve'), to annotate various community activities, and so on. The Egyptian pictographs were both ideographic and phonographic, i.e. they could stand for some concept or for a consonant sound in a word representing a concept. A specific hieroglyphic sign might serve as an ideograph in one word and as a phonograph in another. Most words, moreover, were written with a combination of these two types of signs. Around 2700 BC, the Egyptians replaced hieroglyphic script with a form known as 'hieratic'. This was executed with blunt reed pens and ink on papyrus, rather than inscribed on tablets or on walls. A more cursive and ligatured script, called 'demotic', was developed a little later. Given the greater availability and affordability of papyrus, literacy came to be valued highly among common people, although it continued to be acquired mainly by privileged members of Egyptian society (priests, aristocrats, merchants, etc.).

Once pictographic writing became widely used in the ancient civilizations, it began gradually to evolve into a more stylized system, with 'compressed' pictorial features, so that it could be used more efficiently. From this development, the first true alphabetic system crystallized. An alphabet is a system of abstract symbols, called letters or characters, that stand not for entire concepts, but rather for the sounds that make up words. The most likely 'scenario' to explain the transition from a pictographic to an alphabetic system can be paraphrased somewhat as follows. As the hand movements employed to make pictographs became abbreviated to increase writing efficiency, and as familiarity with the abbreviated pictographs increased in the marketplaces of the ancient world, a more condensed form of pictography emerged to make transactions more efficient. So, for example, instead of drawing the full head of an ox, it became the practice at some point to draw only its bare outline. Eventually, this outline came to stand for the word 'ox' itself (*aleph* in Hebrew), and in due time just for the first sound in the word (*a* for *aleph*). The last stage occurred around 1000 BC. It was the ancient Phoenicians who compiled an abstract system of such signs for recording the consonant sounds that made up words. The Greeks adopted the Phoenician alphabet shortly thereafter, naming each character – *alpha, beta, gamma*, etc. These were imitations of Phoenician words – *aleph* 'ox', *beth* 'house', *gimel* 'camel', etc. The Greeks then introduced characters for vowel sounds, thus producing the first true alphabet, in the modern sense of the word. But, as this hypothetical scenario implies, in every alphabetic character that we use to record our thoughts, there is a pictographic story behind it that has become 'dim' or virtually 'undetectable' because our eyes are no longer accustomed to extracting pictorial content from it.

The alphabet is a truly remarkable achievement. It has made possible the efficient recording, preservation, and transmission of knowledge in the form of books. Whether they are written on parchment, papyrus, paper, or a computer screen, and regardless of what alphabet system is used, books are the basis for sustaining advanced civilizations. The first schools for the masses were, in fact, outgrowths of the invention of efficient print technologies, as were the first mass communications systems.

As McLuhan (1964) remarked, book literacy is also the source of the notion of *objectivity*. Unlike their oral ancestors, literate societies tend to perceive knowledge and ideas as separate from those who transmit them and, thus, that knowledge systems are self-contained collections of *objective* data. When listening to someone speak, McLuhan argued, we are inevitably influenced by the emotion of the human voice, overtly or unconsciously. As a consequence, we tend to perceive a direct link between what the speaker says (= the *object*) and who the speaker is (= the *subject*). On the other hand, when we read a book, we are not influenced by vocalism. What we perceive, as we read, is a written page, with its edges, margins, and sharply defined characters organized in neatly layered rows or columns. This dupes us into perceiving the content of the book (= the *object*) as separable from its author (= the *subject*), as does the additional fact that the author is not present during the reading process. This, McLuhan concluded, is what induces a state of mind, called *objectivity*, that tends to see the *subject* (= the maker of a representation) and the *object* (= the content of the representation) as separate entities.

The Gutenberg Galaxy

As we saw above, the first books were clay tablets. They were hard to produce and circulate. But with the advent of papyrus technology, a little later, books could be produced much more easily and circulated much more widely. Papyrus is a paper-like material made from a pith of reeds, formed into a continuous strip and rolled around a stick. The text was written on the strip with a reed pen in narrow columns on one side. It was unrolled as it was read. A little later, the scroll was subdivided into a number of shorter rolls and stored together in one container. In the first century AD, this method of producing books was replaced by the rectangular *codex*, a small, ringed book consisting of two or more wooden tablets covered with wax, which could be marked with a stylus, smoothed over, and reused many times. In the Middle Ages, codices were used primarily to record texts related to the observance of the Christian liturgy. Literacy remained a realizable goal only for a limited number of privileged people. All this changed, however, with the advent of paper technology and the printing press in the fifteenth century. Since books could be produced quickly and very cheaply, more and more people were encouraged to become educated and literate.

The printing press also led to a major paradigm shift in cultural evolution. As we saw in the opening chapter, McLuhan designated the new world order that it brought into existence, the Gutenberg Galaxy, after the German printer Johann Gutenberg (the inventor of the modern printing press). Through books and other print artefacts (newspapers, pamphlets, etc.) the written word became, after the fifteenth century, the primary means for propagating and storing knowledge and ideas. The printing press was, *ipso facto*, the technological innovation that led to the establishment of a worldwide order, or *metaculture*, based on print literacy, as ideas started to circulate far and wide, crossing political boundaries through the book medium. To this day, the primary means of disseminating new knowledge is through print. Paradoxically, as McLuhan (1962) observed, the emergence of a global print culture did not simultaneously eliminate orality – i.e. the use of the spoken word for a variety of social functions in addition, of course, to oral conversation. We still communicate basic ideas to children orally; and within our mainstream print culture, various groups have formed 'neotribal subcultures' (such as gangs), which are essentially oral in organization.

Books

Because books are material objects, they can be preserved in 'book museums' known as libraries. The latter originated in the Middle East between 3000 and 2000 BC – at about the same time that pictographic writing started playing an increasingly vital role in ancient societies. One of the largest of the ancient libraries was built by the Greeks in Alexandria in the third century. By the second century AD public and private libraries had been established in many parts of the ancient world. A few centuries later, scientific and mathematical texts were copied and preserved in libraries by Muslim scholars, leading to the rise of scholarship and, eventually, to the rise of universities in the late eleventh century.

With the rise of literacy came a concomitant need to organize the knowledge contained in books. This led to the invention of the 'encyclopedia', a term originally referring to instruction in all branches of knowledge. The oldest encyclopedia still in existence is the *Natural History* (79 AD) by Roman writer Pliny the Elder (AD 23–79). The modern type of encyclopedia was largely the result of the Enlightenment movement in the eighteenth century, which entrenched the view of knowledge as information that could be arranged logically according to key words, names, or special topics – clearly, a view of the nature of knowledge that could only have crystallized in the Gutenberg Galaxy.

But knowledge preservation is not the only function that books have served. For at least five centuries, they have also been produced to serve as both literary art forms and mass distraction devices. The innumerable works of fiction known as novels that have come down to us since the medieval period have been read, and continue to be read, by millions of people for the pure enjoyment of it.

Book publishing

The Sumerians and Egyptians introduced many of the conventions that we use today in producing books, such as the use of a 'cover page' with the title and the author's name on it. Professional scribes, who either copied a text or set it down from dictation, were responsible for book reproduction. The ancient Greeks, and later the Romans, became aware of the mass communication potential of books; but the books they produced were prohibitively expensive and thus were owned chiefly by temples, rulers, and a few rich individuals. Most education at the time, and for centuries thereafter, was still conducted by oral repetition and memorization. Literacy remained mainly the privilege of the rich and powerful.

In the early Middle Ages in Europe, books were produced chiefly by clerics for other clerics and for rulers. They were written out with a quill pen by monks working in the *scriptoria* (Latin for 'writing rooms') of monasteries. They were made either with wooden covers fastened with clasps or bound in leather; and often they were adorned with gems. Such books were *objets d'art*. They were commissioned by the very small percentage of the population that could afford them and that knew how to read.

As mentioned, in the fifteenth century two technological developments revolutionized the production and publication of European books. One was paper; the other was the printing press. These simplified book publication and made it economically feasible and relatively easy for people to possess books. As a consequence, public literacy increased greatly. In the sixteenth century, Italian printers adopted certain conventions that have persisted in book publishing practices to this day. These included the use of light pasteboard covers, regularized layouts, Roman and Italic typefaces, a title page, and a preface. Gradually, a table of contents, list of illustrations, explanatory notes, bibliography, and index were added to scholarly books. The idea of book genres also emerged at about the same time, as books were being written not only for religious or scientific purposes, but also more and more for public edification and diversion.

By the time of the Industrial Revolution vast numbers of books could be published at a relatively low cost, as printing and paper technologies became highly efficient. The book had become an item of mass consumption. While other media challenged paper-based books in the twentieth century, they have shown a remarkable 'staying power'. To this day, they remain primary tools for the preservation and dissemination of knowledge, as well as sources for artistic expression and mass distraction.

The novel

The first type of book designed for mass appeal emerged in the medieval period. Known as the 'fiction novel' (from Latin *fingere* 'to form, make, put together'), in the centuries since its invention it has curiously developed into one of the most popular literary art forms of humanity. It also was the first true 'mass distraction artefact' of the emerging pop culture at the start of the twentieth century – an era when 'pulp fiction' novels were written with no other purpose in mind than to appeal to mass audiences and, thus, to be discarded and replaced by new ones regularly. To this day, pulp fiction genres – detective, crime, science fiction, romance, thriller, and adventure novels – fill the shelves of bookstores, and continue to be among the most popular sources of pleasurable reading for vast audiences. And, in the broader contemporary media context, these are the genres that have proven to be the most enduring in cinema and on radio and television.

The novel is a *narrative* text. As such, it tells a story that represents a situation that is supposed to mirror true life or else to stimulate the imagination. Often, it makes direct or indirect reference to other texts in the course of the telling. This imparts upon it a sense of interconnectedness to the larger signifying order within which it is conceived. In recent semiotic theory, this aspect of narrativity is referred to as *intertextuality*. An intertext is another narrative text to which a novel alludes by citation or implication. It is a text from outside the main text, so to speak. A novel may also contain a *subtext*, a story implicit within it that drives the surface narrative. For example, the main text of the movie *Blade Runner* (chapter 5) unfolds as a science fiction detective story, but its subtext is, arguably, a religious one – the search for a Creator. This interpretation is bolstered by the many intertextual allusions to Biblical themes and symbols in the movie.

As mentioned, the first true fiction books were written in the Middle Ages. That was the era in which people started inventing imaginary tales and writing them down for other people to enjoy. Before the Middle Ages, people may have indeed told quasi-fictional stories, such as fables, tales, and legends, but these did not serve the same function that medieval fiction served – the telling of stories for the sake of the telling. The ancient stories, on the other hand, were imaginative portrayals (or satires) of mythic themes and legendary heroes, or else they had some pedagogical function, such as instilling morals and ethics in children and adults alike. Papyri from the fourth Egyptian Dynasty reveal how King Cheops (2590–2567 BC) delighted in hearing the stories that his sons told him about imaginary heroes. The Greek statesman and general Aristides (530?–468? BC) wrote a collection of what we would now call 'short stories' about his hometown, Miletus, to celebrate the Greek victory over the Persians at Salamis. The Roman Apuleius (AD 125?–200?) wrote a collection of stories, called the *Golden Ass*, in order to provide social and moral commentary.

Actually, for the sake of historical accuracy, it should be mentioned that many literary scholars regard the eleventh century *Tale of Genji*, by the Japanese baroness Murasaki Shikibu (AD 978?–1026?), as the first true novel, since it recounts the amorous adventures of a fictional Prince Genji and the staid lives of his descendants. The novel paints a charming and apparently accurate picture of Japanese court life in the Heian period. Its greatest strength lies in its characterization of the women in Prince Genji's life. As the work nears its conclusion, the tone becomes mature and sombre, coloured by Buddhist insights into the fleeting joys of earthly existence.

Fiction became a widespread narrative craft, however, only after the publication of Giovanni Boccaccio's (1313–75) *Decameron* in 1353, a collection of 100 fictional tales set against the gloomy background of the Black Death, as the bubonic plague that swept through Europe in the fourteenth century was called. The *Decameron* is the first real work of fiction in the modern sense of the word. To escape an outbreak of the plague, ten friends decide to take refuge in a country villa outside Florence. There, they entertain one another over a period of ten days by telling made-up stories in turn. Each day's storytelling ends with a *canzone*, a short lyric poem. With the emergence of the so-called *picaresque* genre in sixteenth century Spain – in which a hero is portrayed typically as a vagabond who goes through a series of exciting adventures – the novel became a staple of European society. The classic example of the picaresque genre is the enigmatic novel by Spanish writer Miguel de Cervantes Saavedra (1547–1616), *Don Quixote de la Mancha* (Part I, 1605, Part II, 1615), which is considered by many to be the first novel masterpiece of the Western world.

Ever since, fictional writing has been considered a yardstick for probing human actions and human character. This is probably because we feel intuitively that narrative structure reflects the structure of real-life events as we experience them: i.e. we feel that narrative structure is already implicit in the form of the actions and events that are manifest in actual human lives. We even tend to perceive bestseller novels, Harlequin romances, detective fiction, and the like as telling us something important about ourselves, even though we read them for pure entertainment or titillation.

The novel became a dominant artistic medium in the eighteenth and nineteenth centuries, as more and more writers started devoting their lives to it. Novels became more psychologically real, depicting and often satirizing contemporary life and morals. During the same era, many new genres emerged, including the didactic novel, in which theories of education and politics were expressed, and the Gothic novel, in which the emotion of horror was evoked by depictions of supernatural happenings. The first Gothic novel was *The Castle of Otranto* (1764) by Horace Walpole (1717–97). But perhaps the most well-known example of the genre is *Frankenstein* (1818) by Mary Wollstonecraft Shelley (1797–1851). An enduring genre of the period is the comedy of manners, which is concerned with the clash between characters from different social backgrounds. The novels of Jane Austen (1775–1817) are considered by many to be the finest exemplars of that genre.

Throughout the nineteenth century, and for most of the twentieth, the novel emerged as a powerful medium for probing human nature and human society. Novelists were as popular and well known as media personalities are today. Their critiques of society led to social change; and their portrayal of human behaviours gave the early scientific psychologists key insights into how to investigate human character. The French writer Marcel Proust (1871–1922), for instance, explored the nature of memory; the German author Thomas Mann (1875–1955) searched for the roots of psychic angst in social systems; and English authors Virginia Woolf (1882–1941) and James

Joyce (1882–1941) plumbed the emotional source of human thoughts and motivations. Some writers, like August Strindberg (1849–1912) and Frank Wedekind (1864–1918), even viewed the novel as having no other purpose than to give human concepts and feelings material form. Since the end of the Second World War the novels of an increasing number of writers from developing or socially troubled countries have come to the forefront. Many of these portray, with vivid realism and eloquent language, the clash between classes and races, the search for meaning in a world where materialism reigns supreme, and the desire to reform the world.

Narrative techniques in novels vary from simple first-person storytelling to complex stream-of-consciousness narration, which is designed to reveal a character's hidden feelings, thoughts, and actions. Not to be confused with interior monologue, stream-of-consciousness writing attempts to portray the remote, preconscious state that exists before the mind organizes sensations. Major exponents of the genre are American novelist William Faulkner (1897–1962), British writer Virginia Woolf, and Irish writer James Joyce (mentioned above), who perhaps brought the genre to its highest point of development in *Ulysses* (1922) and *Finnegans Wake* (1939). In these novels, the inaccessible corners of human memory and the hidden repertory of feelings within the psyche are laid bare before us. The conflicts, fantasies, and daydreams of Joyce's characters are those of ordinary people. The French philosopher and writer Jean-Paul Sartre (1905–80) viewed such writing as an 'escape hatch', so to speak, from inner psychic turmoil, because he saw it as eradicating the guilt from which people ordinarily suffer, thus opening the way towards genuine emotional freedom.

The serious study of fiction within semiotics can be traced to the work of Vladimir Propp (1928), who argued persuasively that ordinary discourse was itself built upon narrative structure. According to Propp, there exist a relatively small number of 'narrative units', or plot themes, which go into the make-up of a 'plot grammar' that allows readers to immediately recognize the genre being read. The term sometimes used to refer to these units is *narremes*. For example, fairy tales are recognizable as such because they have the following recurring characteristics:

- They take place in an indeterminate time frame, hence they typically start with *Once upon a time . . .*.
- Imaginary creatures and beings intermingle in the plots.
- The Good fight in a battle with the Evil doers.
- The setting involves both the real world and a supernatural one.
- A hero is tested and must overcome some challenge through trial and persecution.
- Having overcome the test, the story ends *Happily ever after*.

There are actually 31 such characteristics specified by Propp. Propp's theory would, in effect, explain why narrative is the medium through which children learn about the world. Stories of imaginary beings and events allow children to make sense of the real world, providing the intelligible formats that mobilize their natural ability to learn from context. With his pivotal research on early childhood learning, the psychologist Jerome Bruner (1986) showed that narrative thinking underlies how children come to understand their relation to the social world in which they live. Narratives give pattern and continuity to the child's raw perception and experience of things. They impart the sense that there is a *plot* to life, that the *characters* in it serve some meaningful purpose, and that the *setting* of their life is part of the human condition.

After Propp, the scholar who most influenced the study of narrative within semiotics was Algirdas Julien Greimas (1917–92). Greimas claimed that the stories of different cultures were devised with virtually the same stock of actions, characters, motifs, themes, and settings, which he called *actants*. Here are a few of them:

- a *subject* (the hero of the plot)
- who desires an *object* (a sought-after-person, a magic sword, etc.)
- and who encounters an *opponent* (a villain, a false hero, a trial situation, etc.)
- and then finds a *helper* (a donor)
- who then gets an *object* from a *sender* (a dispatcher)
- and gives it to a *receiver*
- and so on.

Several characters can represent an actant, or several actants can be represented by one and the same character. In a mystery novel, for instance, the subject, or hero, may have several enemies, all of whom function actantially as an opponent. In a love story, a male lover may function as both object and sender. An actantial analysis of the novel *Madame Bovary* (1857) by Gustave Flaubert (1821–80), for instance, would start by classifying its characters as follows:

- *subject*   =   Emma
- *object*   =   happiness
- *sender*   =   romantic literature
- *receiver*   =   Emma
- *helper*   =   Léon, Rodolphe
- *opponent*   =   Charles, Yonville, Rodolphe, Homais, L'heureux

The theory of actants is interesting beyond semiotics because it implies that buried deep within us are narrative structures. This might explain why novels have such impact on readers. Children are sometimes named after characters in novels, real places after places described in novels, and so on. The general meaning of the novel, moreover, is often used as an interpretant for evaluating some real-life event or action. This is why we compare people to fictitious characters in novels. It is amazing indeed to contemplate that a text that is essentially a lie (fiction) is used nevertheless to get at the truth, about people, life, and the universe.

Opposed to the view of fictional narrative as a mirror of life created by its author is the French philosopher Jacques Derrida (1930–). In essence, Derrida claims that, because there are an infinite number of legitimate interpretations of a narrative text, it is useless to try to figure out what an author wanted to say. But, contrary to what Derrida believes, common sense tells us that the meaning of a text is not open-ended. Concretely speaking, it is unlikely that anyone today would interpret John Bunyan's (1628–88) novel, the *Pilgrim's Progress*, as an erotic tale. While someone reading it with 'modern eyes' would not see the same kinds of Christian meanings that seventeenth century readers saw in it, one would still not interpret it in vastly different terms.

The novel entered the domain of mass pop culture in the early years of the twentieth century with the rise in popularity of the detective novel and of the many subgenres that it spawned, from spy thrillers to apocalyptic tales. The appeal of this genre lies in how it recycles the hero actant as a private detective or a police officer, through whom the story is told either as a first-person narration or in the third person by the author. The detective interrogates suspects, ferrets out the clues, and tracks down the criminal, sharing all the clues with the reader, but withholding their significance until the end. The detective is a hero for the modern age. He or she is not a 'supernatural being' as was Prometheus, but an ordinary human endowed with extraordinary powers of logic and insight. The detective story thus has a wide appeal because it recycles the basic actantial features of the narrative – hero vs. opponent, etc. – for audiences intrigued by crime and the psychology of evil.

The originator of this genre was American short-story writer Edgar Allan Poe (1809–49), creator of the world's first fictional detective, C. Auguste Dupin. Dupin first appeared in 1841, in Poe's *The Murders in the Rue Morgue*. In England, novelist Wilkie Collins (1824–89) created the detective character Sergeant Cuff in *The Moonstone* (1868). Shortly thereafter, novels about crime, espionage, mystery, and the like could literally not be kept on the bookstore shelves, on account of their rising popularity. Some cultural historians even credit this genre of storytelling as ushering in the era of pop culture. From Sherlock Holmes by British writer Sir Arthur Conan Doyle (1859–1930) and Hercule Poirot by his compatriot Agatha Christie (1891–1976), to the lawyer detective Perry Mason by American writer Erle Stanley Gardner (1889–1970), among many others, the detective hero is a 'representamen' of the modern age.

He or she is human, smart, and out to set things right, not in any metaphysical way, but in a strictly human scientific (forensic) way. Along with romance and science fiction novels, the detective story and its subgenres (the thriller, the espionage tale, etc.) continue to be among the most enduring narrative distraction devices of current-day pop culture. And, as we shall see in chapter 5, they continue to be sources of movie and other media narratives. Indeed, in today's mediated culture, cinema and TV have taken a large part of the novel's narrative appeal. But paper-based novels are still a thriving business. And, in this era of media convergence, more often than not a best-selling novel is the inspiration for a movie script. In many ways, a movie can be defined as a 'visual novel', with the role of the narrator taken over by the camera, and narrative perspective by the camera's angle.

Electronic books

Since the late 1970s, the publishing technologies available in the Digital Galaxy have had an impact on the traditional 'book culture'. Not only has computer-based production largely taken over from traditional typesetting in the publication of paper books, but it is now also becoming more and more frequent to write books directly on the computer and publish them in cyberspace as *e-books* ('electronic books').

E-books and *CD-ROMs* are, by and large, electronic versions of traditional books. However, there is one fundamental difference. Known as *hypertextuality*, e-books and CD-ROMs allow readers to link different texts and images within the main text. Thus, for example, an encyclopedia in CD-ROM form allows a user to go from one topic to another within a page of text by simply clicking on them. If a reader wants to check, say, the meaning of a word on a page in a traditional book, he or she will have to physically consult another source (such as a dictionary). Hypertextuality has made such a task much more practicable and efficient.

Hypertextuality is also leading to a redefinition of the roles of the author and the reader of a text. Hypertextual novels allow for multiple plot twists to be built into a story. They also enable readers to observe the story unfold from the perspective of different characters. Readers may also change the story themselves to suit their interpretive fancies by navigating hypertextually through it as they so please. In such novels, the author sets a framework for the narrative; but the actual narrative is realized by the reader.

CD-ROMs and e-books can store the equivalent of hundreds of paper books. To store the new digital formats, cyber-libraries have already sprung up and may eventually replace traditional libraries. Since anyone can download new books from the Internet directly, the purchase of e-books is also extremely easy and convenient. For this reason, many culture theorists predict that e-books will gradually replace traditional paper-based books. However, for the time being the paper book is still highly popular. For one thing, it is perceived by many as an *objet d'art*. It is something that people apparently want to display in their homes and offices as they would a sculpture or a photograph. It is also still comparatively convenient to hold and carry. So, traditional books will continue to have a market value, so long as paper remains cheap and available. However, the lesson to be learned from studying the development of media technologies is that there is never a 'turning back the clock', once an innovation is introduced into human life that enhances a product's versatility and functionality. For the present time, however, an audience for traditional books will continue to exist, because it seems that people simply continue to enjoy reading and buying them. Purchasing books at a bookstore today, moreover, is a diverting and distracting experience in itself – something that bookstore chains have come to realize, as witnessed by the fact that they have joined forces with coffee chains. There is something cultivated and *recherché* about sipping an espresso coffee and reading a 'real' book.

Newspapers

The main function of newspapers, as the name implies, is to report the news. However, modern-day newspapers provide a lot more than news reporting – they give commentary on the news, express opinion through their editorial sections, pass on special information and advice to readers, and often include features such as comic strips and serialized novels.

Newspapers are big business. In the US, for example, about 1700 daily newspapers print a total of 63 million copies, and almost every copy is read by more than one person. Some 6800 weekly newspapers are also published, with a combined circulation of approximately 40 million. Statistics show that nearly 8 out of 10 adult Americans read a newspaper every day. Similar per capita figures exist for all industrialized countries of the world. Throughout its history, the newspaper medium has been an intrinsic component of mass culture, functioning both as a distraction device (providing entertaining reading of all kinds) and as a source of social consciousness – newspapers such as *The Times* or the *New York Times*, for instance, have managed to maintain a long tradition of press freedom and to raise social consciousness on issues of general concern.

The newspaper is a special kind of text which, for lack of a better word, can be called a *syntext*. This can be defined as a text that imparts the illusion of connectivity among what would otherwise be perceived as fragmented random texts by simply synthesizing them in an organized fashion. As such, newspapers provide reassurance that there is a singular purpose to things, by bringing together crime stories, accident reports, movie and book reviews, advertisements, and many more things that make up daily life. By arranging these neatly into 'rubrics', the newspaper syntext superimposes a logical structure on them, creating a sense that there is pattern to them. Newspaper publishers know this and this is why they provide commentary to their news stories, highlighting the 'human psychology' of certain crimes, the 'metaphysical nature' of certain events such as storms and disasters, and so on.

Newspaper publishing

Handwritten newssheets posted in public places in the ancient world are considered to be the forerunners of newspapers. The earliest known daily newssheet was the *Acta Diurna* ('Daily Events'), which was widely distributed in 59 BC Rome. The world's first true printed newspaper was a Chinese circular called *Dibao*. It was produced on carved wooden blocks around 700 AD. The first regularly published paper-based newspaper in Europe was the *Avisa Relation oder Zeitung*, which started publication in Germany in 1609. The newspaper business started expanding throughout Europe in the seventeenth and eighteenth centuries. By the late 1800s, competing newspapers in large cities tried to outdo one another with sensational reports of crimes, disasters, and scandals.

Newspapers depend for survival on getting as many copies of an issue out quickly, efficiently, and as widely-distributed as possible. Ironically, as popular as the newspaper is as a syntext, today high operating expenses, especially the rising cost of labour and newsprint, have driven many newspapers out of business. Few cities now have competing dailies. In those that do, rival publishers typically print their papers on the same presses to reduce costs. Financial problems have hit major metropolitan papers the hardest, in large part because they face increasing competition from suburban papers and from TV newscasts. Some big-city papers now publish morning and afternoon editions in an effort to gain wider readership.

To remedy the decline in profits, newspapers have adopted digitization technology *en masse* – such as computerized word processing and layout systems – to produce issues. Reporters now typically write stories on portable computers and then send them to the office via a modem. The processes of making up the pages and printing the paper have also changed. For example, in some newspapers, the stories, photographs, and ads are inserted into the layout while it is still on the computer.

In 1980, *The Columbus (Ohio) Dispatch* became the first electronic newspaper in the US. In addition to printing a regular edition, the *Dispatch* began transmitting some of its editorial content to computers in the homes, businesses, and libraries of a small number of subscribers. Today, most papers have followed suit, offering online versions of their regular editions and even entire issues. However, as in the case of books, this has not brought about the end of paper-based newspapers. People still seem to want to read newspapers as they ride on public transport vehicles, as they wait for appointments in offices, as they sip coffee in coffee shops and in their homes, and in many other places. Newspapers will continue to be bought by consumers, so long as they remain cheap.

Newspaper signification systems

Newspapers have always been a powerful force in the Gutenberg Galaxy because, as mentioned above, people read them as meaningful syntexts. This might explain why the press has always been able to influence the opinion of the masses. One of the foremost examples of the 'power of the press' came in 1974 when President Richard Nixon resigned his office after revelations about the Watergate scandal involving his administration, which had first been brought to public attention by the *Washington Post*. No wonder, then, that the Watergate affair led to a rise in the popularity of investigative reporting, establishing it as a new genre in the newspaper syntext.

But perhaps the most prevalent function of newspapers in the world of mass communications today is not to provide a forum for a free flow of ideas, but rather to provide distraction. Indeed, to cope with the competition of instant news reports on radio and television, newspapers have become more diversified and intent on entertaining readers. They now not only give extensive background information to the news, and offer truly well-written documentaries and reviews of books, movies, etc., but they also attempt to embellish these in the same way that TV programmes do (with visual images, with catchy or sensationalistic headlines, etc.). Many people buy newspapers more for their advertising content than for the news; others read them for the comics section; others still cannot wait to solve the crossword puzzle that many newspapers put out daily. So, too, sports, lifestyle trends, classified information, entertainment news, reviews of books and movies, portraits of individuals, and many more rubrics provide an array of genres that rival TV for entertainment value.

Different types of newspapers attract different kinds of audiences. They are thus perceptibly different at the level of the signifier, i.e. in how they are put together, in what kind of language they use (in the headline style and in the actual writing of stories), and in how they present their written text (type font, size of fonts, types of photography used, etc.). Some newspapers, such as tabloids like the *Sun*, are intended to be more 'populist'; broadsheets like *The Times* are designed instead to be much more intellectual (see Table 3.1).

Table 3.1

Sun (populist syntext)	The Times (sophisticated syntext)
Headlines are large and informal.	Headlines are traditional and formal.
Writing style is colloquial and characterized by slang features.	Writing style is more refined and sophisticated.
Reporting is sensationalistic and graphic.	Reporting is subdued and rational.
Many 'bawdy' topics and features are included (such as a 'Sunshine Girl').	Prurient topics and advertising are treated with discretion and prudence.

On average, newspapers devote almost half of their space to advertising. Many adults read a daily newspaper specifically to check the ads for information about products, services, or special sales. The *London Gazette* became the first newspaper to reserve a section exclusively for advertising over three hundred years ago. So successful was this venture that by the end of the seventeenth century several agencies came into existence for the specific purpose of creating newspaper ads for merchants and artisans. In general, they designed the ad texts in the style of modern classifieds, without illustrative support. But the ads nonetheless had all the persuasive rhetorical flavour of their contemporary descendants. The ad makers of the era catered to the wealthy clients who bought and read newspapers, promoting the sale of tea, coffee, wigs, books, theatre tickets, and the like. The following advertisement for toothpaste dates back to a 1660 issue of the *Gazette*. What is captivating about it is the fact that its rhetorical style is virtually identical to the one used today for the promotion of this type of product (cited by Dyer 1982: 16–17):

> Most excellent and proved Dentifrice to scour and cleanse the Teeth, making them white as ivory, preserves the Tooth-ach; so that being constantly used, the Parties using it are never troubled with the Tooth-ach. It fastens the Teeth, sweetens the Breath, and preserves the Gums and Mouth from cankers and Impothumes ... and the right are only to be had at Thomas Rookes, Stationer.

Print advertising spread rapidly throughout the eighteenth century in both Europe and America, proliferating to the point that the writer and lexicographer Samuel Johnson (1709–84) felt impelled to make the following statement in *The Idler*: 'Advertisements are now so numerous that they are very negligently perused, and it is therefore become necessary to gain attention by magnificence of promise and by eloquence sometimes sublime and sometimes pathetic' (cited by Panati 1984: 168).

As print advertising became a fixture of the social landscape in the pre-industrialized world, ad creators began paying more attention to the design and layout of the ad text to be inserted in newspapers. With the spread of newspapers in the nineteenth century, style of presentation became increasingly important in raising the persuasive efficacy of a particular newspaper's advertising pitches. The syntactically cumbersome and visually-uninteresting ads of the previous century were replaced more and more by layouts using words set out in blocks, compact sentences, and contrasting type fonts. New language forms were coined regularly to fit the needs of the advertiser. As a consequence, newspaper advertising was surreptitiously starting to change the very structure and use of language and verbal communication, as more and more people became exposed to advertising not only in newspapers, but also in magazines. Everything from clothes to beverages was being promoted through ingenious new verbal ploys such as:

- strategic repetitions of the firm's name or of the product in the composition of the ad text;
- the use of compact phrases set in eye-catching patterns (vertically, horizontally, diagonally);
- the use of contrasting font styles and formats, along with supporting illustrations;
- the creation of slogans and neologisms designed to highlight some quality of the product.

As the nineteenth century came to a close, newspaper advertisers in particular were, as Dyer (1982: 32) aptly points out, using 'more colloquial, personal and informal language to address the customer' and also exploiting certain effective rhetorical devices including 'the uses of humour to attract attention to a product'. So persuasive had this new form of advertising become that, by the early decades of the twentieth century, it had become a major source of influence in how people communicated with each other.

As the newspaper became a part of mass culture in the late nineteenth century, newspaper writers and advertisers became the new wordsmiths for the larger society. And newspaper reading itself became a kind of prerequisite for being knowledgeable about the world. The overall signified that the newspaper syntext builds into itself is that of 'information savvy'. To this day, there is a widely-held perception that to know what is going on in the world one must read about it in the newspaper. However, the 'credibility' of newspapers varies greatly, from such high-brow papers as *The Times* or the *New York Times*, which purport to explain events in objective terms, to those that have a more grassroots appeal, such as the newspapers in the US and Britain with the term *Sun* in their title (as discussed above), which present the same events in more sensationalistic and populist terms.

The multiplicity of signifieds in a newspaper leads readers typically to perceive its overall content as a blur. Paradoxically, this blur becomes 'focalized' after we have read the newspaper, since from the reading process we still get the sense that we know 'what is going on', even though we hardly remember anything of what we have read.

Magazines

As stimulating and diverting as books and newspapers can be, they can never match the immediate and powerful visual appeal of magazines. So popular are magazines as mass communication and distraction artefacts that, today, they have spawned a unique category of descendants, known as 'fanzines' or simply 'zines', which have started to crop up just about everywhere one looks. These are magazines created by people who are enthusiastic about a topic, usually a hobby.

A magazine is a collection of articles or stories published at regular intervals. Most magazines include illustrations. They provide a wide variety of information, opinion, and entertainment for mass consumption. For example, they may cover current events and fashions, discuss foreign affairs, or describe how to repair appliances or prepare food. Some magazines seek simply to entertain their readers with fiction, poetry, photography, cartoons, or articles about television shows or motion-picture stars; others provide 'professional' information and counselling to those working in certain areas of employment (from automobile mechanics to medical practice).

Magazines, like newspapers, represent the work of various writers, not a single author. But magazines are designed to be kept much longer than newspapers. For this reason, most have a smaller page size and are printed on better paper. In content, magazines often have less concern with daily, rapidly changing events than do newspapers. Most have a cover featuring a photograph or a drawing rather than news stories. Writing of different types – ranging from factual or practical reporting to a more personal or emotional style – is a basic characteristic of the magazine syntext. Some of the best writers have contributed either occasionally or regularly to magazines. And many well-known authors published their early works in them.

Magazine publishing

The earliest magazines published include the German *Erbauliche Monaths-Unterredungen* (1663–68), the French *Journal des Sçavans* (1665), and the

English *Philosophical Transactions* (1665) of the Royal Society of London. They were essentially collections of essays on issues and trends related to art, literature, philosophy, and science. Among the most widely read of the essay periodicals of the seventeenth century were the British publications *The Tatler* (1709–11) and *The Spectator* (1711–14) – creations of the renowned essayists Richard Steele (1672–1729) and Joseph Addison (1672–1719) – and *The Rambler* (1750–52) and *The Idler* (1758–60), founded by Samuel Johnson (1709–84). In the latter part of the eighteenth century, such periodicals developed into general purpose information publications. With the printing of *The Gentleman's Magazine* (1731–1907) in England, the modern-day magazine entered the Gutenberg Galaxy. That event also marked the first use of the word 'magazine', denoting a forum for 'entertaining reading'. It contained reports of political debates, essays, stories, and poems.

By the mid-nineteenth century, the publication of magazines intended for general audiences grew considerably. *Godey's Lady's Book* (1830–98), for example, with its colourful fashion illustrations, was vastly influential in setting the style in women's clothing, manners, and taste. The *Illustrated London News* (1842), the *Fortnightly Review* (1865–1954), *Punch* (1841–) in England, *L'Illustration* in France (1843–1944), *Die Woche* (1899–) in Germany, and *Leslie's Illustrated Newspaper* (1855–1922) and *Harper's Weekly* (1857–) in the United States became regular staples of an emerging affluent middle class of readers. *Youth's Companion* (1827–1929) and later *St Nicholas* (1873–1940) were among several children's magazines published in the same era that became highly popular for imparting literacy skills to children. To this day, children's magazines are published for the same reason. Family magazines such as the *Saturday Evening Post* (1821–) also became vastly popular with the public at large.

With the publication of *Cosmopolitan* (1886–) in the US, the 'fashion magazine' for women came into being. Between 1902 and 1912, this genre dominated American periodical publishing – betraying the fact that women stayed at home and, thus, had the time to engage in pleasurable reading. In addition to *Cosmopolitan*, female readers could choose from *Ladies'* (later *Woman's*) *Home Companion* (1873–1957), *McCall's Magazine* (1876–), *Ladies' Home Journal* (1883–), *Good Housekeeping* (1885–), and *Vogue* (1892–) to while away the leisure hours. Shortly thereafter, the pocket-sized *Reader's Digest* (1922–) began publication, confirming the fact that people had increasingly little time to read entire novels. With the 'digested summaries' that *Reader's Digest* published regularly, readers could indulge their need for narrative and, at the same time, to make up their minds as to whether or not to buy and read an entire novel. Since the 1950s, this periodical has had a monthly circulation in the millions. Two other significant developments, dating from the 1920s and 1930s, were the establishment of weekly news magazines, such as *Time* (1923) and *Newsweek* (1933), and of weekly and biweekly magazines, illustrated with photographs, such as *Life* (1936–72, revived as a monthly in 1978), *Look* (1937–71), and *Ebony* (1946–), which focuses on issues of African American concern.

Today, magazine publishing is firmly established worldwide. In Japan, for instance, several thousand titles of all varieties are published regularly; in Africa periodicals in the African languages as well as in English and French are published on a regular basis. There are also many special-interest magazines today including: *Consumer Reports* (1936–), which offers comparative evaluations of consumer products; *TV Guide* (1953–), which provides weekly TV programme listings; *GQ* (1957–), which focuses on men's concerns; *Rolling Stone* (1967–), which is devoted to rock music; *Ms.* (1970–), which presents topics of concern to women; *People* (1974–), which features contemporary celebrities; *National Geographic* (1975–), which contains updated information on events from the worlds of science, history, and travel; *Discover* (1980–), which is a general audience magazine focusing on science; and *Wired* (1993–), which looks at issues pertaining to digital culture.

Predictably, in today's Digital Galaxy the magazine has converged with other media and has itself been transferred to the digital medium. *E-zines* (magazines published on the Internet) are proliferating. They have various advantages over paper-based magazines. For one thing, they can be put out much more quickly and updated regularly, thus allowing readers to keep constantly abreast of current events. Moreover, given the hypertextuality capacities of e-zines, they can be linked with other sources of information. The Internet also has created 'magazine chat rooms'. In early 2000, *Vogue* and *W* magazines created one of the first magazine chat websites, *Style.com*, where people could log on to get the latest gossip about the fashion industry.

A genre of magazine, which is a cross between a newspaper and a magazine, is the so-called 'tabloid'. This is usually half the ordinary size of a newspaper, with many pictures and short, sensational news stories. Tabloids have the same function as gossip and sensationalistic storytelling that once characterized village square congregations. They entertain audiences by adorning their narrations with sensationalism and exaggeration. Topics treated by tabloids involve such bizarre things as UFOs, alien visitations, religious apparitions, alongside melodramatic exposés of actor love affairs, sexual scandals, and the like.

Textual convergence

Although there are myriads of magazines that glut the market today, there is nevertheless an overriding feature that characterizes virtually all of them. It can be called 'textual convergence' – a feature whereby the content of ads and the content of the magazine are made to converge considerably, creating a sense of continuity between the products advertised and the articles of the magazine. For example, a photography magazine attracts camera fans who will undoubtedly find its ads helpful in choosing certain photographic equipment and, thus, who read the magazine in such terms. Advertisers of such equipment can thus reach many potential customers through the magazine by integrating their ad texts with the magazine's contents. But this convergence of product advertising with magazine contents is found not only in specialized magazines, but even in those that advertise different types of products:

- *Chanel* products, for instance, are related to the interests of female audiences who read magazines such as *Vogue*;
- *Nike* shoes are related to the interests of trendy adolescent and young adult audiences who read magazines such as *Seventeen*;
- *Audis* and *BMWs* are related to the interests of an up-scale class of automobile customers who read magazines such as *Esquire*;
- *Dodge* vans are related to the interests of a middle-class suburban consumer population who read magazines such as *Look*;
- and so on.

In no other genre is convergence so obvious as it is in the fashion magazine. The articles, illustrations, ads, and features in such magazines are concerned primarily with body image. In the late 1990s, women's magazines projected images of models in ads with a 'tough look' about them, similar to the one expected of their male counterparts in men's magazines, thus reflecting a new 'girl power' look that was manifest in other areas of pop culture, as for example in the look adopted by such pop music artists as the Spice Girls, Da Brat, Foxy Brown, L'il Kim, Courtney Love, Joan Jett, Patti Smith, and the members of L7. The girl power look was also embodied by female stars seen in television programmes and Hollywood movies, such as *Buffy the Vampire Slayer*, *Xena*, *Charlie's Angels*, and the like.

Just as interesting, in the same period some men's magazines started becoming more concerned about aspects of body image that, in previous generations, would have been considered 'girlish'. For example, *MH-18*, a male teen magazine that started publishing in the late 1990s, contained advice to boys on how to bleach or dye their hair and on what kind of cologne and jewellery to wear in certain situations – mirroring a concern about body image that, once, was considered to be purely within the domain of the female gender. Moreover, the popularity of boy bands such as 'N Synch, 98 Degrees, and Backstreet Boys, as well as Latino artists such as Ricky Martin and Julio Iglesias, Jr, made it acceptable for male teens to worry openly about their looks. Many magazines incorporated this new gender imagery effectively to boost sales.

The comics

In closing this chapter, a brief commentary on a type of paper-based magazine known as the 'comic book' is in order, for the reason that even today it stands out as a kind of overarching symbol of pop culture. Its predecessors are the caricatures or satirical portraits of famous people that became popular in seventeenth century Italy. Caricature art spread quickly throughout Europe shortly thereafter. In the early nineteenth century, these were expanded to include speech balloons, giving birth to the modern comic form, which had its 'golden age' between 1938 and 1945.

Comics are narratives told by means of a series of drawings arranged in horizontal lines, strips, or rectangles, called 'panels', and read like a verbal text from left to right. The term applies especially to comic strips in newspapers but also to comic books. Comics usually depict the adventures of one or more characters in a limited time sequence. Dialogue is represented by words encircled by a line, called a 'balloon', which issues typically from the mouth or head of the character speaking.

One of the first American works with the essential characteristics of a comic strip was created by Richard Felton Outcault and appeared in the series *Hogan's Alley*, first published on 5 May 1895, in the New York *Sunday World*. The setting the comic strip portrayed was squalid city tenements and backyards filled with dogs and cats, tough-looking characters, and ragamuffins. One of the urchins was a flap-eared, bald-headed, Oriental-looking child with a quizzical, yet shrewd, smile. He was dressed in a long, dirty nightshirt, which Outcault often used as a placard to comment on the cartoon itself. Two other early comics were the *Little Bears* by James Guilford Swinnerton, which first appeared in the San Francisco *Examiner* in 1892, and *The Katzenjammer Kids* by Rudolph Dirks, which first appeared in *The American Humorist* in 1897. Newly formed newspaper syndicates, such as King Features, founded in 1914, made the mass circulation of comics possible. Every small-town newspaper could obtain, for reprinting, templates of the strips from the syndicates, which employed comic-strip artists. Eventually American comic strips were distributed worldwide. *Blondie* by Chic Young became the most widely syndicated comic strip of the mid-twentieth century.

Mutt and Jeff first appeared as *Mr A. Mutt* in a November 1907 issue of the *San Francisco Chronicle*. That comic strip subsequently was introduced to a wide audience by newly formed newspaper syndicates, and it became the first successful daily comic strip in the United States. To satisfy demand, newspapers published collections of the cartoons, and a 1911 *Mutt and Jeff* collection was one of the first comic books to be published. But the first comic book published independently of any newspaper, containing material specially prepared for it, was *The Funnies*, which ran for thirteen issues in 1929. Starting in 1933, a number of comic books, which were reprints of well-known newspaper comic strips such as *Joe Palooka* and *Connie*, were published and distributed as premiums with certain merchandise. The first comic book to be sold on news-stands was the *Famous Funnies*. It appeared in 1934.

While the Sunday comics were primarily for children, the daily comic strip attracted adult audiences. Harry Hershfield's *Abie the Agent*, first published in 1914, has been called the first truly adult American comic strip, capitalizing on the popularity of the detective and mystery genre. One of the earliest and most influential contributors to the genre's evolution was Roy Crane, who created *Wash Tubbs* in 1924. The adventure genre began with the publication in 1929 of *Tarzan* and *Buck Rogers* – the former adapted from the novels of writer Edgar Rice Burroughs (1875–1950). *Gasoline Alley* by Frank O. King, marked a departure from the comic strip tradition that the cast of characters never ages; its characters aged day by day.

A great impetus was given to the publication of comic books by the phenomenal success in 1938 of *Action Comics,* of which the principal feature was the *Superman* comic strip, later published in *Superman* comic books. This was, as comic book historian Bradford W. Wright (2000) has argued, the comic-book industry's 'Big Bang'. Indeed, only a year after, *Superman* became a fixture not only on magazine stands, but on radio programmes. *Superman's* popularity spawned a series of comic-book hero clones in the early 1940s – the decade which saw the debuts of *Batman, The Flash, Green Lantern, Wonder Woman*, and *Captain America*. Since that time hundreds of comic books have been published, some containing collections of noted comic strips, others consisting of new material. Some deal with contemporary life; some are condensations of literary classics; still others are adventure stories.

Even before the advent of television, comics set the style for clothing, coiffure, food, manners, and mores. They have inspired plays, musicals, ballets, motion pictures, radio and television series, popular songs, books, and toys. Modern discourse is permeated with idioms and words created for the comics. For example, the code word for the Allied Forces on D-Day was 'Mickey Mouse', and the password for the Norwegian Underground was 'The Phantom'. Numerous contemporary painters and sculptors have incorporated comic-book figures into their art works; motion picture directors have adapted techniques of the comics into their films.

A number of strips have also found a devoted following among intellectuals. *Krazy Kat*, for instance, has been regarded by many as one of the most amusing and imaginative works of narrative art ever produced in America. The art of the late Charles Schultz (1922–99), too, falls into this category. His comic strip *Peanuts*, which was originally titled *Li'l Folks*, debuted in 1950, becoming one of the most popular comic strips of history, appearing in more than 2000 newspapers and translated into more than 24 languages. Schultz's characters – Charlie Brown, his sister Sally, his dog Snoopy, his friends Lucy, Linus, Schroeder, Peppermint Patty, and Marcie, and the bird Woodstock – have become icons of the modern world.

The comic book has also gone digital. Many online *e-toons*, as they are called, are essentially animated comics, featuring or parodying various traditional representations. For example, the e-toon *Gary the Rat* (Mediatrip.com) is about a ruthless New York lawyer who gets turned into a huge rat, in obvious parodic imitation of Franz Kafka's (1883–1924) horrifying masterpiece *Metamorphosis*. The rat is hated by his landlord, who wants to evict him, and chased by an exterminator who is out to eliminate him. Yet, Gary the rat is adored by his boss because clients are eager to work with him. *Queer Duck* (Icebox.com) satirizes the gullibility of people in listening to 'radio shrinks'. It is about a gay duck and his animal pals who are frequent crank callers to a well-known 'radio psychologist'. *The God and Devil Show* (Entertaindom.com) is a cartoon talk show hosted by a bearded ruler of heaven and a sexy leader of hell. Other popular online e-toons are: *The producer* (Thethreshold.com), which parodies media producers and production; *Kung Fu 3D* (Entertaindom.com), which is a web animation update of the American TV series starring David Carradine (1972–75); *The Critic* (Shockwave.com), which features an animated film critic who comments satirically on current movies and actors; and *Star Wars Network* (Atomfilms.com), which spoofs the whole distraction subculture spawned by the *Star Wars* movies of the late 1970s.

To conclude this chapter, it is obvious that print products continue to be popular, as we start the first decade of the twenty-first century, despite predictions of their demise. In 1732, Benjamin Franklin fingered booksellers as bringing about the demise of 'true books' because of the 'trash' they dealt in. More recently, tirades against a 'dumbing-down' of reading materials by social critics have led to similar dire predictions of literacy's demise (Epstein 2000).

If traditional print products are indeed ever going to vanish, it will not be on account of the qualities (or lack thereof) of writing itself, but because of the inevitable paradigm shifts that technology brings about. And that would be indeed ironic, for the shift from orality to writing that occurred barely five millennia ago was at first denounced as a threat to reason, memory, and the soul by philosophers such as Plato. As Eric Jager (2000: 15) has recently observed, the signs of literacy's demise may ironically have been captured by a media slogan of a late 1990s literacy campaign, 'Find Yourself in a Book', which signalled 'not only the book's demise as an actual medium for understanding ourselves and the world but also its fading relevance as a symbol in our collective imagination'.

4   Audio media

I am fond of music I think because it is so amoral. Everything else is moral
and I am after something that isn't. I have always found moralizing
intolerable.

Hermann Hesse (1877–1962)

From the swing dancing of the 1930s to the 'moshing' scenes of the 1990s,
where teens hurled themselves from the stage into the crowd, passed hand
over hand in front of the stage, the essence of so-called 'pop' music has always
been, as its name implies, entertainment for the masses. The rise of music as a
mass distraction art was made possible by the advent of recording and radio
broadcasting technologies at the start of the twentieth century. These brought
the Electronic Galaxy *ipso facto* into existence. In this Galaxy, records and
radio have made music available to large audiences, transforming it as
essentially an art for the élite to a commodity for all. What print technology
did for the written word, recordings and radio did for music – they made it
available cheaply to one and all, not just a privileged few.

Despite its apparent lack of 'classical good taste', people have always loved
pop music, no matter how controversial or crass it appeared to be to some.
But ultimately, most pop music is designed to be highly ephemeral, so that
new songs and new musical styles can be sold to mass audiences virtually
overnight. With few exceptions, along with TV programmes, blockbuster
movies, bestseller novels, fashion shows, and most commercial products, pop
songs and styles come and go quickly. Discussing the reason for this is one of
the objectives of this chapter. As in previous chapters, the focus of semiotic
analysis is on the meanings of audio genres, and especially the larger signifying
order systems of meaning that these entail.

Recorded music

Thomas Edison (1847–1931) invented the phonograph in 1877. A decade
later, in 1887, the German-born American inventor Emile Berliner

(1851–1929) improved Edison's model, producing the flat-disk phonograph, or gramophone, which was used shortly thereafter for recording music. About 1920, Berliner's mechanical technology began to be replaced by electrical recording and reproduction, in which the vibrations of the phonograph needle were amplified by electromagnetic devices.

By the 1920s, the cheapness and availability of mass-produced vinyl records led to a true paradigm shift in musical art – the entrenchment of pop music as mainstream music. New musical styles and idioms such as jazz, swing, country-and-western, soul, and rock are among the best known genres that recording technology helped to institutionalize. Since the 1920s, in fact, music has been perceived as a source of entertainment and distraction for mass audiences, not primarily as an art for the cognoscenti. Inevitably, as pop music styles proliferated throughout the century, so too did the tendency for audience fragmentation. Today, with so much music 'out there', music artists and producers know full well that their music will appeal primarily to specific audiences. As in the case of modern-day print media (chapter 3), the fragmentation of music audiences is a salient characteristic of the mediated culture in which we live.

The emergence of pop music

The origin of pop music can be traced to late eighteenth century America, when catchy tuneful music was composed on purpose by professional musicians for performance in parks in front of large gatherings of people (generally on Sunday afternoons). By the early nineteenth century, Italian opera had also become popular, influencing the development of the soft, sentimental type of singing known as 'crooning', which became widespread in the century. Before the advent of sound recordings, the primary medium of disseminating such music was printed sheet music. At the threshold of the twentieth century, the growing popularity of the pop music idiom created a flourishing music-publishing business centralized in New York City, in an area of lower Manhattan called Tin Pan Alley. The first Tin Pan Alley song to sell one million copies, *After the Ball* (1892) by Charles K. Harris, inspired rapid growth in the music-publishing industry. The early pop songs were simple, memorable, and emotionally appealing, attracting large audiences. Vaudeville became the most popular form of entertainment in American society, for the simple reason that one of its central components was the use of popular songs. At about the same time, so-called 'ragtime' pieces written by professional composers such as Scott Joplin (1868–1917) also became popular, introducing a truly powerful creative force that was to influence the development of mainstream pop music subsequently – namely, African American musical art.

A small cadre of composers and lyricists based in New York City produced the best-known songs of the 1920s and 1930s. In most cases, the two worked in pairs (George Gershwin and Ira Gershwin, Richard Rodgers and Oscar Hammerstein, Richard Rodgers and Lorenz Hart, etc.). Their songs were popularized in Broadway musical comedies, and by well-known singers accompanied by dance orchestras throughout society. With the growing popularity of vinyl recordings, such music quickly spread throughout the social landscape. Affordable and better-quality gramophone discs made recordings more popular than sheet music. Relatively unknown singers such as Bing Crosby and, later, Frank Sinatra became social icons overnight through the medium of records and radio broadcasts.

The African American influence on mainstream popular music became particularly evident during what came to be known as the Jazz Age, which preceded the Great Depression of the 1930s. In 1935, white jazz musician Benny Goodman boosted the popularity of the style with his band's recordings of jazz works. From 1935 to 1945, the dominant type of popular music was, in fact, big band swing, a style modelled on the innovations of black jazz orchestras. The 'big band era' ended after the Second World War (1939–45), although the influence of swing music could still be heard in the so-called 'jump band' rhythm and blues and swing music of the 1940s.

Important shifts in popular music after the Second World War were tied to social and technological changes. The massive migration of Southern musicians and audiences to urban areas and the use of the electric guitar were particularly influential in shifting the paradigm in American pop music. These set the stage for the hard-edged Chicago blues of Muddy Waters, the honky-tonk or 'hard-country' style of Hank Williams and, in the mid-1950s, the rise of rock-and-roll music.

Rock grew out of the intermingling of several streams of postwar popular music styles, including rhythm and blues, the recordings of blues 'shouters' such as Big Joe Turner, gospel-based vocal styles, boogie-woogie piano blues, and honky-tonk music. Promoted by entrepreneurs such as Alan Freed – who coined the term 'rock and roll' as a commercial pop music category – and recorded by small independent labels, rock was an unexpected success, attracting a newly affluent teenage audience in the mid-1950s. The pioneers of rock came from varied backgrounds. Bill Haley and the Comets, whose *Rock Around the Clock* (1955) was the first rock song to gain wide popularity through the medium of records, was a country-and-western bandleader; Fats Domino was a rhythm-and-blues artist; Chuck Berry was a hairdresser; and Elvis Presley was a truck driver. As will be discussed in more detail below, the 'golden era' of rock and roll – defined by the exuberant recordings of Haley, Berry, Domino, Presley, Little Richard, Jerry Lee Lewis, and Buddy Holly –

lasted from 1954 to 1959. The most successful artists wrote and performed songs about love, sexuality, identity crises, personal freedom, and other issues that were (and continue to be) of central concern to teenagers.

By the early 1960s most of what the music industry promoted as rock and roll was an imitation of the original form. The period also saw the development of distinctive regional styles, such as the sound of the southern California band the Beach Boys, the Greenwich Village urban folk movement that included the art of Bob Dylan, the Kingston Trio, and Peter, Paul, and Mary; and the rugged sound of Northwest groups such as the Sonics. Certainly, by this decade, audiences for crooning music, jazz, and other pop music forms were in decline. Rock was becoming the musical voice of larger and larger segments of the entire society. In one short decade, it had made its way to centre stage.

This became especially noticeable when the so-called 'British Invasion' began in 1964 with the arrival of the Beatles in New York City, and with the emergence of the 'rock group' as an artistic force. British pop bands, raised on the influence of blues, rhythm and blues, and early rock and roll, invigorated mainstream popular music, in part by reinterpreting the early classics of American rock. Each group developed a distinctive style: the Beatles combined Chuck Berry's guitar-based rock and roll into a sophisticated new style; the Animals combined blues and rhythm-and-blues styles to produce a hard-driving musical idiom; and the Rolling Stones incorporated aspects of Chicago urban blues into their distinctive, thrusting sound.

The late 1960s was a period of corporate expansion and stylistic diversification in the record industry. Pop music generally was being defined more and more as music for young people. Styles included not only the influential experiments of the Beatles, but also San Francisco psychedelia, guitar rock by Jimi Hendrix and Eric Clapton, Southern rock, hard rock, jazz rock, folk rock, and other styles. Soul music, the successor to rhythm and blues, covered a wide range of styles, including the gospel-based performances of Aretha Franklin, the funk techniques of James Brown, and the soulful crooning of Marvin Gaye. Country-and-western music – firmly centered in Nashville, Tennessee – produced a new generation of stars who combined elements of old country-and-western music standards with rock and roll. Johnny Cash, Waylon Jennings, and Dolly Parton helped contribute to the rising popularity of such music.

In the 1970s, glamorous superstars playing to massive crowds in sports arenas defined a new trend. A plethora of distinctive new styles – disco, glam rock, punk rock, new wave, reggae, funk, etc. – were pioneered by independent labels and creative musicians. As a consequence, by the end of the decade pop music became highly fragmented and thus much less profitable for record companies to sell to large homogeneous audiences. The music industry became cautious due to a drop in sales of recorded music by almost $1 billion between 1978 and 1982 and a similarly precipitous decline in income from live concerts.

A number of factors contributed to an economic revival in pop music during the mid-1980s. The advent of the music video – marked by the debut in 1981 of Music Television (MTV), a 24-hour music video channel – and the introduction of the digitally recorded compact disc in 1983 stimulated demand for popular music. The video-album *Thriller* (1982) by Michael Jackson became the biggest-selling artefact in pop music history up to that time, and it established a pattern by which record companies relied upon a few big hits to generate profits. Popular musicians of this period included Bruce Springsteen, the working-class bar-band hero; the artist formerly known as Prince, whose 1984 single *When Doves Cry* was the first song in more than twenty years to top both the mainstream pop charts and the black music charts; and Madonna, the iconoclastic performer from a working-class background who transformed herself into a controversial 'sex-kitten' pop icon.

Audiences for pop music became even more fragmented in the 1990s. Bands such as Blur, Oasis, Pearl Jam, REM and Radiohead continued the tradition of rock music. But it was rap and hip-hop, along with a recycling of jazz and other previous musical styles, that dominated the scene. Today, it is becoming increasingly obvious that each new pop music style and craze comes and goes quickly. Unlike the music of classical composers and perhaps of some jazz greats such as Louis Armstrong (1901–71), pop music generally has a very brief 'musical battery life', so to speak. This does not imply that many types of pop music are not highly influential and important art forms. However, the commercialization of such forms requires that they have a short life span, so that the economics of music recordings can be constantly renewed and thus made to be profitable. Simply put, most pop music is not designed to last.

For this reason, it is little wonder that jazz and even classical music made an unexpected comeback in the 1990s. The number of newly-formed record labels devoted to reissuing the classical music repertoire on CD was unprecedented. Their success was fuelled in large part by the repeated use of classical music by the movies. Labels such as Naxos and Chandos, for instance, became profitable. The renewed interest in jazz was highlighted by a brilliant 10-part television documentary on American PBS, by director Ken Burns, in early 2001. The main point made by the programme was that the jazz phenomenon not only dictated all subsequent pop music trends, but was also a mirror of twentieth century musical art. The TV programme was followed by a coffee-table book, a DVD boxed set, a five-disc CD companion, and a special series of 22 essential jazz artist compilations.

Pop music genres

Although music genres, recording stars, and hit songs change constantly, strong continuities can be detected within popular music. Most music genres today still draw upon: (1) the smooth, romantic vocal style of Tin Pan Alley; (2) the strong rhythms and emotional intensity of African American jazz, gospel, and blues music; and (3) the poetic themes and ballad forms of crooning and swing music. These are the elements of the pop music code that contemporary musicians incorporate, in one way or other, and to varying degrees, in the making of their music texts (whether they are consciously aware of it or not).

The promotion of jazz, blues, swing, show tunes, and Tin Pan Alley pop music from the 1920s to the 1950s was bolstered largely through the medium of radio, which broadcast music to large audiences, creating crazes overnight for new songs and performers. Especially influential in this regard was the advent of the 'Top 40' programme in the early 1950s, a radio format that played only top single records – the top 40 on record sales charts. This became the dominant radio format from the 1950s to the 1970s, uniting musical tastes across audiences, by promoting mainly rock and roll. As mentioned, by the 1980s audiences became highly fragmented. So, Top 40 radio gave way to many top 40 formats, one for each diverse style, from country to rap. Today, there are dozens of genres, each with its own 'hit parade' and each one promoted by specific record labels. They include the following:

- *Adult Contemporary:* a mix of oldies and softer rock hits (Celine Dion, the Backstreet Boys)
- *Contemporary Hit Radio:* mostly current hits, usually mixing pop (Mariah Carey) and rock (Metallica)
- *Country:* subdivided into traditional country (Dolly Parton), urban country (Dixie Chicks, Lee Ann Womack), and rock country (Shania Twain)
- *Modern rock:* current rock music split into its various branches: e.g. hard rock (Hole, Korn), industrial rock (Marilyn Manson), etc.
- *Rap and Hip-hop:* current works by rap and hip-hop stars such as Eminem, Will Smith, and many others
- *Oldies:* 1950s and 1960s rock songs
- *Classic Rock:* rock songs of the late 1960s (The Rolling Stones), 1970s (The Cars), and 1980s (Elvis Costello, The Police)
- *Rhythm and Blues:* rhythm and blues music by classic and contemporary performers (Tina Turner, Luther Vandross)
- *Experimental:* rock and folk promoted mainly by college and university radio stations

- *Latin:* music composed and performed by Hispanic artists (Pepe Aguilar, Ricky Martin, Christina Aguilera, Jennifer Lopez)
- *Classical music:* music intended for lovers of the great composers (Bach, Mozart, Beethoven, etc.)
- *Jazz and Blues:* jazz and blues music intended to appeal to lovers of both current (Herbie Hancock) and traditional (Louis Armstrong) jazz and blues artists
- *Gospel:* gospel music intended to appeal to lovers of both current and traditional gospel performers

In addition to the above largely American-based typology, the music styles of other countries has started gaining widespread appeal through recordings, radio, and television. The Argentine tango gained worldwide popularity during the 1910s, initiating a craze for Latin ballroom dancing in Paris, London, and New York City. Similarly, the Cuban rumba became popular around the world in the 1930s primarily through recordings and radio. In the post-Top 40 era, such styles have made a comeback, becoming popular with new audiences across the world. Another emerging pop music genre is Indian film music, which is produced in studios in New Delhi and Mumbai. Although it gets very little attention from the mainstream Anglo-American media, it nevertheless has a very large audience. African music too is popular in today's diverse society with individual audiences. It includes a number of distinctive regional styles, such as the *juju* music of Nigerian bandleader King Sunny Adé; central African *soukous*, a blend of indigenous songs and dance rhythms with Afro-Cuban music; and South African *isicathamiya*, the Zulu choral singing style performed by Ladysmith Black Mambazo.

The list of new trends for specific audiences could go on and on. Never before has music of all types been so available to whoever wants to listen to it. From classical music and jazz to the latest teen music craze, the recording industry has literally brought music to the people. The expressions and themes that pop music expounds quickly pass into general discourse, and the clothing fashions that pop musicians wear quickly become general fashion trends. Music has become an intrinsic part of modern-day signifying orders, thanks to the mass media. The *William Tell* overture gallop movement by the eighteenth century opera composer Gioacchino Rossini (1792–1868), for instance, has become so closely linked with the *Lone Ranger* TV series of the 1950s that the two are hardly ever perceived as separate by those who grew up in that era; similarly, another Rossini overture, the one he composed for the opera *The Barber of Seville*, has become so associated with a famous *Bugs Bunny* cartoon that the two are now inseparable in many people's minds.

Rock music

The swing music that became the rage between 1935 and 1945 appealed mainly to the young people of the era, who saw it as a way to survive the stark economic realities of the post-Depression era and the moral ravages of world war. The juvenilization of music became even more pronounced when, in 1942, Frank Sinatra wowed 'bobby-soxers' at the Paramount in New York, giving America a foretaste of the teenage hysteria that was just around the corner. The marriage of pop music with teenagers was officially consummated a little more than a decade later when rock-and-roll, a term clearly connoting the sexual impulses connected with adolescence, emerged as a music designed to appeal exclusively to teenagers.

As mentioned above, the birth of 'commercial rock' is usually traced to the 1955 hit song by Bill Haley and the Comets, *Rock Around the Clock*, although in actual fact the first true rock song is Elvis Presley's *Good Rockin' Tonight*, which he recorded in 1954 – itself a remake of Wynonie Harris' 1947 rendition of the same song. Haley's song, incidentally, was the theme music of *The Blackboard Jungle*, a motion picture about teenagers and the many problems associated with coming of age. The movie made it obvious to all that adolescence had emerged as a social force to be reckoned with – it provoked riots in South London on its original release, as did *Rock Around the Clock*.

As an amalgam of a vocal-group style known as 'doo wop', of a piano-based rhythmic style of jazz known as 'boogie woogie', and a country-music idiom known as 'honky tonk', rock quickly developed its own recognizable musical style that teenagers could call theirs, and theirs alone. In addition to recordings and radio, the rising popularity of television in the mid-1950s helped to turn rock songs and stars into overnight successes. Through this new and powerful medium, the first rock musicians introduced clothing and hairstyle fashions, and started dance crazes. In 1956, Elvis Presley became the 'king' of rock, after appearing on the *Ed Sullivan Show*, symbolizing the new youth rebelliousness with his hip swinging and brash attitude before a national audience of viewers.

Semiotically speaking, rock music had a truly distinctive style from, say, crooning music because it formed an opposition to it. For instance, whereas crooning music was to be sung and played softly and tenderly, rock music was intended instead to be sung loudly and roughly (see Table 4.1).

Table 4.1

Crooning music	Rock music
Soft and tender	Loud and rough
Restrained rhythms	Hard-driving rhythms
Flowing melodies	Hard-edged melodies
Romantic lyrics	Lyrics tinged with allusions to sexuality

The instrument that truly set rock apart from all its pop music predecessors was the electric guitar. Rock-and-roll guitarist Chuck Berry established a style of playing in the late 1950s that remains a great influence on rock music to this day. Beginning in the late 1960s a new generation of rock guitarists, including Jimi Hendrix, Eric Clapton, and Carlos Santana, experimented with amplification and various electronic devices, extending the musical potential of the instrument. Other instruments commonly used in early rock music included the 'stand-up' bass, the electric bass guitar, keyboard instruments, and the drum set.

A Brief History of Rock

The recordings of Chuck Berry, Elvis Presley, Little Richard, and Buddy Holly exemplified the 'golden age' of rock-and-roll in the mid-1950s. These artists gave the music its emotional power. Presley's *Hound Dog* (1956) and *All Shook Up* (1956), Little Richard's *Tutti Frutti* (1955) and *Lucille* (1957), and Berry's *Maybellene* (1955) and *Johnny B. Goode* (1958) established, in fact, the main features of the rock style – loudness, hard-driving rhythms, etc.

An incident that occurred in the winter of 1959 brought out the emotional sway that rock-and-roll musicians held over the 'first generation' of rock-and-roll teenagers. Three highly popular singers, Buddy Holly, Ritchie Valens, and the Big Bopper were killed, in that year, in an airplane crash on their way to a rock concert. The media portrayed their death as a tragedy of mythical proportions. Their songs, which would have faded away into the 'oldies' category forthwith, became legendary classics. Television news and documentary programmes projected images of teenage girls crying inconsolably as they listened to their fallen heroes daily. Posters and magazine photos of the three were transformed into icons of veneration and hung on bedroom walls throughout North America.

But all this did not last for very long. By the early 1960s Elvis, the 'king', was dethroned. The Beatles emerged to take his place on the throne. Several hit parades, instead of just one as in the 1950s, reflected a new diversity and growing sophistication in musical tastes. Rock and roll became a medium for expressing revolutionary social and political ideas. It was no longer just music 'to dance to' or 'to fall in love by'. The radical hippie movement of the mid-1960s was, in fact, propelled by rock and roll. Its artistic voices denounced apathy, warmongering, racism, stereotyping, and other social ills. By the end of the decade, it became obvious to society at large that the 'second generation' of teens was quite different from the previous one, and certainly much more committed to social issues.

In the 1960s rock had, in effect, entered its second critical period, now known as the 'classic' era. Motown music emerged in that era, as did distinctive regional styles, such as the California style made popular by the Beach Boys and the Greenwich Village urban folk movement that included the music of Bob Dylan. The British Invasion began in 1964 with the arrival of the Beatles in New York City. The Beatles' 1967 album *Sgt Pepper's Lonely Hearts Club Band* established new standards for studio recording and helped perpetrate the image of the long-haired rock musician as a creative artist. This image was further enshrined by the media with the advent of 'psychedelic rock', which promoted the use of hallucinogenic drugs, psychedelic art, light shows, and an emphasis on spontaneity and communitarian values. Musicians such as Jerry Garcia and the Grateful Dead, Jim Morrison and the Doors, and Frank Zappa developed a unique blend of complex rock genres and styles, catapulting rock into the domain of true musical art. Jimi Hendrix gained exposure and became an instant legend at the first large-scale rock festivals in the United States – Monterey Pop (1967) and Woodstock (1969). Soul music became part of the mainstream, with the widespread appeal of such African American artists as Aretha Franklin, James Brown, and Marvin Gaye. Paradoxically, despite the 'anti-establishment orientation' of the music, and its rejection of traditional bourgeois goals, artists signed lucrative contracts with major recording companies.

The music of the classic era continues to attract musical audiences to this day. This was confirmed by a VH1 poll released in 2001. Of the 100 albums chosen by 500 journalists, music executives, and artists as the most influential and important of rock history, most were recorded in the 1960s and 1970s. The top one chosen was the 1966 *Revolver* album with which the Beatles initiated their experiment to transform the simple hard-driving form of early rock into a genre of 'serious music'. With few exceptions – e.g. Nirvana's *Nevermind* album (1991), which came in second, Lauryn Hill's *The Miseducation of Lauryn Hill* album (1998), which came in thirty-seventh, and U2's *Achtung Baby* album (1991), which came in sixty-fifth – the majority of the albums selected were recorded during the classic era of rock. No albums from the golden era made it to the list, except for Elvis Presley's *Sun Sessions*, recorded in 1954–55, although the album was not released until 1976. It was rated twenty-first. Dominating the list are the Beatles, the Rolling Stones, Bob

Dylan, Led Zeppelin, the Who, Aretha Franklin, David Bowie, and other stars of the classic era.

The shift away from classic rock came in the mid-1970s with the appearance of disco and punk as opposing styles in teenage musical tastes. Initially associated with the gay subculture of New York City, disco drew upon black popular music and attracted a large teen following. Although despised by many teens, disco had a substantial impact on rock music, especially after the release of the motion picture *Saturday Night Fever* (1977) and its hugely successful disco soundtrack featuring the group called the Bee Gees. Disco lifestyle was based on unabashed sexual dancing and glittering fashion.

Punk music culture originated around 1976 in New York City and London as a reaction against the commercialism of disco and the 'artistic pretentiousness' of 1960s rock, even though two precursors to punk rock were 1960s 'surf' rock bands and 'garage' bands such as The Standells and The Seeds. Punk rock music was raw, abrasive, and rude. Early punk groups included the Sex Pistols, the Clash, and the Ramones. A variant, less coarse form of punk culture, new wave, was represented by Elvis Costello, and the Jam. Alienating themselves visibly from mainstream culture, the followers of punk music and new wave emerged as a more menacing threat to the social order than the one posed by their hippie predecessors. The stage performances of punk musicians were deliberately violent and confrontational. They spat on their audiences, mutilated themselves with knives, damaged the props on stage and in the hall, shouted, burped, urinated, and bellowed at will to a basic rhythmic pulsating beat, inciting their fans to follow suit. The fashion trends they introduced – chains, dog collars, black clothes, army boots, and hairstyles, which ranged from shaved heads to the wild-looking 'Mohawk' hairdos of every colour imaginable – emphasized degradation, mockery, social caricature, and insubordination at once. Punk teens rejected disco culture with the expression 'disco sucks', seeing it as too superficial and much too acceptable to the adult world.

By the late 1970s, both disco and punk vanished from the mainstream, although snippets of the musical forms they introduced have remained influential to this day. Among the new trends, one of the most popular favoured makeup, cross-dressing, and an overall blurring of the lines between the sexes. The hard rock band, Kiss, whose performances on stage were designed to shock adults, symbolized this new trend perfectly. Each musician assumed a mock comic-book role – a glamour boy, an alien from outer space, a kitty cat, and a sex-crazed Kabuki monster. Band members wore makeup and their stage act included fire-eating, smoke-bombs, hydraulic lifts, and the smashing of instruments. Two performers – Michael Jackson and Madonna – challenged prevailing gender attitudes even more than Kiss had done in the

1980s. Madonna's songs *Like a Virgin, Material Girl,* and *Dress You Up* blatantly portrayed femininity as objectified sexuality. These topped the hit-parade charts to the chagrin and dismay of leading feminists of the day. Madonna openly defied the political correctness of the era by adopting a Marilyn Monroe 'sex-kitten' peep-show pose as her performance trademark. Michael Jackson assumed both male and female sexual characteristics for his stage persona. He achieved this through extensive cosmetic surgery.

The advent of MTV and of music videos in the 1980s highlighted the role that television has always played in the propagation of rock as mainstream music. The whole rock-and-roll craze was, in effect, first introduced into society at large by *The Ed Sullivan Show* after it hosted Elvis Presley and early rock stars on Sunday evenings in the mid-1950s. The same programme catapulted the Beatles to fame in 1964. An estimated 73 million people watched that show. The moments that link TV with the diffusion and promotion of pop music are now part of pop culture history. In addition to the Elvis Presley and Beatle TV debuts, here are a few other highlights of the TV–rock music partnership:

- In 1957, Dick Clark's *American Bandstand* was launched, spreading teen trends in music, fashion, and dance through daily exposure on television.
- In 1967, The Who included explosives in their musical act on the *Smothers Brothers Comedy Hour*, introducing 'crudeness' into rock performances long before the advent of punk rock.
- In 1968, Elvis Presley made a comeback with his special on NBC, entrenching an 'Elvis subculture' after his death in 1977.
- In 1975, *Saturday Night Live* introduced rock musical acts into its programmes, entrenching rock music more and more into the mainstream.
- In 1981, MTV was launched with the video, *Video Killed the Radio Star*, by the Buggies, merging recorded music and television once and for all.
- In 1983, the *Motown 25* special featured Michael Jackson's first 'moonwalk', the signature move of his dance style, bringing rock music even more into the domain of mainstream pop culture.
- In 1984, Madonna shocked everyone by appearing in a wedding gown singing *Like a Virgin* on the MTV Video Awards, emphasizing that rock music and pop culture trends were one and the same thing.
- In 1985, the *Live Aid* concert was aired by ABC and MTV, rekindling interest in rock as a vehicle of political and social commentary.
- In the early 1990s, MTV started its own 'reality TV' programme, called *Real World*. The programme – which is still ongoing as I write – depicts the lives, loves, and other personal issues confronting the 'MTV generation'. A recent rating showed that it was first among basic cable offerings for viewers from 12 to 34 years of age.

In the 1990s, pop music became even more eclectic and fragmented, as hip-hop musicians, girl-power music groups (such as the Spice Girls and subsequent clone groups), and Latino artists vied for 'musical airtime' with artists representing a vast array of grunge, techno, and other styles. Fan loyalties were also split among artists of previous eras and those who represented a new type of crooning music such as Celine Dion and Elton John. Moreover, pop music faced a new source of competition for the 'music dollar' – a renewed interest in classical music and opera brought about mainly by the use of such music by movies of that era.

The emergence of hip-hop culture

Of all the trends of the 1990s, the one that gained the largest following among teenage audiences was hip-hop music, which traces its roots to the mid-1970s reggae and rap music styles. The superstar of the reggae style was Bob Marley, who by the time of his death in 1981 had become one of the most popular musicians in the world. During the 1980s rap music made its way to the centre of the pop music entertainment stage. Rock superstars, such as Peter Gabriel, David Byrne, and Paul Simon, whose 1985 album *Graceland* featured musicians from Africa and Latin America, played an important role in bringing this about by exposing the works of African American musicians to audiences in the United States and Europe. Rap is a genre in which vocalists perform rhythmic speech, usually accompanied by music snippets, called 'samples', from pre-recorded material or from music created by synthesizers. The first rap records were made in 1979 by small, independent record companies. Although artists such as the Sugarhill Gang had national hits during the early 1980s, rap music did not enter the pop music mainstream until 1986, when rappers Run-D.M.C. and the hard-rock band Aerosmith collaborated on a version of the song *Walk This Way*, creating a new audience for rap among white, suburban, middle-class rock fans. By the end of the 1980s, MTV had established a programme dedicated solely to rap. This made it possible for artists such as M.C. Hammer and the Beastie Boys to achieve success.

The term 'rap' is often used interchangeably with 'hip-hop'. But the latter was derived from a phrase used in the rap recording *Rapper's Delight* (1979) by Sugarhill Gang. The term 'hop' has been around a long time to describe virtually the same kind of movements involved in hip-hop dancing. For example, the Lindy hop style originated in Harlem in the 1920s. It is probably better known in its 'jitterbug' version. It was characterized by energetic body rhythms and the improvisational moves of the dancer. Lindy hop dancers created a heightened energy level and excitement by performing daring aerial movements. The hop dance of early rock and roll, too, was a high-energy acrobatic form of dance. The most famous example of this style was the dance performed to Danny and the Juniors' 1958 hit *At the Hop*.

The rise of rap and hip-hop in many ways parallels the birth of rock-and-roll in the 1950s. Both originated within the African American community and both were initially recorded by small, independent record labels and marketed almost exclusively to black audiences. In both cases, the new style gradually attracted white musicians, a few of whom began performing it. For rock and roll it was a white American from Mississippi, Elvis Presley, who broke into the Billboard magazine popular music charts. For rap it was a white group from New York City, the Beastie Boys. Their release of *You Gotta Fight for Your Right to Party* (1986) was one of the first two rap records to reach the Billboard top-10 list of popular hits. The other was *Walk This Way* (1986). Soon after 1986, the use of samples and declaimed vocal styles became widespread in the popular music of both black and white performers, significantly altering previous notions of what constitutes a legitimate song, composition, or musical accompaniment.

Hip-hop music typically emphasizes lyrics and wordplay over melody and harmony, achieving interest through rhythmic complexity and variations in the timing of the lyrics. Hip-hop is not unlike the popular musical form of the late medieval era, the madrigal – an unaccompanied vocal composition for two or three voices in simple harmony, following a strict poetic form, developed in Italy in the late thirteenth and early fourteenth centuries. Hip-hop was, in my view, the madrigal music of the 1990s. Its lyric themes can be broadly categorized under three headings: (1) those that concern human relationships, (2) those that chronicle and often embrace the so-called 'gangsta' lifestyle of youths who live in inner cities, and (3) those that address contemporary political issues or aspects of black history. Underpinning the rapper's vocals is the separately recorded musical accompaniment, known as a backing track. In 1982, computer-generated sounds from synthesizers were used along with snippets from pre-existing recordings. With the arrival of digital technology in 1983, sampling began to replace the turntable style of cutting and mixing. DJs were thus able to access precise digital sound bites and reconstruct them into new sound collages. Sampling eventually facilitated the layering of sound, enabling rap artists such as Public Enemy to place seven or eight samples on top of each other.

By the 1990s any sound source was considered fair game and rap artists borrowed sounds from such disparate sources as folk music, jazz records, and television news broadcasts. Rap moved from the fringes of pop music culture to the mainstream as more and more white musicians began to embrace the new style. Particularly worrisome to many adults was the rise of gangsta rap, which depicted an outlaw lifestyle of sex, drugs, and violence in inner-city America. In 1988 the first major album of gangsta rap was released, *Straight*

Outta Compton by the rap group NWA (Niggaz With Attitude). Songs from the album generated an extraordinary amount of controversy for their violent attitudes and inspired protests from a number of organizations, including the FBI. However, attempts to censor gangsta rap only served to publicize the music and make it more attractive to youths generally.

Hip-hop culture in the late 1990s became a widespread source of identity construction and self-definition for many teens. It introduced the practice of using nicknames, known as 'tags', as part of self-definition. These were commonly etched on the urban landscape – on bus shelters, buses, subways, signs, walls, freeway overpasses, mailboxes, etc. – with markers, spray paint, or shoe polish (*Futura 2000, Phase 2, Zephyr, Crash*). In this way, hip-hop teens advertised their new identity to everyone. To symbolize the event, the tag was decorated with crowns, stars, arrows, underlines, halos, etc. There were two main forms of decoration: throw-ups and pieces. The former consisted in spray-painting one's new name in bubble, block, or some other expansive style; the latter in decorating it with characters from cartoons or with proverbs. In such cities as Los Angeles and New York hip-hop teens made thousands of murals.

So interesting had hip-hop tagging art become by the late 1990s that some traditional art galleries even started putting it on display. In December 2000, the Brooklyn Museum of Art organized an exposition of 400 pieces of urban street art, called *Hip-Hop Nation: Roots, Rhymes and Rage*, reflecting more than three decades of hip-hop art. In a city where nearly 2000 arrests for graffiti offences were carried out in the same year, the art gallery had taken on the role previously confined to the streets.

Pop music took on a seemingly harder edge as the 1990s came to an end. That was the era when, for a brief period of time, heavy metal and rap joined forces to produce rap-metal music. The style was directed primarily at macho male types known as 'mooks'. Its message was a combination of rage, profanity, and blatant sexuality. Groups such as Korn and Limp Bizkit, as well as the controversial metal-rapper Eminem, symbolized this new trend. Along with the music of gangsta rappers such as Ice-T, DrDre, and Snoop Doggy Dogg, rap-metal music became particularly worrisome to parents, who fretted especially over the brutal and hardcore sexual lyrics of the music. At the start of the year 2000, female rap-metal bands also came into the spotlight, showing as much rage and profanity as their male counterparts, adding to the uneasiness felt by many adults about the whole hip-hop movement.

Why all the rage? Was it a legitimate response to a consumer-crazed world? Was it a way to let off steam, much safer than walking through a high school corridor with a weapon under one's coat? Was it rage against family breakups and divorce? Maybe. But, by and large, the mooks were products of the mediated culture in which they were reared. They were hardly individuals caught in an underclass situation, or teens who felt oppressed and victimized. Rather, like the 'rebels without a cause' of the 1950s, they were primarily middle-class bored youths who espoused rage music as a veiled attempt to eschew the responsibilities of growing up. This is perhaps why all the rage got channelled fairly quickly into marketable niches where it could be appreciated without any undue impact on the larger society.

Rock subcodes

As I write, change is occurring all over the pop music world. 'Techno' groups, who combine computer-generated, disco-like rhythms with digital sounds, and acid jazz bands, who combine rock, soul, rhythm-and-blues, and jazz influences into an eclectic style have become popular. But they are competing with artists representing a plethora of new and recycled music styles. The only 'constant' in pop music is that of 'constant change'. Perhaps in no other area of pop culture is Barthes' notion of neomania more applicable than it is to the domain of pop music.

Essentially, the underlying meaning of the rock music code, or *meta-code*, is that it is music *for*, *about*, and *by* teenagers. But teenagers, like adults, are different. This is why a plethora of rock subcodes have crystallized since the 1950s, each with its system of connotative meanings, to suit different interpretants (i.e. meanings that specific audiences extract from a particular musical code). A few of them are listed in Table 4.2.

Table 4.2

Music genre	Connotations
Golden rock (1950s)	Sexuality, rebellion, romance . . .
Classic rock (1960s–early 1970s)	Rebellion, anti-establishment, social issues, revolution, individuality, free love . . .
Disco (mid-1970s)	Free spiritedness, glamour, sexuality, cool appearance . . .
Punk (mid-1970s)	Anti-establishment, disruption of traditional values, blatant carnality, sexuality, weirdness, toughness . . .
Hip-hop (mid-1980s–early 2000s)	Street savvy, self-styled identity, 'brotherhood' with other hip-hoppers . . .

Sexuality still dominates pop music themes. And, as in the hippie 1960s, protest and a general critique of society can still be found in many songs. Groups such as Rage Against the Machine continue the tradition of Dylan and

Crosby, Stills, Nash, and Young, expressing rage against the 'system'. But although such music remains an important vehicle for conveying and debating ideas, like all other things in modern society, it seems either to pass much too quickly from public consciousness, or else to have very little impact other than to get teens to buy CDs and music videos.

Another disconcerting trend is the fact that some former teen pop stars refuse to grow up. Cher and Michael Jackson, for instance, are continually undergoing cosmetic surgery in order to maintain a pseudo-adolescent appearance. Madonna is always experimenting with new kinds of contemporary music styles, from metallic to hip-hop, in order to maintain her place in the spotlight. Even rap and hip-hop musicians have been afflicted by the 'forever young' syndrome. Many older rappers showed up in movies and TV programmes in the late 1990s dressed up and acting as they did years before when their music meant something. The paradox of modern pop culture is, in fact, that its artistic voices have become intrinsically intertwined with its economic system. Hip-hop music is rebellious music, to be sure, but it is also about gold rings, gold chains, and brand-name sneakers. The hip-hop subculture, like the hippie and punk subcultures before it, started out as genuine rebellion. But the instant that hippie, punk, and hip-hop musical styles and fashions were adopted by the mainstream culture, the rebellion faded and economics took over.

Every musical style has, of course, a lifecycle. Baroque music survived for a century as the dominant style from about 1650 to 1750; the classical forms of Haydn and Mozart persisted from the 1770s to well into the nineteenth century, when Beethoven and other composers radically altered them to bring about the so-called 'romantic movement'; and serious composers in the twentieth century, from Shostakovich and Bartok to Stravinsky and Glass, constantly experimented with new ways to make music. But pop music has shown itself to be particularly inclined to change rapidly and to pass from communal memory. Its ephemerality or 'short-life' is, no doubt, a sign of the pop culture it mirrors. As emotionally powerful as any given pop music genre is to a particular group of people, it quickly loses its sway over subsequent generations. The music of Bach, Mozart, Beethoven, Bartok, and Glass, on the other hand, will continue to appeal to people in the future.

In a recent book titled *If It Ain't Got that Swing* (2000), Mark Gauvreau Judge argues that Chuck Berry's 1950s song *Roll Over Beethoven* signalled the end of the more traditional forms of music. As a consequence, it also heralded the demise of adult popular culture. Ironically, rock music may have itself run its course, becoming increasingly an object of nostalgia, as indicated by various events that took place in the 1990s. In 1995, the Rock and Roll Hall of Fame opened in Cleveland, Ohio – a sure sign that it may have become 'museum music'. Also in the 1990s, several major television documentaries were produced on the history of rock-and-roll, and historical box-set recordings were reissued featuring rock artists from the past – further signs that rock music had become more a part of history than of current interest. Today, oldies stations have as large, if not a larger, following than do those promoting contemporary music.

The radio

In 1837, the telegraph became the first electronic system of international communications. However, it was soon found to be inefficient because it depended on a complex system of receiving stations wired to each other along a fixed route. In 1895, the American engineer Guglielmo Marconi (1874–1937) transmitted an electronic signal successfully to a receiving device that had no wired connection to his transmitter, thus demonstrating that a signal could be sent through space so that devices at random points could receive it. He called his invention a radiotelegraph (later shortened to radio), because of the fact that its signal moved outward in all directions, i.e. radially, from the point of transmission. This is how radio was introduced, technologically-speaking, into the world.

Evidence of a plan for radio broadcasting to the general public can be found in a 1916 memorandum written by David Sarnoff (1891–1971), an employee of Marconi's US branch, American Marconi, which would eventually become the Radio Corporation of America (RCA). In it, Sarnoff recommended that radio be made into a household 'utility'. Sarnoff's memo was not given any consideration by management at first. After the First World War ended in 1918, however, several manufacturing companies began to explore Sarnoff's idea for the mass-marketing of home radio receivers very seriously.

In an effort to boost radio sales in peacetime, the Westinghouse Electric Corporation of Pittsburgh established what many culture historians consider to be the first commercially-owned radio station to offer a schedule of programming to the general public. It came to be known by the call letters KDKA, after it received its license from the Department of Commerce (which held regulatory power following the end of the war) in October of 1920. KDKA aired various kinds of entertainment programmes, including recorded music, which was generated by a phonograph placed within the range of a microphone. The station did not charge user fees to listeners, nor did it carry paid advertisements. Westinghouse used KDKA simply as an enticement for people to purchase home radio receivers.

Other radio manufacturers soon followed Westinghouse's example. The General Electric Company, for example, broadcast its own programmes on station WGY in Schenectady, New York. RCA eventually gave Sarnoff permission to develop company sales of radios for home entertainment. Sarnoff opened stations in New York City and Washington, DC, and in 1926 he founded the National Broadcasting Company (NBC), an RCA subsidiary created for the specific purpose of broadcasting programmes via a cross-country network of stations. The Columbia Broadcasting System (CBS) radio service was established shortly thereafter in 1928, becoming a dominant force in American broadcasting industry over the subsequent 50 years. In contrast to the Westinghouse Corporation, AT&T began exploring in 1922 the possibilities of toll broadcasting, i.e. of charging fees in return for the airing of commercial advertisements on its stations. Fearing legal action, however, the telephone company sold its stations to RCA and left the broadcasting business. In return, AT&T was granted the exclusive right to provide the connections that would link local stations to the NBC network.

The sale of radios more than justified the expense to manufacturers of operating broadcasting services. According to estimates by the National Association of Broadcasters, in 1922 there were 60 000 households in the United States with radios; by 1929 the number had topped 10 million. But increases in sales of radio receivers could not continue forever. The sale of advertising time loomed, consequently, as the only viable solution for American radio broadcasting. The merger of advertising with radio programming was the event that, arguably, brought the Electronic Galaxy into existence. In that Galaxy, non-commercial broadcasting would play only a minor role and, in fact, there would not be a coast-to-coast non-commercial radio network in the United States until the formation of National Public Radio (NPR) in 1970. In Great Britain, on the other hand, radio has always been funded by license fees, collected by the government, which are turned over directly to the British Broadcasting Corporation (BBC).

Radio broadcasting reached the pinnacle of its popularity and influence during the Second World War. In that period, American commentator Edward R. Murrow (1908–65) changed the nature of news reporting permanently with his sensational descriptions of street scenes during the German bombing raids of London, which he delivered as an eyewitness from the rooftop of the CBS news bureau there. American president Franklin D. Roosevelt was among the first politicians to understand the power of radio as a propaganda device. He would frequently use the radio medium to bypass the press and directly address the American people with his so-called 'fireside chats' during the Great Depression. Roosevelt knew that the emotional power of the voice would be much more persuasive than would any logical argument he might put into print. The chats continue to this day as part and parcel of the American presidency. Adolf Hitler, too, saw the radio as a propaganda medium, using it to persuade millions to follow him. And the radio appeal from Japanese emperor Hirohito to his nation for unconditional surrender helped end the Second World War following the atomic bombings of Hiroshima and Nagasaki.

Radio broadcasting dramatically changed social life wherever it was introduced. It brought news, information, and the arts directly into homes. Historically a privilege of the élite, the arts could be enjoyed by members of the general public, most of whom would otherwise not have access to venues such as the concert hall and the theatre. The parallel growth of network radio and Hollywood cinema, both of which were launched as commercial enterprises in 1927, created an unprecedented mass culture for people of all social classes and educational backgrounds. The 'democratization process' started by the novel in the domain of print, and by the gramophone in the domain of music, was extended by the radio medium considerably in the Electronic Galaxy to encompass virtually all cultural domains.

Radio genres

At first, radio was no more than a new audio medium for print and theatrical genres. For example, it adapted the various genres of traditional stage drama, transforming them into radio dramas, action serials, situation comedies (or *sitcoms*), and so-called soap operas. It looked to vaudeville to garner and adapt material for its comedy-variety programming. And it modelled its news coverage on the format of daily newspapers – announcers would, in fact, often simply read articles from the local newspaper over the air. Nevertheless, because of its capacity to reach large numbers of people, from the 1920s to the early 1950s radio broadcasting evolved into society's primary medium of information, arts appreciation, and, above all else, distraction. Only after the advent of television in the 1950s did radio's hegemony in this domain begin to erode, as its audiences split into smaller, distinct segments. Today, radio is primarily a medium for automobile and office use. People listen to it mainly in their cars as they drive from location to location, or in their offices (or other places of work) as they do something else. Aware of this, radio stations typically present traffic information in a regular interspersed fashion throughout their broadcasts, or else present uninterrupted stretches of music during certain periods of the working day.

Despite the obvious differences between radio and television, the development of programming for both broadcast media is best understood as a single history comprised of two stages. Early radio broadcasting was dominated, as mentioned, by adaptations of older media. The sitcom, for example, was adapted from theatrical genres that originated in the *Commedia dell'Arte* – a comedy developed in Italy in the sixteenth and seventeenth centuries characterized by improvisation from a standard plot outline and the use of stock characters. Sitcoms adapted this genre for new radio audiences by using familiar characters and conditions to explore life in the home, the workplace, and other common locations. It became one of the more popular of the early radio programmes. The most highly rated sitcom in radio history was *Amos 'n Andy*, in which actors performed the stereotypical roles of African American characters in outrageous caricature. The series premiered on NBC in 1928, and ran for 20 years on radio before moving to television, where it ran from 1951 to 1953. Similarly, *The Goldbergs* (1929–50), *Life with Luigi* (1948–53), and other ethnically-based family sitcoms successfully exploited the aural character of the radio medium, as actors used thick immigrant accents and malapropisms (misuse of words) to carve out their roles and characters. Lucille Ball's radio show *My Favorite Husband* (1948–51) was a notable exception, developing sitcom artistry considerably. It established dramatic elements such as battles between the sexes, arguments among neighbours, and other mundane conflicts that became fundamental to the TV version of this genre.

Radio variety shows were adapted from vaudeville. Popular comedy-variety radio stars such as Jack Benny, Fred Allen, and Edgar Bergen were, originally, vaudeville actors and comedians. A radio comedy-variety hour typically consisted of short monologues and skits featuring the host. These alternated with various show-business acts, including singers, musicians, comedians, and others.

Radio drama also became highly popular. The genre was presented in one of two formats – in anthology and serial format. The *anthology* format showcased individual plays, such as one would expect to see on stage or in motion pictures. This was highly popular in the 1930s and 1940s and included *Mercury Theatre on the Air* (1938–41), created by American actor and director Orson Welles (1915–85), and *Theatre Guild of the Air* (1945–54). Radio series, using recurring characters, situations, and settings, were more popular, however. Genres in this format included urban police dramas, such as *Gangbusters* (1935–57), private eye mysteries, such as *The Shadow* (1930–54), and Westerns, such as *The Lone Ranger* (1933–55). These were adaptations of adventure novels or comic book narratives. The radio narratives became quickly the narratives of the whole society. They provided reference points (signifieds) to which people could turn in their everyday discourse. Radio drama virtually disappeared by the mid-1950s as its biggest stars and most popular programmes were transferred by the networks from radio to television.

Soap opera, or daily serial drama, was originally developed as a daytime genre aimed specifically at a female audience. Soap operas explored romance, friendship, and familial relations in emotionally-involving narrative formats. The invention of the soap opera is credited to Irna Phillips, who began developing the genre for local radio broadcast in Chicago during the 1920s.

Many of her radio shows were adapted for television, with some running first on radio and then on television for more than 25 years.

In the area of news reporting, radio could offer its audiences live coverage of events – something that newspapers could not do. The immediacy with which radio news reports reached people redefined the role of news reporting in society. Print journalism became a supplemental medium, focusing on in-depth coverage and editorial opinion. Today, radio continues to be a primary source of news reporting. So-called 'drive time' (7–9 a.m. and 4–7 p.m.) – the time most commuters travel to and from work – has become radio's 'prime time'. Programming consists mainly of traffic bulletins, weather reports, news items, and time checks. Some stations have now even adopted 'news-only formats', reflecting the radio's need to cultivate specialized audiences for economic survival. National Public Radio's *All Things Considered* (1971–) and *Morning Edition* (1979–), for example, were developed as morning and evening on-air newspapers for sophisticated audiences.

Needless to say, radio has always been a promoter of pop music. The jazz, swing, rock, and hip-hop movements would not have become as dominant as they did without radio. Radio hit parades have always showcased new and old tunes, spurring consumers to buy records. Today, a host of radio stations provide specialized pop music broadcasting, from adult contemporary to classical music and jazz.

Barthes argued that mass media spectacles, from movie blockbusters to wrestling matches, were emotionally powerful because they were drafted on the basis of mythic themes. To distinguish between the original myths and their modern-day versions, Barthes (1957) designated the latter *mythologies*. In early movie Hollywood westerns, for instance, the mythic theme of Good vs. Evil manifested itself in various symbolic and expressive ways: e.g. cowboy heroes wore white hats and villains black ones; cowboy heroes were, like mythic heroes, honest and strong; etc.

Radio genres, too, were imbued with mythological elements. For example, radio sports broadcasts, such as boxing matches, were portrayed by announcers as epic battles pitting Good against Evil. The whole fanfare associated with preparing for the big boxing match had a ritualistic quality similar to the pomp and circumstance that the mythic armies engaged in before going out to battle, as announcers interviewed the boxers, recounted their life stories dramatically, and drew moral lessons from their lives. To the listener, the distinction between the mythical and the real became a blurry one. The term used to refer to this phenomenon is 'reification'. An event that showed the reifying power of radio was a 1938 broadcast by Orson Welles. His radio version of *The War of the Worlds* by English author H.G. Wells (1866–1946) was so realistic that thousands believed an alien attack was actually occurring. Consequently, the police and the army were notified by concerned citizens; people ran onto the streets shouting hysterically; and some even contemplated suicide.

In the Digital Galaxy, radio has shown itself to have staying power and to be an adaptive medium. It is estimated that there are about 1.6 billion radio sets in use worldwide, with more than half concentrated in North America, the European Union countries, and Japan. In developing societies, too, nearly all citizens own or have access to a radio. All-digital stations are springing up in many places. Programmes and commercials are being transferred to digital databases for broadcasting. Some advertising agencies send in commercials on digital audiotape (DAT) cassettes; other companies send their commercials to the stations' computer via high-speed Internet links.

Two-thirds of Americans aged 12 and over listen to radio at least briefly each day, and nearly everyone listens at least once a week. Most listen to local programmes, but audiences for certain kinds of syndicated or network programmes, such as talk shows, are growing. In sum, the radio is not yet a relic in the Digital Galaxy. It may have come down from its top perch, but it continues, nevertheless, to be an integral part of the distraction factory.

Radio and advertising

Like magazines, a radio programme or genre is integrated with advertising. The soap opera genre was even named for the type of advertiser – soap companies – that sponsored them. In the United States advertising agencies produced almost all network radio shows before the development of network television. Stations often sold agencies full sponsorship, which included placing the product name in a programme's title, as with *Palmolive Beauty Box Theatre* (1927–37) or *The Texaco Star Theatre* (1948–53) on early television. Entire radio programmes became associated with products. The ratings system arose, in fact, from the sponsors' desire to know how many people they were reaching with their advertising. In 1929 Archibald Crossley launched *Crossley's Cooperative Analysis of Broadcasting*, using telephone surveys to project daily estimates of audience size for the national radio networks. The A.C. Nielsen Company, which had been surveying audience size in radio since the mid-1930s, eventually became the dominant ratings service. The resulting projections, or ratings, helped determine the price of advertisements and, ultimately, whether the programme would stay on the air or be cancelled. Only public radio stations are exempt from the 'ratings game', for the reason that they are financed by government subsidies, individual donations, and corporate grants.

Radio introduced the 'commercial' into advertising – a mini-narrative or musical jingle revolving around a product or service and its uses. The commercial became a highly persuasive form of advertising, because it could reach masses of potential customers, print literate or not, instantaneously through the persuasive capacity of the human voice – which could be seductive, friendly, cheery, insistent, or foreboding, as required by the nature of the product. Radio commercials of the day consisted of pseudoscientific sales pitches, satires of movies, and snappy jingles. They became so familiar that perception of the product became inextricably intertwined with the style and content of the commercials created to promote it. The commercial also created the first advertising personalities, from Mr Clean (representing a detergent product of the same name) to Speedy (a personified Alka-Seltzer indigestion tablet); and it became a source of dissemination of recognizable tunes throughout society, from 'Mr Clean in a just a minute' (for the Mr Clean detergent product) to 'Plop, plop, fizz, fizz oh what a relief it is' (for the Alka-Seltzer stomach product).

From the outset, it was obvious that radio advertising both reflected and set social trends. A 'synergy' thus quickly developed between advertising campaigns and general lifestyle trends, as advertisers attempted to keep in step with changing trends and shape them at the same time. Pepsi advertising, for example, has always tried to maintain this synergy by emphasizing the changing social climate in its ad campaigns. A 'time capsule' of some of its famous campaigns highlights how that company has capitalized on the change from print to electronic media throughout the years with great success:

- 1898: American pharmacist Caleb Bradham gives the brand name *Pepsi-Cola* to his carbonated invention.
- 1903: Bradham produced the first print ads with a pharmacological subtext to them: *Exhilarating, Invigorating, Aids Digestion.*
- 1906: Ad headlines were changed to: *The Original Pure Food Drink.* This was designed to intimate that the drink was not some chemical concoction, but a 'pure' one, as consumers started to challenge the nutritional quality of pop drinks.
- 1920: As society became more affluent, Pepsi changed its campaign to: *Drink Pepsi-Cola: It Will Satisfy You.* This slogan became part of its early radio commercials.
- 1939: The Depression years forced Pepsi to change its slogan to: *Twice as Much for a Nickel*, a theme introduced cleverly by the cartoon called *Peter & Pete.* This theme was reinforced through radio commercials.
- 1940: Pepsi's radio jingle *Nickel, Nickel* was so popular that it became a hit on its own.
- 1943: A new jingle, *Bigger Drink, Better Taste*, was designed to tap into the new affluence of the era, becoming one of the most popular tunes on radio.
- 1949: The radio slogan *Why Take Less When Pepsi's Best?* reflected a

concern over the increasing takeover of the market share by other soft drink companies.

- 1950: With its *More Bounce to the Ounce*, Pepsi changed its strategy to reflect a new emphasis on vigorous lifestyle. This slogan was heard on a daily basis on all kinds of radio programmes.

- 1953–54: With the growing concern over obesity in society, Pepsi started a new weight-conscious campaign with its *The Light Refreshment* and *Refreshing without Filling* radio and TV commercials.

- 1958: Pepsi revitalized its image, tapping into the new 'teen market' with *Be Sociable, Have a Pepsi* on radio and TV commercials.

- 1963: Ever more aware of the economic potential of the teen generation Pepsi renamed it outright *The Pepsi Generation* and developed catchy tunes for radio and TV.

- 1966: A Pepsi jingle called *Girlwatchers*, which is self-explanatory in its emphasis on a growing openness in sexual mores, became a top-40 hit on radio.

- 1967: Pepsi's *Taste that Beats the Others Cold: Pepsi Pours it On* campaign was designed to reflect a growing competitiveness in society.

- 1969: The hippie movement and its emphasis on giving and helping others was captured with its new radio and TV slogan: *You've Got a Lot to Live. Pepsi's Got a Lot to Give.*

- 1973: The themes of freedom and youth tribalism that the hippie movement had spawned were encapsulated in Pepsi's new *Join the Pepsi People, Feelin' Free* campaign.

- 1975: The growing challenges facing society were reflected in its *Pepsi Challenge* campaign.

- 1976: With its *Have a Pepsi Day* campaign, featuring a little boy, Pepsi tapped into a growing sensitivity to the issues of childhood in society at large.

- 1979–82: Two campaigns – *Catch the Pepsi Spirit, Drink it In!* and *Pepsi's Got the Taste for Life* – were designed to capture the growing 'selfishness' of the times, now characterized as the 'Me Generation'.

- 1984–85: Pepsi co-opted pop culture stars, reflecting the growing power of the media in society and the fact that young people of the era were the first generation to have grown up as 'TV's babies'. Michael Jackson declared Pepsi *The Choice of a New Generation*, and Tina Turner, Gloria Estefan, Lionel Ritchie, Joe Montana, Dan Marino, Teri Garr, and Billy Crystal were featured in *New Generation* commercials on radio and television. Michael J. Fox starred in the classic commercial *Apartment 10G*. TV had replaced radio as the primary medium through which the soft drink company promoted its product. Nevertheless, parallel radio commercials were developed for the 'prime time drive' audience.

- 1987–93: In 1987 Pepsi called itself *America's Choice*, with Michael Jackson as the star of its episodic four-part *Chase* commercial. In 1990 teen stars Fred Savage and Kirk Cameron were featured in commercials entreating their peers to join the *New Generation*. And music legend Ray Charles grooved to the times with *You Got the Right One, Baby, Uh-Huh!* Other celebrities declared *Gotta Have It* and *Been There, Done That, Tried That* on radio and TV commercial slots, tapping into the growing *ennui* among affluent teenagers of the era. This campaign culminated in 1993 with basketball star Shaquille O'Neal exhorting his viewers to *Be Young, Have Fun*.
- 1995–97: With its *Nothing Else Is a Pepsi* and *Security Camera* campaigns, the pop drink company reflected a growing stress on individuality and Self-identity in society. With *GeneratioNext* in which the Spice Girls were featured, Pepsi revamped its *Pepsi Generation* theme, with this clever bit of self-reference.
- 1998: Pepsi's *Dancing Bears* campaign, with its humorous tone, tapped into a growing emphasis on sitcom-style behaviour in society at large.
- 1999: Aware of the constantly growing power of classic pop culture stars, Pepsi's *Joy of Cola* campaign featured Marlon Brando, Isaac Hayes, Aretha Franklin, and Jeff Gordon.

Radio programmes and commercials today are totally integrated. Commercials are interspersed throughout a programme, informing listeners of products that they want to hear about. Radio advertising has the advantage that people can listen to programmes while doing other things, such as driving a car or working at home. Another advantage is that radio audiences, in general, are more highly selectable by programme genre than are television audiences. For example, stations that feature country music attract different kinds of listeners than do those that play rock. By selecting the station, advertisers can reach the people most likely to buy their products.

5 Film

The first successful 'moving photographs' were made in 1877 by Eadweard Muybridge, a British photographer working in California. Muybridge took a series of photographs of a running horse, setting up a row of cameras with strings attached to their shutters. When the horse ran by, it broke each string in succession, tripping the shutters. Muybridge's procedure influenced inventors in several countries to work toward developing devices for recording moving images. Among them was Thomas Edison (1847–1931) who invented the first functional motion picture camera in 1888 when he filmed 15 seconds of one of the assistants sneezing. Shortly thereafter, in 1895, Auguste Marie Louis Nicolas Lumière (1862–1954) and his brother Louis Jean Lumière (1864–1948) gave the first public showing of a cinematic film in a Paris café.

Thus was born the technology and art of the motion picture, perhaps the most influential art form of the last century. If we live today in a 'visually-mediated' world – a world where visual images shape lifestyle and inculcate values – we owe it first and foremost to the movies. Vision-based and vision-enhancing media are so common that we hardly realize how intrinsic they have become to modern-day signifying orders. Photography, for instance, is the medium through which, by and large, we remember people, events, and things. Photographs capture a fleeting and irretrievable moment in time, extracting it from the flux of change that characterizes human life. Such 'captured' moments have strong appeal because they allow us literally to reflect upon them by 're-seeing' them. The photographs that adorn the tables and walls in our homes are visual mementos and testimonials of who we are. This reifying power of the photograph was brought out by Michelangelo Antonioni in his 1966 movie masterpiece, *Blow-Up*. The search for 'clues' to a crime in a blow-up of a photograph in that movie constituted a metaphor for the search for clues to our own existence.

At the level of the signifier, the film is a text consisting of a chain of photographic images that create the illusion of real-life motion and action. At the level of the signified, movies are metaphorical mirrors of life. The topic of cinema is, clearly, a central one for media semiotics because movie genres constitute signification systems to which most people today respond and to which they look for recreation, inspiration, and insight at the level of the interpretant.

Motion pictures

The three main categories of motion pictures are feature films, documentaries, and animated films, commonly called 'cartoons'. The feature film is a work of fiction, almost always narrative in structure, which is produced in three stages. The pre-production stage is the period of time when the script is procured. The script may be an adaptation from a novel or short story, a play, or some other print work; it may also be something written specifically for the screen. The production stage is the period of time when the filming of the script occurs. Finally, the post-production (editing) stage is the phase when all the parts of the film, which have been shot out of sequence, are put together to make one cohesive story.

The documentary is a non-fiction film depicting real-life situations with individuals often describing their feelings and experiences in an unrehearsed manner to a camera or an interviewer. Documentaries are frequently shot without a script and are rarely shown in theatres that exhibit feature films. They are seen regularly on television, however. Documentaries can be shot on location or simply assembled from archival material.

Animation is the technique of using film to create the illusion of movement from a series of two-dimensional drawings or three-dimensional objects. The traditional creation of an animated motion picture nearly always begins with the preparation of a storyboard, a series of sketches that portray the important parts of the story. Additional sketches are then prepared to illustrate backgrounds, décor, and the appearance and temperaments of the characters. Today, most (if not all) animated films are produced digitally on computers.

Whereas in print fiction the author (or authors) can be easily identified as the writer/creator of the text, in feature films the question of authorship is a much more complex one. In this case, there is both a screenwriter and a director who are responsible for various dimensions of the text and its artistic delivery. The function of screenwriters varies greatly with the type of film being produced. The screenwriter may be called upon to develop an idea or to adapt a novel, stage play, or musical to the special requirements of the screen. But the writer is not the key individual in the production of the film – that person is the director, the individual who visualizes the script and guides the production crew and actors in carrying out that vision. In theory, the director has artistic control over everything from the script itself to the final cut of the film, although in reality various circumstances compromise this ideal of the director's absolute artistic authority. Nonetheless, it is the director's sense of the dramatic, along with his or her creative visualization of the script, that transforms a script into a motion picture. The movie *Amadeus* is a case-in-point. This 1984 movie was directed by Milos Forman (1932–). It is based on the 1979 play by British playwright Peter Shaffer (1926–) about the eighteenth-century rivalry between Austrian composer Wolfgang Amadeus Mozart and Italian composer Antonio Salieri. The play plumbs the meaning of art, genius, and the important role of music in the spiritual life of human beings. The film captures these themes visually and acoustically by juxtaposing the emotionally powerful music of Mozart against the backdrop of dramatized events in his life and the truly splendid commentaries of Salieri, who guides the audience through the musical repertoire with remarkable insight and perspicacity. Now, Forman's camera shots, close-ups, angle shots, tracking shots (which capture horizontal movement), and zooming actions allow us to see Mozart's moods (his passions, his tragedies, etc.) on his face as he conducts or plays his music, as well as those of his commentator Salieri (his envy, his deep understanding of Mozart's art, etc.) as he speaks to his confessor. Forman thus blends music, plot, and commentary through brilliant camera artistry to create a truly effective *mise-en-scène* that is perceived as narrative, drama, musical performance, and historical documentary at once. Forman's cinematic touch is what delivers Shaffer's message powerfully, offering possibilities that the theatrical play cannot possibly do on its own.

Interestingly, Shaffer comments in a postcript to the published version of the play (Shaffer 1993: 108) that the

> cinema is a worrying medium for the stage playwright to work in. Its unverbal essence offers difficulties to anyone living largely by the spoken word. Increasingly, as American films grow ever more popular around the world, it is apparent that the most successful are being spoken in Screenspeak, a kind of cinematic esperanto equally comprehensible in Bogotà and Bulaway.

Shaffer perceptively indicates, with this statement, that cinema has, in fact, introduced a new language into social discourse, which is based on the image and on a general popularization of colloquial speech. The implications of Screenspeak in the development of theatre and cinema is self-evident.

Alongside the screenwriter and director is the musical composer. For many feature films, composers are assigned the task of creating a musical score to accompany scenes in the story. The composer works with the director to enhance the dramatic content of the individual scenes, since music can establish a mood as well as conjure up any number of emotions. For example, music can identify a person as being suspicious when there is nothing visible on the screen to suggest such a thing. Music can also function as a bridge from one scene to another in order to prepare the audience for an impending change of mood. One or two characters may also be associated with their own musical themes, either related to or separate from the main theme. Film music has, in effect, become a genre of its own and, in some cases, it even eclipses the film itself.

Combining images, narrative, and music, cinema creates representations that are among the most powerful ever devised by human ingenuity. Today, the images and sounds that movies project in a theatre are overwhelming, thanks to digitization. Digital effects have now become an intrinsic component in the production and editing of all movies. The first completely computer-generated film, *Toy Story*, was released in 1995.

Early cinema

Most cinema historians trace the origin of the movies to the year 1896 when the French magician Georges Méliès made a series of films that explored the narrative potential of the new medium. In 1899, in a studio on the outskirts of Paris, Méliès reconstructed a ten-part version of the trial of French army officer *Alfred Dreyfus*, and in 1900 he filmed *Cinderella* in 20 scenes. He is chiefly remembered, however, for his clever fantasy *A Trip to the Moon* (1902), in which he exploited the new possibilities of the movie camera for portraying narrative visually. His short film was an instant hit with the public and was shown internationally. Although considered little more than a curiosity today, it remains a significant precursor of an art form that was not even in its infancy at the time.

One year later, in 1903, American inventor Edwin S. Porter produced the first American silent movie, *The Great Train Robbery*, a twelve-minute film that greatly influenced the development of motion pictures, establishing many of cinema's basic techniques – movement of the camera close to the action, the use of separate shots, and editing of the shots to cut back and forth among different actions to form a unified narrative. He used these techniques to shape a story, rather than present a spectacle as earlier silent films had tended to do.

With the release of D.W. Griffith's *The Birth of a Nation* (1915), small theatres sprang up throughout the United States, and cinema emerged as a *de facto* art form. Griffith invented the close-up, with the camera showing the actor's emotions. His *Birth of a Nation*, a dazzling spectacle lasting three hours, stunned audiences and established cinema as an art form for cultured spectators. Yet the film's racist ideology – especially its defense of white supremacy to protect racial purity – was controversial in its own time and remains repugnant to this day. Simply put, the movie is racist, but is nonetheless an essential part of movie history.

Between 1915 and 1920, grandiose movie palaces were built throughout the United States and Europe. Hollywood started producing hundreds of films a year to satisfy an ever-increasing demand from a fanatical movie-going public. The vast majority of the films were Westerns, slapstick comedies, and romantic melodramas such as Cecil B. DeMille's *Male and Female* (1919). By the mid-1920s, movie studios had become distraction factories themselves, taking people's minds off daily problems. Movies were also perfect antidotes against boredom. The film medium had, in effect, emerged as a major force in the development of pop culture – a culture whose defining characteristic is an eclectic blending and mixing of the artistic and the diversionary.

Despite the stylistic innovations introduced by Griffith and others, which made narrative feature films highly popular, comedy remained the main staple of silent cinema. After the risqué comedies of the early years, a new comic style called 'slapstick' emerged. This boisterous, physical comedy was named for the stick wielded by clowns in Punch-and-Judy puppet shows. American Mack Sennett formed a new company, *Keystone*, in 1912 that played an important role in developing the genre. Sennett employed a host of talented comedians, the most notable of whom was the English actor Charlie Chaplin. At Keystone, Chaplin developed his signature zany character. He then went on to direct, produce, write, and star in his own movie productions. By the time of the First World War, such classic short comedies as *Easy Street* (1917) and *The Immigrant* (1917) brought him international acclaim greater than that of any other movie performer. In the 1920s, he began making feature-length comedies, such as *The Kid* (1921) and *The Gold Rush* (1925). Chaplin's comedy was firmly rooted in common life, and thus appealed to most audiences. Two other cinema comedians during the same era, Buster Keaton and Harold Lloyd, diversified and enlarged the slapstick genre, portraying young men coping with the conundrums of modern life.

Actually, throughout the early era it was not Hollywood, but Germany, who had the strongest film industry, even as American films made inroads there. Filmmaking in Germany emphasized cinema as an art form, not a 'distraction spectacle', with particular attention paid to visual representation in itself, conveyed through lighting and set design. Director Robert Wiene's *The Cabinet of Dr Caligari* (1919), with its disfigured sets and twisted narrative of a sleepwalking murderer who is controlled by a mysterious doctor, is an exemplar of early German cinematic art. Other leading German filmmakers during the 1920s included Fritz Lang, F.W. Murnau, and G.W. Pabst. Lang's films projected extraordinarily macabre visions of contemporary life and portentous ones of the future. His most famous silent film was *Metropolis* (1927), a stunning depiction of a futuristic city with railway bridges running between upper stories of skyscrapers, while workers toiled at huge machines underground. Murnau made works of deep psychological complexity, including the classic vampire film *Nosferatu* (1922) and *The Last Laugh* (1924), which portrayed the morbid thoughts of an aging doorman demoted to a washroom attendant. Pabst, known as a realist filmmaker, directed the highly popular sexual tragedy *Pandora's Box* (1928).

In the former Soviet Union, the works of filmmakers such as Sergei Eisenstein and Dziga Vertov were far ahead of their time, posing challenging questions about the relationship between politics and art. Eisenstein's *Strike* (1925) and *October* (1928) are still viewable today as emotionally powerful testaments to human perseverance. Vertov produced persuasive documentaries, rather than feature films, developing 'montage' as part of an emerging cinematic code. Montage refers to the composition of images by juxtaposing or superimposing them in some way to create a rapid succession of different shots in a scene.

In France, filmmakers introduced surrealism into movie-making art – a form of representation that incorporates bizarre images in order to portray the grotesque nature of everyday reality. For example, *Entr'acte* (1924), directed by René Clair, used early trick camera photography to produce surrealist images on the screen with animated designs and objects. In like fashion, Fernand Léger made *Le ballet mécanique* (1924) and Marcel Duchamp *Anemic Cinema* (1926). A filmmaker who brought even more creative ambitions to the screen was Abel Gance, whose five-hour film *Napoléon* (1927) showed images in different combinations on three side-by-side screens. Filmmakers from other countries also produced important movies in France. Carl-Theodor Dreyer of Denmark directed *The Passion of Joan of Arc* (1928), considered a classic for its unprecedented psychological realism. The Spaniards Luis Buñuel and Salvador Dalí produced a surrealist film, *An Andalusian Dog* (1929), which became famous for its unusual and disturbing imagery.

The power of the new film medium caught everyone's attention. Many nations sought to establish their own film production as a matter of importance to national culture, sometimes by placing quotas on film imports. Meanwhile, film became an international medium, with filmmakers creating works outside their homeland or emigrating to take up their careers elsewhere. The 'global culture' called into existence by paper print technology in the Gutenberg Galaxy was given some of its contemporary finishing touches by the film medium in the Electronic Galaxy. The consequences for society of this proliferating new medium were much debated. Movie stars such as Charlie Chaplin, Greta Garbo, and Rudolph Valentino were seen, admired, and imitated by millions. Censorship bodies tried to control the influence of films by editing them before exhibition, or by proposing rules and standards for producers to follow.

Movies adopted genres from print and from earlier entertainment domains. These included comedy, the Western, mystery, horror, romance, melodrama, and the war story. Cinema came up with many of its own variations and combinations as, for example, the comedy-drama. The hallmark of the early cinematic genres was their familiarity – spectators could easily identify a genre easily since its story, character, setting, and costume conventions were highly predictable.

The transition from silent to sound films was so rapid that many movies released in 1928 and 1929 had begun production as silent films but were hastily turned into 'talkies', as they were called, to meet the growing demand. The first talkie was *The Jazz Singer*, released in 1927, starring the legendary actor Al Jolson. However, it was with the release of *Applause* (1929), by American director Rouben Mamoulian, that the power of the talkie manifested itself to all. Mamoulian overlapped sound from different sources. The impressionistic effects he created contrasted with efforts to develop a natural or realistic standard for film sound. Gangster films and musicals dominated the new 'talking screen' of the early 1930s. These created a great stir among politicians and self-appointed moral guardians, who believed that they had too much of an impact on audiences. As a consequence, the American politician and motion-picture executive William Harrison Hays established a *Production Code* (1930), as president of the Motion Picture Producers and Distributors of America (1922–45), which prescribed the moral content of American films from 1930 to 1966. The vogue of filming novels reached a peak in the late 1930s with expensively mounted productions of classic novels, and one of the most popular films in motion-picture history, *Gone with the Wind* (1939).

The golden age

Escaping from the dreariness of everyday life through motion pictures became a veritable vogue in the 1930s and 1940s – the period of time now called cinema's 'golden age'. Moreover, going to the movies was developing into much more than just a 'night out', but rather something that seemed strangely to unify people in a ritualistic way. People started naming their children after movie actors and movie characters. The musical soundtracks of certain movies became hits on their own and were played on radio and sold through recordings.

The golden age started with a cycle of classic horror films, including

Dracula (1931), *Frankenstein* (1931), and *The Mummy* (1932), which spawned a series of sequels and spin-offs that lasted throughout the 1930s. One of the most enduring films of the decade was the musical fantasy *The Wizard of Oz* (1939), based on a book by L. Frank Baum (1856–1919) – a children's movie with a frightful theme that reflected the emerging cynicism of society at large – namely, that all human aspirations are ultimately make-believe, that the 'Wizard' at the end of the 'road of life' is really a fraud, a charlatan. The fun of living is getting to Oz, not finding out the truth about Oz.

One American filmmaker who came to Hollywood from radio in 1940 was the writer-director-actor Orson Welles, who experimented with new camera angles and sound effects that greatly extended the representational power of film. His *Citizen Kane* (1941) and *The Magnificent Ambersons* (1942) influenced the subsequent work of virtually every major filmmaker in the world. Welles' originality resulted from unusual techniques, such as maintaining deep focus (in which all objects in the sets, both near to and far from the camera, are in focus), employing low and high camera angles and long takes (periods of uninterrupted filming), and deploying sound and lighting as editing devices.

The growing artistic value of cinema came to the forefront in the late 1940s, when Italian cineastes, such as Roberto Rossellini with *Open City* (1945) and Vittorio De Sica with *Bicycle Thieves* (1949), achieved an intimacy and depth of emotion that radically transformed motion pictures. Known as 'neorealism', the style was continued well into the 1950s, 1960s and 1970s which saw the release of such classic films as Pier Paolo Pasolini's *The Gospel According to Saint Matthew* (1966), Federico Fellini's *La Strada* (1954), *La Dolce Vita* (1960), *8 1/2* (1963), and *Juliet of the Spirits* (1965), Michelangelo Antonioni's *L'Avventura* (1959) and *Red Desert* (1964), Bernardo Bertolucci's *The Conformist* (1970) and *1900* (1977), and Lina Wertmuller's *Swept Away* (1975) and *Seven Beauties* (1976).

Two genres that flourished with the coming of sound were gangster films and musicals. The gangster movie capitalized on public concern over increasing crime as well as the notoriety of famous criminal gang leaders. *Little Caesar* (1930) made actor Edward G. Robinson a star in the role of Italian-American Rico Bandello, and actor James Cagney won acclaim portraying Irish-American Tom Powers in *The Public Enemy* (1931). Musical films were a logical outcome of recordings. They gained wide popular appeal after Warner Brothers released a series of musicals that broke with stage conventions, filming large groups of dancers from multiple viewpoints to create unique cinematic spectacles. These included *42nd Street, Gold Diggers of 1933*, and *Footlight Parade* (all 1933), choreographed by American Busby Berkeley. Perhaps the most popular cinematic musicals of all time were those that featured individual performers, in particular the dance team of Fred Astaire and Ginger Rogers in such films as *Top Hat* (1935) and *Swing Time* (1937).

An older genre that gained new vitality with the coming of sound was the horror film. The heavy voice of Hungarian-born actor Bela Lugosi gave new thrills to audiences in the vampire film *Dracula* (1931), directed by American Tod Browning. In *Frankenstein* (1931), directed by British-born filmmaker James Whale, actor Boris Karloff created a remarkably compassionate portrayal of the blundering monster brought to life by an ambitious scientist.

In Britain, producer-director Alexander Korda made a worldwide impact with his *The Private Life of Henry VIII* (1933), starring Charles Laughton. Alfred Hitchcock directed popular thrillers and espionage films such as *The 39 Steps* (1935). Britain also developed a significant government-sponsored documentary film practice under the leadership of John Grierson. In France, there emerged a distinctive style of filmmaking called 'poetic realism', which focused on ordinary people struggling with the banality of their existence. Leading directors of the movement included Jean Vigo with *L'atalante* (1934) and Marcel Carné with *Daybreak* (1939). However, the most versatile and prolific director was Jean Renoir, whose best-known works from the period include *The Grand Illusion* (1937) and *Rules of the Game* (1939). In Germany, Fritz Lang and G.W. Pabst, leading directors of the silent period, made innovative early sound films – Lang with *M* (1931) and Pabst with *Comradeship* (1931).

During World War II Frank Capra, John Ford, William Wyler, John Huston, and other Hollywood directors joined the armed forces and made war-related documentaries. Capra supervised the *Why We Fight* series (1942–45), seven films which sought to explain the reason for war, and Huston directed *The Battle of San Pietro* (1945), which depicted the grim consequences of warfare on the human spirit.

Film animation gained enormously in popularity during the golden age. Walt Disney made the first animated cartoon with synchronized sound, *Steamboat Willie*, in 1928. It was the third film to feature the popular Mickey Mouse character. Disney also pioneered the use of colour animation, producing *Flowers and Trees* (1932), the first film released in the three-colour Technicolor process. He began making feature-length animated films in colour with *Snow White and the Seven Dwarfs* (1937). Colour was used in only a minority of films until the 1950s, when Hollywood turned more frequently to colour in an effort to differentiate cinema from the increasingly popular medium of television, then available only in black-and-white. Further simplification and improvements in colour technology meant that colour movies had become the standard and black-and-white the exception by the 1960s.

Contemporary movie-making

Contemporary movie-making can be said to have started after World War II. The advent of television caused the greatest threat to the hegemony of the cinema after the War. Although motion-picture attendance had begun to decline before television became widely available, the rapid spread of home television sets in the 1950s was accompanied by a steady decrease in movie-going that continued right into the 1960s. In an effort to offset television's appeal, movie studios adopted new technologies – such as wide-screen and three-dimensional processes – that offered a more spectacular screen image. These briefly stemmed attendance loss following their introduction in 1953, but they could not halt the longer-term transformation of the TV-mediated pop culture. Three-dimensionality, or 3-D, was achieved by recording multiple images through filters that directed light and required viewers to wear specially designed spectacles to observe the three-dimensional effects. In 1954, dozens of 3-D films were released by Hollywood, featuring effects that were purported by movie trailers to 'come off the screen right at you'. But the popularity of this gimmick film soon waned, and it quickly dropped (no pun intended) from sight.

In the 1970s, cinema made a veritable comeback. No doubt, the 'pop culture savvy' of such Hollywood directors as Francis Ford Coppola, George Lucas, Martin Scorsese, and Steven Spielberg had a lot to do with this. Coppola directed a huge hit of the early 1970s, *The Godfather* (1972), a film that showed the first concrete signs of cinema's revival. Lucas made *American Graffiti* (1973), a highly popular film about teenagers that looked back nostalgically to the previous decade. Scorsese's *Mean Streets* (1973), set in the ethnic milieu of New York City's Little Italy neighbourhood, garnered much interest and stimulated much debate. After directing several small films, Spielberg, the youngest of the group, directed the film whose enormous success was to change the American movie landscape, *Jaws* (1975). As a movie about a killer shark that terrorizes a small beach community, it became the model for a number of films in which fear-inspiring creatures threatened helpless victims.

Many of these directors continued as important filmmakers following the 1970s revival. For example, Spielberg has made a host of other multimillion-dollar blockbusters since the 1980s. With *Close Encounters of the Third Kind* (1977) and *E.T.* (1982), he capitalized on a widespread fascination with extraterrestrial life. His *Raiders of the Lost Ark* (1981), *Indiana Jones and the Temple of Doom* (1984), and *Indiana Jones and the Last Crusade* (1989) were clever remakes of the popular serial cliffhangers of the 1930s – recycling the same mythological themes in new technologically-effective ways. Most of Spielberg's films rely, in fact, heavily on high-tech special effects. His *Jurassic*

Park (1993), for instance, featured frighteningly realistic computer-generated dinosaurs. Within the first four weeks of its release, it became the highest-grossing film up to that time, only to be surpassed by *Titanic* (1998) five years later.

Other directors also helped to bring the film medium back to centre stage. Woody Allen made wry urban comedies, such as the Academy Award-winning *Annie Hall* (1977), that appealed to the 'baby-boomer' generation. Michael Cimino won an Academy Award for *The Deer Hunter* (1978), a critically acclaimed cinematic exploration of the Vietnam War – another favourite baby-boomer theme. British director Ridley Scott made two highly significant films, *Blade Runner* (1982), a futuristic film praised for its visual effects, and *Thelma and Louise* (1991), about two women on the run from a male-dominated society. More recently, he directed the thriller *Hannibal* (2001), emphasizing the 'humanity' that harbours even within heinous, twisted psychopaths. *Blue Velvet* (1986), directed by David Lynch, a surreal film set in a small American town, was ranked by critics as one of the top American films of the 1980s. Similarly ranked was *Do the Right Thing* (1989) by filmmaker Spike Lee, who also directed a biographical film about a militant and controversial black leader of the 1960s, *Malcolm X* (1992). Lee's film followed another polemical film examining recent history, *JFK* (1991), directed by Oliver Stone, which claimed that a conspiracy among government officials lay behind the 1963 assassination of President John F. Kennedy. Actor-director Clint Eastwood gained recognition as a major filmmaker with *Unforgiven* (1992), a Western that won Academy Awards for best picture and director.

By the mid-1990s, movie-going had once again become the 'thing to do' for vast audiences. Cinema had regained its status as a pop culture trend-setter. It cleverly promoted the 'girl power' trend in society at large with an end-of-decade fare of movies that often featured female actors dressed in leather, stiletto-heeled boots, with minds like a steel trap and bodies to match. This representational trend continues to this day. Female heroes abound and, often, outmatch their male opponents on the silver screen, who are overwhelmed by their toughness and beauty all wrapped into one. For instance, the film *Crouching Tiger, Hidden Dragon* (2001), a martial arts fantasy set in nineteenth-century China, focused on three generations of warrior women, the youngest of whom could wipe out an army of male thugs without even sweating. However, as we saw in the opening chapter with the Airoldi watch ad, the idea of a 'feral woman' is really nothing more than pop culture's recycling of an ancient mythic idea – as expressed for example in the mythic character of Diana the huntress.

At the same time that Hollywood regained its bearings in the home pop culture market, the cinematic traditions of other countries continued to flourish. One of the most distinctive and original directors to emerge in the post-Second World War international cinema stage was Sweden's Ingmar Bergman, who brought an intense philosophical and intellectual depth to his films, treating the themes of personal isolation, sexual conflict, and religious obsession with stark cinematic imagery. In *The Seventh Seal* (1956) he probed the mystery of life and spirituality through the trials of a medieval knight playing a game of chess with Death. In *Wild Strawberries* (1957) he highlighted the role of memory in the creation of Selfhood, using a series of poetic flashbacks through which an elderly professor reviewed his life. He dissected the human condition starkly in a series of subsequent films – *Persona* (1966), *Cries and Whispers* (1972), *Scenes from a Marriage* (1973), and *Autumn Sonata* (1978) – which mocked the penchant in the human species to search for meaning to its existence.

Italian cinema introduced the *on location* type of film – i.e. the film that captured events in city streets and other authentic settings, rather than on studio lots – with post-synchronized sound (the dubbing of dialogue in the studio after filming) that made it possible to utilize a more fluid camera movement amid realistic settings. Director Luchino Visconti made what is often considered to be the first such film, *Obsession* (1942), during the war years. He was followed by Federico Fellini, who got his start in the neorealist movement as a scriptwriter, becoming a director in the 1950s. Fellini's movies became influential worldwide, especially among filmmakers in Asia, Africa, and Latin America, who saw his mould of cinema-making as an alternative to Hollywood's dream and distraction factory and a means of making inexpensive films about their own histories and peoples.

In late 1950s France, a similar type of movement, known as 'new wave', was spearheaded by François Truffaut, whose first feature *The 400 Blows* (1959) remains a classic of stark realism. With *Breathless* (1961), Jean-Luc Godard challenged narrative conventions by utilizing 'jump cuts', gaps used for breaking the temporal continuity of a scene. His innovation signalled a desire among filmmakers to reconceptualize cinema, while at the same time paying homage to Hollywood and cinematic pop culture.

The most prolific and controversial among the post-war German directors was Rainer Werner Fassbinder, who made nearly 40 films over a 13-year career before his death in 1982. Fassbinder's films dealt primarily with power and desire in sexual relationships. A significant aspect of the postwar German scene was the prominence of women filmmakers such as Helke Sander and Helma Sanders-Brahms, who approached history and modern life from a refreshing feminist viewpoint.

In Britain, veteran directors such as Michael Powell, David Lean, and Carol Reed, as well as such newcomers as Laurence Olivier, contributed to an extraordinary period of creativity in British cinema that ended only in the late

1950s. Lean won Hollywood awards for best picture and best director with *The Bridge on the River Kwai* (1957) and *Lawrence of Arabia* (1962). Karel Reisz's *Saturday Night and Sunday Morning* (1960), Lindsay Anderson's *This Sporting Life* (1963) and Tony Richardson's *The Loneliness of the Long Distance Runner* (1962) emphasized social realism. Feminist directors such as Sally Potter, and filmmakers representing black and gay cultures, such as Isaac Julien and Derek Jarman, set British filmmaking apart from that of other countries in the 1960s. In subsequent decades, Irish cinema started gaining attention, culminating in *The Crying Game* (1992) by Neil Jordan, which became an international hit.

The period of *glasnost* in the 1980s led to the release in Russia of older films that the Soviet government had suppressed, as well as new films that dealt with the previously off-limits topics of politics and private life. With the end of the Soviet Union in the late 1980s, some Russian filmmakers began to examine the burdens of their recent social experiment. Eastern European countries too started gaining international prestige with their cinematic art, and continue to receive international attention to this day. Poland was perhaps the first to make its mark internationally with the films of Andrzej Wajda. Czechoslovakia produced its own new wave cinema with such directors as Milos Forman and Jirí Menzel. In Yugoslavia, filmmaker Dusan Makavejev gained prominence with *Man Is Not a Bird* (1966). In Hungary, Miklós Jancsó gained worldwide attention with his meticulously choreographed *Red Psalm* (1972), a work in the form of a folk ballet depicting historical events. In Romania, Lucien Pintilie made *The Oak* (1992) and other films about the region's recent history that captured wide audiences across the globe.

International recognition for the film culture of Japan came after 1945, beginning with acclaim for Japanese directors Mizoguchi Kenji, Ozu Yasujiro, and Kurosawa Akira, who are now acknowledged as leading filmmakers of the 1950s. Ozu made intricate, intimate films representing the pitiable aspects of domestic life. In the 1960s, Japan had its own new wave movement with the films of Oshima Nagisa, Imamura Shohei, and Shinoda Masahiro.

Since the 1930s, filmmaking in India was perceived primarily as a musical art. In a country with dozens of major languages, film music reached across linguistic barriers. Cinema performers gained celebrity from follow-up recordings and radio broadcasts of their music. The first Indian filmmaker to be appreciated internationally as a cinema stylist was Satyajit Ray. The Indian film industry is the largest, in terms of numbers, in the world.

In China, filmmaking became an important art form in the 1980s. A new generation of directors, including Chen Kaige, Zhang Yimou, and Tian Zhuangzhuang, led the way towards the establishment of an indigenous Chinese cinematic art form. They did this by breaking with the tradition of studio filmmaking, going to rural China to make films of daily life there.

The English-speaking nations of Canada, Australia, and New Zealand had difficulty establishing their own film cultures after the war, because American and British films filled their theatres. In Canada, filmmakers Chantal Akerman, David Cronenberg, and Atom Egoyan have recently won international acclaim for their art. In Australia, Peter Weir earned acclaim for *Picnic at Hanging Rock* (1975) and *The Last Wave* (1977), Fred Schepisi for *The Chant of Jimmie Blacksmith* (1978), Gillian Armstrong for *My Brilliant Career* (1979), and Bruce Beresford for *Breaker Morant* (1980).

Although Egypt and a few other Arab and African countries had produced films for decades previously, filmmaking generally began to develop on the continent of Africa only after the 1960s, following the withdrawal of European colonial powers. Egyptian cinema experienced a surge as political changes made it possible for filmmakers such as Youssef Chahine to produce social commentaries in a neorealist style. In other parts of Africa, the importance and role of indigenous cinema grew steadily from the mid-1960s onwards. For example, African filmmaker Ousmane Sembéne of Senegal, a novelist turned film director, has become a leading director with movies such as *La noire* (1966), the first black African feature film. Other important African filmmakers to emerge include Souleymane Cisse of Mali and Idrissa Ouedraogo of Burkina Faso.

A prominent film movement, known as *cinema novo* ('new cinema'), took a foothold in Brazil with works that dramatized the nation's social ills. Directors Glauber Rocha and Nelson Pereira dos Santos made powerful films set in remote regions of the country depicting the dire dehumanizing effects of systemic poverty. In Cuba, filmmakers Tomás Gutiérrez Alea and Humberto Solas made films that challenged the status quo with regards to human rights and the role of women in society. In Mexico, Paul LeDuc's *Frida* (1984), which dramatized the life of painter Frida Kahlo and Alfonso Arau's *Como agua para chocolate* (1991) became highly popular both within and outside Mexico, as works blending realistic detail with elements of fantasy and magic.

Video and disc

The late 1980s saw a revolution in the way people perceived movies, with major releases being made available for home video viewing almost immediately after they left the movie theatre. This development, combined with the advent of cable television featuring relatively current films on special channels, seemed to threaten the long-term survival of movie theatres and created a climate of uneasiness in movie studios throughout the world similar to that of the early 1950s, when television began to challenge the hegemony of motion pictures. As a result, film companies started increasingly favouring large spectacle movies with fantastic special effects in the hope of luring the public away from home videos and back to the big screen. But their fears turned out to be unfounded. As in the early days of cinema, going to the movies is still perceived as a communal event, something that is to be shared with others, albeit in a strangely silent and uncommunicative way. Being at a movie theatre is a social act. So, despite the challenge from video cassettes and more recently video discs, the traditional movie theatre has remained as popular as ever.

The first home videotape recorder to be sold was the Beta machine invented by the Sony Corporation in the late 1970s. The popularity of that device was quickly eclipsed by the VHS videotape format, introduced into the market through clever advertising by the Radio Corporation of America, becoming the industry videotape standard. Sony's Betacam system, however, is still the standard in commercial broadcasting equipment.

The videocassette recorder (VCR), with its capacity to play prerecorded videotapes that can be rented or purchased at video shops, and to record programmes shown on television for later playback, made an inevitable dint at first in movie-going. So too, as mentioned, did the cable television systems that emerged at about the same time, vastly expanding the number of channels available to the home viewer and providing access to recent movies via a pay-TV format. As these new technologies came into widespread use, movie studios were understandably worried. But, as mentioned above, it was all for naught. The studios had forgotten a major lesson of cinematic history – being in a movie theatre with a real audience is part of the whole communal effect that cinema is intended to create.

As it has turned out, the advent of video has actually fostered a much wider audience for movies. All kinds of films, past and present, are now available to the home viewer; cassette rental and sales earn new revenue for motion-picture companies (in some cases, more than their theatrical releases); and advance sales of video rights enable small production companies to finance the creation of low-budget films. With cable networks as additional sources of revenue, and functioning in some cases as producers themselves, a substantial increase in independent feature-film production has ensued. Digital video discs (DVDs), invented in the 1990s, have stimulated even more interest in movies. Although they make it possible to enjoy movies in the home with all the technological splendour offered by movie theatres (given the right equipment), DVDs are in fact entrenching movie-going even more so in social life, not replacing it.

Cinema and postmodernism

Most feature films are, essentially, visual narratives. This is why, according to some cinema semioticians (e.g. Metz 1974), they can be viewed as having the same structural features of language. In my opinion, this is true only in part. It is more accurate to say that the cinematic text expands the categories of language by blending dialogue, music, scenery, and action in a cohesive way. For this reason, it can be characterized as a composite sign made up of verbal and non-verbal signifiers.

Its composite nature is what makes cinematic representation powerful. A detective movie, for instance, is made up of dialogue between the actors. The narration of the action unfolds through camera shots, montage, and other types of cinematic techniques. Music may be added to emphasize dramatic and emotional aspects of the text. Together, the experience of the text is synesthetic, blending different sensory modalities.

One technique for which cinema is especially well-suited is called 'postmodern' – a hotly discussed and debated topic in semiotic criticism throughout the 1980s and 1990s. There are two main ways in which cineastes have used postmodern technique: (1) creating scenery to reinforce the irony or nihilism of the modern world; (2) using only scenery to deliver the message. Two classic examples of the first type are the movies *Clockwork Orange* and *Blade Runner*; a well-known example of the second is *Koyaaniskatsi*. These will be discussed shortly below.

Postmodern art did not originate in cinema. Its origins can be traced to the theatre of Irish-born playwright and novelist, Samuel Beckett (1906–89), a leading figure of the movement known as the *theatre of the absurd*. In his novels and plays, Beckett focused on the wretchedness of existence, exposing the essential frightfulness of the human condition, which he ultimately reduced to the solitary Self. His late 1940s play, *Waiting for Godot*, is a remarkable work of 'proto-postmodern' drama. People reacted strongly to the play, becoming an instant classic of the Western theatre soon after its debut on television in 1951. *Waiting for Godot* appeals to the modern imagination because, like the two tramps in it, many people have become sceptical about the presence of any 'purpose' to human existence. The play challenges the age-old belief that there is a 'meaning to life', insinuating instead that all our meaning structures and systems (language, religious concepts, etc.) are no more than illusory screens we have set up to avoid the 'truth' – that life is an absurd moment of consciousness on its way to extinction.

But despite its nihilism, people seem paradoxically to discover 'meaning' in Beckett's play. The tramps in his masterpiece are perpetually waiting for a character named Godot – a name coined in obvious reference to God. Godot never comes in the play. But deep inside us, as audience members, we yearningly hope that Beckett is wrong, and that on some other stage, in some other play, the design of things will become known to us – that God will indeed come. That is the ambiguity and dilemma of the human condition that postmodern art explores. It is a highly absurdist, nihilistic, and ironic form of representation that attacks traditions and value systems as concoctions of human fancy, rather than as systems reflecting a mysterious purpose. But in so doing, it forces us nonetheless to think about the very systems it decries.

The term *postmodernism* is rarely applied to Beckett's play for the simple reason that it was coined by architects after the play in the 1960s to designate an architectural movement that rejected the earlier modernist style (characterized by the building of monolithic corporation skyscrapers and tall apartment buildings, etc.) that had degenerated into sterile and monotonous formulas, reintroducing traditional and classical elements. Postmodern architects called for greater individuality, complexity, and eccentricity in design, while also demanding acknowledgment of historical precedent and continuity. Shortly after its adoption in architecture, the notion of postmodernism started to catch on more broadly, becoming a catchphrase for a more general movement in philosophy and the arts. But Beckett's play clearly anticipates the whole postmodern movement in the arts.

Clockwork Orange and *Blade Runner*

In no other art form did postmodern technique find such a welcoming home as the cinema. One of the first movies designed in a postmodern way was Stanley Kubrick's (1928–2000) cinematic masterpiece of 1971, *A Clockwork Orange.* The setting for the movie is Britain in the future (which many critics claim foreshadowed the world as we know it today). A teenage thug, Alex De Large, lives a life of crime and sex in a wanton and reckless fashion. Caught and imprisoned for murder, he volunteers to undergo an experimental shock treatment therapy designed to brainwash him to become nauseated by his previous lifestyle. However, Mr Alexander, one of Alex's victims, traps him with the aim of avenging himself. He hopes to drive Alex to commit suicide ironically to the strains of Beethoven's ninth symphony. But Alex is supported by the media and soon after he is released and restored to health through therapy.

The movie ends in typical postmodern fashion with no true resolution. But the scenario of senseless, aimless violence that a teenager is capable of perpetrating is a typical postmodern portrait of contemporary life. Alex is a goalless and ruthless creature trapped in a weary, decaying environment. His only way out is through intimidation and physicality. He is a 'ticking timebomb' ready to explode at any instant. Alex feels an acute and urgent need to change – indeed to 'save' – the world. But he does not know what to save it from! The rage in Alex's eyes is the rage shown by contemporary street youths.

The film's fragmented images of life on the streets reinforce Alex's overall view that reality is illusory, thus bolstering the movie's subtext that life is absurd, without a purpose, and that human actions are a montage of illusory ready-made stories with no real substance behind them, concocted simply to help us wait for our inevitable extinction and return to nothingness.

Some of the movie's scenic techniques were emulated by Ridley Scott in his 1982 masterpiece, *Blade Runner*, based on a science fiction story titled *Do Androids Dream of Electric Sheep?* by Philip K. Dick (1928–82). The movie still attracts considerable interest from movie aficionados. Before discussing the movie, it is necessary to discuss briefly the science fiction genre itself.

Unlike traditional forms of fiction, this genre deals typically with the effects of science or future events on human beings. Although it has ancient roots – e.g. in his *True History* (160 AD) Lucian of Samosata described a trip to the moon; the seventeenth century British prelate and historian Francis Godwin also wrote of travel to the moon; and the English statesman Sir Thomas More wrote about a futuristic world in *Utopia* (1516) – science fiction as we now know it traces its origins to the period after the Industrial Revolution when, in her novel *Frankenstein* (1818), the British novelist Mary Shelley (1797–1851) explored the potential of science and technology for doing good or evil. Right after the publication of her novel, the science-fiction genre emerged as a new form of popular fiction. The first writer to specialize in the new genre was French author Jules Verne (1828–1905). His highly popular novels included *Journey to the Centre of the Earth* (1864) and *Around the World in Eighty Days* (1873). The first major English writer of science fiction was H.G. Wells (1866–1946), whose *Time Machine* (1895), *The Island of Dr Moreau* (1896), and *The War of the Worlds* (1898) became classics the instant they were published.

In the twentieth century the popularity of science fiction grew with the publication of *Brave New World* (1932) by Aldous Huxley (1894–1963) and *Nineteen Eighty-four* (1949) by George Orwell (1903-1950), with the advent of movie sci-fi thrillers, starting with Méliès' *A Trip to the Moon* (1902), and with the rise of TV science fiction programmes such as *The Twilight Zone* (1959–64, revived 1985–87), *Lost in Space* (1965–68), *Star Trek* (1966–69), *Dr Who* (1963–91), and the *X-Files* (1993–).

The movie *Blade Runner* was scripted in a 1980s' style of science-fiction writing known as 'cyberpunk'. The target of cyberpunk writers was dehumanized societies dominated by technology and science, emphasizing the fallibility of scientists. *Blade Runner* deals with the following typical cyberpunk theme: what if we could bring machines to life? What would they be like? Would they be more 'human' than humans?

Against the depressing backdrop of a contemporary choking urban landscape, Rick Deckard is one of a select few futuristic law-enforcement officers, nicknamed 'blade runners', who have been trained to detect and track down 'replicants', powerful humanoid robots who have been engineered to do the work of people in space. But the replicants have gone amok. They have somehow developed the mental characteristics of humans and have started to ask fundamental philosophical questions about their own existence, made all the more urgent by the limited lifespan programmed into them. A desperate band of these killer replicants has made its way back to earth seeking to have their programs changed. They are looking desperately for the sinister corporate tycoon responsible for their creation so that he can give them eternal life. Deckard's assignment is to track down these runaway replicants and terminate them.

His search takes place in an urban wasteland where punk mutants control the streets while the pathetic inhabitants of endless blocks of gloomy high-rises remain glued to their TV sets. Deckard relies on a VCR, complete with stop action and precision image-enhancers, to find the replicants through dark alleys abandoned to the forces of anarchy.

The method used by Deckard to identify a suspect as being either 'human' or 'replicant' is reminiscent of the classic Turing test used by artificial intelligence theorists. The British mathematician Alan Turing (1912–54) suggested, shortly before his untimely death, that one could program a computer in such a way that it would be virtually impossible to discriminate between its answers and those contrived by a human being. His notion has become immortalized as the Turing test. It goes somewhat like this. Suppose a human observer is placed in a room that hides a programmed computer on one side and, on the other, another human being. The computer and hidden human being can only respond to questions in writing on pieces of paper which are passed back and forth from the observer to the computer and human being through slits in the wall. If the observer cannot identify, on the basis of the written responses, who is the computer and who the human being, then he or she can only conclude that the machine is 'intelligent'. It has passed the Turing test. Deckard's detection technique rejects the validity of the Turing test because he focuses on the reactions of his interviewee's eyes.

The eye is an obvious symbol of humanity. The replicants and the various mannequins seen in the movie are, clearly, icons of the human form. One of the replicants is even killed ironically by a mannequin. Human-like toys are also seen from time to time. But there is one feature that differentiates human anatomy from artificially-made anatomies – the eye. Replicants use their 'eyes' exclusively to see; humans use them as well to show feeling. Aware of the mysterious power of the human eye, the replicants kill their maker by poking out his eyes. Interestingly, we are never sure throughout the movie if Deckard is a human or a replicant himself, since the camera never provides a close-up of his eyes.

In this postmodern scenario the replicants, paradoxically, are more 'human' than the human characters. Deckard even falls in love with one of them, Rachel, whose name has obvious intertextual connections with the Biblical character of the same name. She helps him track down his prey, falling in love with him. The film makes many other references to the Bible. For example, near the end, a naked replicant Roy, with only a white cloth around his waist, in obvious allusion to the Crucifixion scene, saves Deckard's life at the cost of his own. The white dove that appears when Roy 'expires' is reminiscent of the dove that was sent to Noah's ark in the midst of torrential rain to help the ark find a safe place away from the deluge – a symbolic quest for a safer future. That is, in fact, what happens right after Roy's demise, as Deckard and Rachel escape the gruesome city scene to fly off into the countryside. The dark, gloomy postmodern atmosphere suddenly clears up, the sun comes out, and a 'new dawn' rises. These are images that call to mind the Garden of Eden scene. For the sake of historical accuracy, however, it should be mentioned that this was not the original ending of the movie, but one that the producers insisted upon. Nevertheless, in my view, it is as valid as the director's cut version.

Blade Runner asks the fundamental questions of philosophy in a new way: What is a human being? What is real? Is there any meaning to existence? By making the replicants the iconic simulacra of human beings, and by transforming their struggle to survive and to know who they are into a reflection of our own struggle, the movie is about the nature and meaning of human life.

Koyaanisqatsi

American director Godfrey Reggio's brilliant 1983 film *Koyaanisqatsi* is both an exemplar of the second type of postmodern technique in cinema described above and a scathing critique of industrialized society. It is a film without words that unfolds through a series of discontinuous images. On the one hand, this emphasizes how disjointed the contemporary world has become. On the other hand, it is an example of what postmodern art is like – a parody of documentary-style films and TV programmes. The film has no characters, plot, dialogue, or commentary – in a word, nothing recognizable as a narrative. The camera juxtaposes contrasting images of cars on freeways, atomic blasts, litter on urban streets, people shopping in malls, housing complexes, buildings being demolished, etc. We see the world as the camera sees it. And it is a turgid, gloomy world with no purpose or apparent meaning whatsoever. People walk in crowds, or perform routine tasks, like mindless creatures. To emphasize the insanity and absurdity of this world Reggio incorporates the mesmerizing music of Philip Glass (1937–) into his cinematic text. The music acts as a guide to understanding the images, interpreting them melodically and rhythmically. We can 'feel' the senselessness of human actions in such a world in the contrasting melodies and rhythms of Glass's music. His slow rhythms tire us with their heaviness, and his *prestissimi* – which accompany a demented chorus of singers chanting in the background – assault our senses. When this musical-imagistic frenzy finally ends, we feel an enormous sense of relief.

In a certain sense, the whole film can be conceived as a musical sonata with an opening part, or exposition, a middle developmental section, and a final recapitulation with coda. The film starts off with a glimpse into a vastly different world – the world of the Hopi tribes of Arizona. This is a world firmly implanted in a holistic mythical view of existence, a view that does not separate human achievement from Nature. Glass's choral music in this exposition is spiritual, sacred, and profound. It inspires reverence for human spirituality. This stands in dark contrast to the development of the filmic sonata, which consists of a cornucopia of dissonant images of a decaying, senseless, industrialized world. Then, we are taken back, at the end, to the Hopi world. As in any recapitulation, the opening profound strains of the choir come back, hauntingly, awesomely, and with a warning this time (the coda) which is projected onto the screen:

> *koyaanisqatsi* (from the Hopi language) (1) crazy life, (2) life in turmoil, (3) life out of balance, (4) life disintegrating, (5) a state of life that calls for another way of living.

We are left, in this way, with no resolution and no dramatic blockbuster ending. The movie presents a bleak portrait of the contemporary world in cinematic language without words. Like *Waiting for Godot*, we leave the theatre without any *catharsis*, as Aristotle called the 'purging effects' of a great play. That is the trademark of all postmodern movies.

Primarily through cinema, postmodern art tends to destabilize the status quo and, ironically, the hegemony of the Hollywood distraction factory that itself allows directors to make postmodern art. As social critic Jean-François Lyotard (1984: xxiv) states, postmodernism impugns the status quo because it shows that the 'narrative function is losing its functors, its great heroes, its great dangers, its great voyages, its great goal'. Some, especially radical critics, see postmodernism as a welcome relief, a liberation from the 'great white male story' that has guided the course of Western civilization since its inception. These critics are essentially correct. In parodying traditional language and narrative, postmodern art has done humanity a service. However, in making Western culture more aware of its illusory past, it has concomitantly engendered a kind of ahistoricity and nihilism that is of little value to the progress of the human species. The postmodern perspective is itself a product of a self-deprecating ironic worldview.

Postmodern cinema is powerful because it is so critical and reflective. But ultimately, the human spirit cries out for something more emotionally satisfying, something more *poetic*. Indeed, today movies such as *Koyaanisqatsi* are no longer being produced, except maybe by small experimental production companies. Nevertheless, postmodernism has left its mark in the cinema. Thrillers and mystery stories now dominate the movie-going scene, and most of these use cinematic techniques that are reminiscent of *Clockwork Orange* and *Blade Runner*. So, while postmodernism may have run its course as a widespread artistic movement, it has left many residues.

One recent example of its legacy is *The Matrix* (1999), a truly brilliant science fiction narrative that struck a resounding chord with young audiences brought up in a rapidly expanding Digital Galaxy. The movie exposes the artificial world of the computer screen, with intertextual allusions to the Bible. It critiques those 'technophiles' who are totally engrossed in their 'e-lives'. The 'computer nerds' rule – implies the movie – but what kind of world have they generated? The search for a higher state of consciousness, free of objects, is ultimately what satisfies humanity.

Cinema genres

Early filmmakers drew upon novels, vaudeville, the circus and other sources for their film scripts. But they also created their own genres that still greatly influence film production. Current films, television series, made-for-TV movies, mini-series, and even new forms of video and multimedia productions often follow the genre formulae of mainstream cinema.

The signification system that undergirds how we extract meaning from movies is yet another metaphor of our fragmented life experiences. Movies allow us to interconnect crime stories, mysterious happenings, romance and sex, and many more things that make up social reality through the camera's ever-probing eye.

The traditional genres

The most popular film genres of today derive their ancestry from the various early and golden age eras of filmmaking. These included:

- *Crime drama:* such as *Little Caesar* (1930)
- *Sci-fi:* such as *A Trip to the Moon* (1902)
- *Animation:* such as *Snow White and the Seven Dwarfs* (1937)
- *Comedy:* such as *It Happened One Night* (1934)
- *Character drama:* such as *Citizen Kane* (1941)
- *Historical drama:* such as *Intolerance* (1916)
- *Documentaries:* such as *Nanook of the North* (1921)
- *Detective movies:* such as *The Maltese Falcon* (1941)
- *Suspense movies:* such as *M* (1931)
- *Monster movies:* such as *King Kong* (1933)
- *Horror films:* such as *Nosferatu* (1922) and *Dracula* (1931)
- *Musicals:* such as *Flying Down to Rio* (1933) and *The Wizard of Oz* (1939)
- *War films:* such as *Birth of a Nation* (1915) and *Wings* (1931)
- *Action-adventure:* such as *Thief of Baghdad* (1921)
- *Film noir:* such as *Double Indemnity* (1944)
- *Westerns:* such as *The Great Train Robbery* (1903)
- *Romances:* such as *The Sheik* (1921)
- *Melodrama:* such as *The Perils of Pauline* (1914)

From the outset, movies were able to enter the world of mass culture easily because they made fiction available to large audiences, including audiences who previously had restricted access to printed works of fiction because of illiteracy. The central objective of all such early genres was, in fact, to provide the same kind of narrative distraction that print fiction had traditionally supplied. However, as mentioned above, unlike the novel, which is written by an author, or group of authors, and to which the reader has direct access, the film story is mediated by the director, adding a different level of signification to the text. In effect, whereas the interpretant level of print narrative – the act of deriving a meaning from a text – unfolds as an interplay between author and reader, in cinema it is mediated by another set of eyes, so to speak – those of the director. The director is, in fact, the one who sets the parameters of the interpretant for the movie viewer.

Take the case of Alfred Hitchcock (1899-1980), the British-born American motion-picture director, noted for his technically innovative and psychologically complex thrillers. Hitchcock entered the movie-making business in 1920 as a designer of silent-film title cards and worked as an art director, scriptwriter, and assistant director before directing his first picture, *The Pleasure Garden*, in 1925. However, it was not until his third picture, *The Lodger* (1926), about a man suspected of being Jack the Ripper, that he became identified with thrillers. In 1929, Hitchcock made his first talking film, *Blackmail*, which was acclaimed for its imaginative use of sound. In that movie, Hitchcock used a continually clanging shop bell to convey the heroine's feelings of guilt. During the 1930s he gained international fame with a series of immensely popular suspense dramas, including *The Man Who Knew Too Much* (1934), *The 39 Steps* (1935), and *The Lady Vanishes* (1938).

Hitchcock went to Hollywood in 1939. His first American film, *Rebecca* (1940), was adapted from a novel by British writer Daphne du Maurier and won an Academy Award for best picture. Afterwards, he returned to the thriller genre, becoming inextricably associated with it, creating expectations in his audiences of a specific kind. These included *Suspicion* (1941), about a woman who imagines that her husband is a murderer, and two widely praised suspense movies, *Shadow of a Doubt* (1943) and *Notorious* (1946).

Hitchcock embarked upon the most creative period of his career in the 1950s. In rapid succession, he produced and directed a series of inventive films, beginning with *Strangers on a Train* (1951) and continuing with *Rear Window* (1954), a remake of *The Man Who Knew Too Much* (1956), *Vertigo* (1958), *North by Northwest* (1959), *Psycho* (1960), and *The Birds* (1963). The plots of these pictures have been likened to dreams or nightmares that take place in daylight – a small town appears calm on the surface but reveals dark tensions underneath; an innocent man finds himself suddenly the object of suspicion; a wholesome-looking motel clerk is actually a psychotic killer who impersonates his dead mother; and so on. Hitchcock's movies are also notable for their techniques, which were clearly influenced by the montage experiments of Russian director Sergei Eisenstein – arranging a series of quick shots to evoke strong emotions in the viewer. In addition to montage, Hitchcock manipulates his audience with his unusual camera angles and carefully placed sound effects. He meticulously planned each shot in his films and treated the actor as just another element on the set, leaving the impression that nothing on the screen had been put there by chance.

So powerful was Hitchcock's art that all subsequent thriller movies are now cast in his shadow. Every new thriller movie is either implicitly or explicitly compared to his work; and the adjective 'Hitchcockian' has entered the movie lexicon permanently. The *Hitchcock = thriller* formula is now part of cinema lore and a permanent page in its historical evolution. Such is the power of the director. Incidentally, the American Film Institute's 2001 listing of the 100 most popular thrillers of all time, voted on by 1800 cinema-goers, showed that Hitchcock's *Psycho* (1960) was number one. Two other Hitchcock films made the top 10: *North by Northwest* (1959) at number four and *The Birds* (1963) at number seven.

The blockbuster

Given the type of artistic possibilities that cinema affords, it should come as little surprise to find that it has spawned its own genres, in addition to those mentioned above. Since the 1950s, cinema has, in fact, generated the following *sui generis* film categories:

- *Youth rebellion:* such as *The Wild One* (1954) and *Rebel Without a Cause* (1955)
- *Adventure spy films:* such as the James Bond series of movies, e.g. *Goldfinger* (1964)
- *Romantic comedies:* such as *Pillow Talk* (1959)
- *Science fiction:* which already existed but has been developed greatly by digital techniques, e.g. *The Matrix* (1999)
- *Slasher movies:* such as *Friday the Thirteenth* (1980) and *I Know What You Did Last Summer* (1997)
- *Rock music movies:* such as *Jailhouse Rock* (1957), *A Hard Day's Night* (1964), and *Spice World* (1998)
- *African American theme movies:* such as *Superfly* (1972)
- *Spanish-language movies:* such as *El Mariachi* (1992)
- *Coming-of-age movies:* such as *The Breakfast Club* (1985)
- *Antiwar movies:* such as *Apocalypse Now* (1979)
- *Sword and sorcery movies:* such as *Conan the Barbarian* (1982)
- *Disaster movies:* such as *The Towering Inferno* (1974) and *The Perfect Storm* (2000)
- *Apocalyptic thrillers:* such as *Lost Souls* (2000) and *Left Behind* (2001)
- *Blockbuster movies:* such as *Jaws* (1975)

Of these, the blockbuster requires some commentary. Although it has come to the forefront since the mid-1970s, its originator was, arguably, Cecil B. DeMille (1881–1959), the early American motion-picture director and producer, whose spectacular historical epics and Biblical film extravaganzas have inspired all contemporary blockbuster movie-making. In the 1910s, DeMille made a number of distinctive silent films, including *The Warrens of Virginia* (1915), *Joan the Woman* (1916), and *The Whispering Chorus* (1918). In a short time, he carved out, through his own persona, the image of the dashing Hollywood director that prevailed for many decades. He also helped to establish the idea that movies are extravaganzas, not unlike the mythical spectacles of yore.

In 1923, he created the 'proto-blockbuster' with *The Ten Commandments,* an overblown spectacle that contained the germ of the blockbuster formula. The movie was enormously successful at the box office. He followed this success in the subsequent decade with many others, including *The Sign of the Cross* (1932), *Cleopatra* (1934), and *The Crusades* (1935). Subsequently, DeMille's larger-than-life, big-budget films became legendary with a string of pictures that included *The Plainsman* (1936), *The Buccaneer* (1938), *Union*

Pacific (1939), *Northwest Mounted Police* (1940), *Reap the Wild Wind* (1942), *Samson and Delilah* (1949), *The Greatest Show on Earth* (1952), and a sensationalistic remake of *The Ten Commandments* (1958).

There is very little doubt that DeMille's successor in this domain of movie-making is Steven Spielberg (1947–). Spielberg began making movies at the age of 12, and by the time he finished college he had at least eight amateur filmic works to his credit. Spielberg's earliest commercial efforts were television movies, among them *Duel* (1971), a suspense film about 'road rage' that brought him wider recognition. *Sugarland Express* (1974), Spielberg's first theatrical feature film, was an expertly crafted variant of *Duel*. He soon followed it up with *Jaws* (1975), a thriller based on American author Peter Benchley's novel of the same name. *Jaws* proved a tremendous success and quickly established Spielberg's reputation and fame. It also heralded a new era of blockbuster films with large gross revenues.

Jaws marked a turning point in the fortunes of the American film industry. Blockbuster-type films had always been part of the Hollywood production mix, as we saw above, but *Jaws* rewrote the formula and, above all else, proved that in conjunction with effective marketing strategies a movie could produce unprecedented revenues. Although it was based on a best-selling novel, *Jaws* lacked big-name stars; it had, instead, a frightening special-effects mechanical monster shark. The movie also impressed upon Hollywood that the most important segment of the movie-going audience was young people. This was further corroborated by the film that surpassed *Jaws* at the box office, George Lucas's *Star Wars* (1977), a science-fantasy film that displayed the most spectacular special effects of space flight ever seen in cinema up to that time.

Star Wars shaped the blockbuster phenomenon over the next two decades. In a juvenilized culture, blockbuster films based on comic-book characters or adventure heroes tend to blur the dividing line between young and mature audiences. Aware of this, Lucas produced two additional titles in the *Star Wars* series: *The Empire Strikes Back* (1980), directed by Irvin Kershner, and *Return of the Jedi* (1983), directed by Richard Marquand, which attracted children and parents together to the movie theatre, something that would have been unthinkable in the early and golden eras of cinema. Spielberg then directed and Lucas produced three films about an intrepid archaeologist, Indiana Jones, that attracted the same mixed-age audiences: *Raiders of the Lost Ark* (1981), *Indiana Jones and the Temple of Doom* (1984), and *Indiana Jones and the Last Crusade* (1989). Similarly, Spielberg's *E.T.* (1982), about an alien left behind on Earth by his spaceship, and *Jurassic Park* (1993), a work combining computer-generated animations of dinosaurs with human actions, became huge successes because they attracted mixed audiences.

The blockbuster has, in fact, been a major contributor to the further entrenchment of juvenilization in society. Prior to the advent of the blockbuster, most movies were hardly perceived as suitable for children. The phenomenal commercial success of movies such as *Star Wars,* the 'teenage mutant ninja' movies and many others since can only be explained as the successful result of a Hollywood marketing ploy, tapping successfully into the spreading juvenilization of pop culture. The big success of cinema as an art form for the young and old alike is a good illustration of how energetically the movie distraction factory has overrun the lines that once separated children from adults. Just as many modern grown-ups enjoy Disney movies and such major motion-picture-superheroes as Batman, Superman, and Dick Tracy (all once considered strictly kids' stuff), as do their children. The cultural subtext of such movies is that childhood isn't as childish as it used to be, and adulthood tends to be a lot less mature.

But there are signs that this trend might have run its course. Several mixed-age action films fared poorly at the box office in the late 1990s. In the same year as *Jurassic Park*, Spielberg himself also released *Schindler's List* (1993), a film about one man's efforts to save European Jews from Nazi death camps during World War II. This work, shot almost completely in black-and-white, earned Spielberg his first Academy Award. It was hardly intended for mixed-age audiences.

Movies will continue to attract large audiences, for the simple reason that they are 'easy to process'. A novel takes time to read; a movie can be seen in under three hours. Movies have, in effect, reintroduced a modern form of orality. We feel that the movie 'tells us' the story, in much the same way that village storytellers once did. The impact is immediate and to the point. Movies will thus remain an intrinsic component of the Digital Galaxy for time to come.

6 Television

Television hangs on the questionable theory that whatever happens anywhere should be sensed everywhere. If everyone is going to be able to see everything, in the long run all sights may lose whatever rarity value they once possessed, and it may well turn out that people, being able to see and hear practically everything, will be specially interested in almost nothing.

E.B. White (1899–1985)

Studying TV has become pivotal for understanding modern-day signifying orders. TV has created its own form of literacy that informs and engages more people than any other medium has been capable of doing at any other time in human history. It has also become *the* medium that many people blame for helping to entrench our materialistic and shallow culture. Since the 1970s scientific research papers on the effects television has purportedly had on society have proliferated. Today, it is common to accuse television of causing virtually everything that is bad, from obesity to street violence. Are the social critics right? Has television spawned a 'psychologically toxic' world? Are the victims of TV programmes, as Key (1989: 13) suggests, people who 'scream and shout hysterically at rock concerts and later in life at religious revival meetings'? There is no doubt that TV has had an impact on people's behaviours, but so has every other form of representation – from religious texts inscribed on clay tablets to the paperback novel. In actual fact, the TV text is hardly ever innovative or inspiring, as are some religious texts for instance. It produces programmes that reinforce already-forged lifestyle trends. TV moguls are more intent on adopting and recycling such trends than in spreading commercially risky innovations of their own.

TV genres and the codes that underlie them constitute the subject matter of this chapter. Semiotically, TV can be characterized, as will be discussed below, as a *social text*. This can be defined as an overarching representamen that guides and informs the wider society on issues of current concern.

The advent of TV

As mentioned in the opening chapter, television owes its origins to the 1884 scanning disk invented by engineer Paul Nipkow. Nipkow's device was used from 1923 to 1925 in experimental television systems. In 1926 the Scottish scientist John Logie Baird perfected the scanning method, and in 1931 the Russian-born engineer Vladimir Zworykin built the electronic scanning system that became the prototype of the modern TV camera. American inventor Ernst F.W. Alexanderson actually exhibited the first home television receiver in Schenectady, New York, in 1928. The images his device transmitted were small, poor, and unsteady, but astute business people present at the exhibition saw it nonetheless as having great commercial potential.

By the late 1930s, television service was in place in several Western countries. The British BBC, for example, started a regular service in 1936. By the early 1940s there were 23 television stations operating in the United States. But it was not until the early 1950s that technology had advanced to the point that made it possible for virtually every North American household to afford a television set. Immediately thereafter, television personages became household names, and people began more and more to plan their daily lives around television programmes.

Since the 1960s television programming has developed into much more than an assortment of disconnected fact and fiction shows. Like the newspaper, it has become a syntext (chapter 3) for the larger society. The TV syntext can be characterized more specifically as a social text (as shall be discussed below), functioning as a kind of meta-text through which people glean a large portion of their information, intellectual stimulation, and distraction. TV's total integration into the social system can be seen by the fact that TV sets are now ubiquitous in society – in hotel rooms, airports, schools, elevators, office waiting rooms, cafeterias, washrooms, and TV cameras have even been taken to outer space. The successful US manned landing on the moon in July 1969 was documented with live broadcasts made from the surface of the moon. The world, it would seem, has become one big television monitor.

Technology, moreover, has constantly improved TV viewing. Today, digital television receivers, which convert the analogue, or continuous, electronic television signals received by an antenna into an electronic digital code (a series of ones and zeros), are doing to television what the compact disc did to sound recording in the 1980s. Known as high-definition television (HDTV), the technology was developed originally in the mid-1980s. HDTV offers sharper pictures on wider screens, with cinema-quality images. A fully digital system was put on display in the United States in the early 1990s. Recently, engineers have devised ways of making HDTV compatible with computers and telecommunications equipment so that HDTV technology can be applied to other systems besides home television, such as medical devices, security systems, and computer-aided manufacturing.

TV has, like all other mass distraction media, been a two-edged sword. On the positive side, it has been instrumental in bringing about significant and important changes in society. For instance, the TV images of the Vietnam War broadcast daily in the late 1960s and early 1970s brought about protest and ultimately an end to the war. The constant exposure and treatment of sexual themes on sitcoms has also, through the years, greatly reduced the puritanical hypocrisy that previously existed with regard to sexual matters in society at large. The protests and changes in sexual mores were successful because they did not involve just 'intellectuals', but large segments of the populace. On the other hand, whereas reading books or watching artistic movies require various degrees of critical reflection on the signifieds being conveyed, processing TV images does not. This has led, as Baudrillard (1988, 1998) has emphasized, to a generalized passiveness and unreflectiveness in how people receive and understand messages. TV has thus surreptitiously induced a kind of intellectual lethargy in society at large.

The term *image*, as used by Baudrillard, can be defined simply as an iconic sign that stands directly for some referent. It is something prototypical (a fashion style, a certain look such as the 'girl power' one, etc.) based on cultural norms and on personal experiences with the referent it entails. The image of womanhood portrayed by Lucille Ball in her sitcom *I Love Lucy* was vastly different than the one portrayed by, say, the mother in *Father Knows Best*; the former image showed the female as a highly intelligent and independent-minded persona; the latter as a passive and subservient one.

TV broadcasting

As mentioned in chapter 4, after World War I the Westinghouse Electric Corporation established the first commercially owned radio station, KDKA, to offer programming to the general public. As we saw, early radio broadcasting was dominated by adaptations of novels, comic book stories, newspaper reports, stage dramas, and vaudeville, which were redesigned for radio in the form of weekly action serials, situation comedies, soap operas, and the like. In like fashion, many of the early TV programmes came directly from radio. These included Westerns such as *Gunsmoke*, soap operas such as *The Guiding Light*, and sitcoms such as *The Jack Benny Show*. The TV variety show also evolved in large part from its radio counterpart. So, it is reasonable to say that TV at first was little more than 'visual radio'. In the same way that radio extended print and theatrical genres into the audio domain, television extended radio genres into the visual domain.

The Radio Corporation of America (RCA) showed the American public how effective and appealing TV was with its live coverage of the 1939 New York World's Fair. Immediately thereafter, the National Broadcasting Company (NBC), the Columbia Broadcasting System (CBS), the American Broadcasting Company (ABC), and the DuMont Television Network (which went out of business in 1955) became the first TV networks in the US. *Networks* are groups of stations that centralize the production and distribution of programming. By the mid-1950s NBC, CBS, and ABC – collectively known as the Big Three in television history – had successfully secured American television audiences as their exclusive domain. In the mid-1980s the Fox television network went on the air, capturing a segment of that domain. So, before cable television ended channel scarcity in the late 1980s, viewing choices were largely limited to the programming that the major networks provided.

As is the case in all the other media discussed so far, advertising is the fuel that propels TV. In the United States and Europe advertising agencies produce nearly all network shows. Only in the area of public broadcasting is this not the case. Public TV services are generally supported by government funding, contributions from viewers, corporate gifts, and foundation grants. Direct-broadcast satellite (DBS) now provides viewers with an antenna system capable of bypassing closed-circuit systems to capture satellite signals. Most channels available from satellites, however, require subscription fees and licences.

TV genres

As we saw in previous chapters, the parallel growth of network radio and Hollywood sound cinema in the late 1920s created an unprecedented mass pop culture for people belonging to a wide range of social classes and educational backgrounds. This culture was entrenched further with the rise of television in the 1950s.

Despite the obvious differences between radio and television, the development of programming genres for both broadcast media constitutes a single history. *I Love Lucy* (1951–57), which starred Lucille Ball, for example, was adapted from her radio show *My Favorite Husband* (1948–51). It became the first veritable 'hit programme' in American television history, finishing first in the national ratings for three seasons in a row (1951–54) and establishing dramatic elements that have been adopted by subsequent sitcoms – such as the battle between the sexes, arguments among neighbours or work colleagues, and other mundane conflicts. Some television sitcoms, such as *Father Knows Best* (1954–60) and *The Cosby Show* (1984–92), leaned instead toward the moralistic narrative as their underlying code, often focusing on child rearing. Others raised the 'critical coefficient' of their contents considerably by providing controversial social commentary. Prime examples of such sitcoms were *All in the Family* (1971–79) and *M*A*S*H* (1972–83). Some sitcoms have also occasionally used fantasy characters as vehicles for comedy – e.g. *Bewitched* (1964–72) and *I Dream of Jeannie* (1965–69). Currently, sitcoms – from *Dawson's Creek* to *Malcolm in the Middle* (to mention two that are currently popular on American TV as I write) – have become highly parodic and ironic, appealing primarily to young adults. Most deal openly with problems of sexuality and romance, typically perpetuating a juvenilized view of human relations (see Table 6.1).

Table 6.1

Sitcom	Underlying code
I Love Lucy	Battle between the sexes, arguments among people, mundane conflicts
Father Knows Best/Bill Cosby Show	Moralistic narrative, family problems
All in the Family/M*A*S*H	Social commentary and critique
Bewitched/I Dream of Jeannie	Fantasy characters who solve human problems
Dawson's Creek/Malcolm in the Middle	Parody of human relations

An interesting exception to this fare was a short-lived American sitcom of the early 1960s called *It's a Man's World*, which was much more accurate in its representation of the angst of young adults than any of the glibly contrived juvenilized sitcoms that pass for realism today. *It's a Man's World* premiered on NBC in 1962. It followed the daily lives of four young men: a refugee from a rich Chicago family, a folk singer, and two orphaned brothers. The themes of the sitcom were truly iconoclastic for the era. They dealt with premarital sex, feminism, and the generation gap much more intelligently and artistically than any of the current sitcoms can claim to do. Mass audiences were not ready for this type of programme, however, and after only 19 episodes, NBC cancelled it.

The TV comedy-variety genre is a hybrid of vaudeville and nightclub entertainment. In the early years of television, many of the medium's first great stars were, as a matter of fact, comedy-variety performers, including Milton Berle, Sid Caesar, Jackie Gleason, Martha Raye, and Red Skelton. A comedy-variety hour typically consisted of short monologues and skits featuring the host, which alternated with various show-business acts, including singers, bands, stand-up comedians, trained animal acts, and other novelties. The variety show – a related genre in which the host served only as master of ceremonies – emerged in the early period of TV. The *Ed Sullivan Show* (1948–71), for example, hosted by newspaper columnist Ed Sullivan on CBS, featured entertainers as diverse as the rock group the Beatles and the Bolshoi Ballet.

The early years of television offered many highly regarded anthology dramas. Hour-long works by Paddy Chayefsky (1923–81), Rod Serling (1924–75), and other television playwrights were presented live on such programmes as *Goodyear-Philco Playhouse* (1951–60) and *Studio One* (1948–58). As with radio, however, serial dramas proved to be much more popular and, therefore, the anthologies gradually disappeared. Filmed series had mass appeal. They included police dramas, such as *Dragnet* (1952–59, 1967–70), *The Mod Squad* (1968–73), and *Hawaii Five-O* (1968–80); private-eye series, such as *77 Sunset Strip* (1958–64), *The Rockford Files* (1974–80), and *Magnum, P.I.* (1980–88), in which the personality of the detective was as important as the criminal investigation; and westerns, such as *Gunsmoke* (1955–75), *Wagon Train* (1957–65), and *Bonanza* (1959–73), which focused on the settling of the Western United States. Other distinct types of TV series have included war programmes, such as *Rat Patrol* (1966–67); spy series, such as *The Man from U.N.C.L.E.* (1964–68); and science-fiction series, such as *Star Trek* (1966–69). Many dramatic series have also been based on the exploits of lawyers, doctors, or rich business entrepreneurs. These have included *Perry Mason* (1957–66), *L.A. Law* (1986–94), *Ben Casey* (1961–66), *Marcus Welby, M.D.* (1969–76), and *Dallas* (1978–91).

TV soap operas, like their radio counterparts, have always explored romance, friendship, and familial relations in narrative form. Among the most popular of the early TV era were *The Guiding Light* (1952–), which is still ongoing, and *The Edge of Night* (1956–84). The history of the TV soap opera is also the history of gender relations in society. At first, the soaps were no more than afternoon 'romance interludes' for stay-at-home wives; now they appeal to male and female audiences alike, dealing with many other aspects of relationships. Clearly, as a social text, TV now functions both as society's 'mirror', reflecting its trends and also, in a kind of strange synergy, shaping them.

From the outset, news broadcasting has held a wide appeal for television audiences. The speed with which TV broadcasting can reach entire populations has, in fact, redefined the role of news reporting in society. Print journalism has, as a consequence, become a supplemental medium to radio and TV, focusing on in-depth coverage and editorial opinion. Actually, the earliest years of television offered little in the way of news coverage. But this changed in the mid-1950s. In 1956, NBC introduced *The Huntley-Brinkley Report*, a half-hour national telecast presented in the early evening and featuring filmed reports of the day's events. The other networks followed suit shortly thereafter. With the invention of videotape, the cost of such coverage dropped significantly, allowing individual stations to initiate and expand local news coverage. Network and local news programming has now become an integral part of the TV syntext.

In addition to daily news coverage, the networks capitalized on the popularity of news reporting by developing weekly prime-time news magazine series, such as *60 Minutes* (1968–) and *20/20* (1978–). Such shows consist of a mixture of cultural reporting, investigative reporting, and human-interest stories. They have proliferated in prime-time broadcasting. And, of course, all-news cable channels have become popular since the mid-1980s. The first of these, CNN (Cable News Network), was founded in 1980 by American businessman Ted Turner. CNN was the first 24-hour television network devoted entirely to news broadcasts. In 1991, the network received wide publicity when its reporter Peter Arnett remained in Iraq during the Persian Gulf War to broadcast his reports. In effect, Arnett gave a 'play-by-play' account of the conflict, not unlike what a TV sportscaster does in describing a football or baseball match. Clearly, TV news reporting is as much entertainment and 'reality drama' as it is information programming. The war was real; the broadcasts, however, transformed the events of the war into a daily adventure serial imbued with all the elements of a fictional narrative. The addictive need for information broadcasting among a steadily growing segment of the population was rendered obvious by CNN's establishment of its *Headline News*, a channel running television news programmes consecutively throughout the day, and CNN Radio, a 24-hour syndicated service.

In the United States, news television has had a noticeable effect on electoral politics and public opinion. For example, in 1960 presidential candidates Richard M. Nixon and John F. Kennedy agreed to a series of debates, which were broadcast simultaneously on television and radio. According to surveys, most radio listeners felt that Nixon had won the debates, while television viewers picked Kennedy. Kennedy won the general election that fall. This showed the power of the visual image over any other type of signifier in media events – as Baudrillard has consistently remarked, incidentally, in his writings (e.g. 1973, 1998). Television coverage of the Vietnam War (1959–75) helped change the rules of American politics. By the mid-1960s the Big Three networks were broadcasting daily images of the war into virtually every home in the United States. For many viewers, the horrors they saw on television were emotionally disconcerting, overshadowing the optimistic reports of impending victory issued by government officials to radio and print media.

Other TV genres that have proven to be durable include: talk shows (providing a daily dose of gossip, scandal, and information, all mixed into one), sports coverage, children's programming, game shows, music programmes, animation programmes, and religious programmes. One recent genre that requires special comment is the so-called 'reality' programme. Today, various Cops and Rescue programmes clutter the prime time airwaves, as do unscripted programmes such as the series of *Survivor* programmes of the early 2000s, which pitted real-life people, not actors, into situations involving all the dramatic elements of the soaps – intrigue, danger, betrayal, and sex. The appeal of the unscripted programme, which blurs the difference between reality and fiction, lies in its 'text-in-the-making' nature. As with Luigi Pirandello's (1867–1936) great 1921 play *Six Characters in Search of an Author*, the audience is presented with real-life characters in search of a script and a narrative. The fun is in figuring out how this will come about.

Early 2001 unscripted TV added a new twist to its 'real-life = text-in-the-making' formula by introducing *Temptation Island* (on the Fox network). Set on an idyllic island, a group of people in bathing suits were put there so that their emotional and romantic lives could be wrecked on purpose through 'temptation' schemes. The reason the couples in the show agreed to be in it was, purportedly, so that they could test their devotion to each other. But, in my view, the people in the show, along with the audiences that viewed them, were enticed by the power of reification. Andy Warhol's (1930–87) prediction that everyone would have their '15 minutes of fame' in the media age has been superseded considerably by unscripted television. People now, it would seem, perceive little difference between what happens on TV and in real life. Unscripted programmes simply reify this. But what strikes one in watching such programmes critically is the absolute silliness of the whole idea. Author-less scripts are indeed interesting. But the result is hardly breathtaking drama. It is 'people-watching' gone 'virtual'.

Unscripted TV is not new. It has been a staple of cable networks and some public broadcasting outlets for years. Britain's Channel 4's fine series *1900 House*, for instance, was much more intriguing than any *Survivor* or *Temptation Island* format, since it followed the misadventures of a family that agreed to live as the Victorians did for three months. The series combined elements of narrative with those of documentary and drama producing a TV sociology of family life that was truly powerful. Similarly, the American 1971 documentary of the Loud family – involving seven months of uninterrupted shooting and 300 hours of nonstop broadcasting – created a text-in-the-making that reflected the banality of the family life of the protagonists. The hyperreal Loud family fell apart, which leads to the question: did the TV cameras cause this?

Reality TV is voyeurism for the Digital age. It inheres in the making of pseudo-events for the sake of the making. With the use of webcams (cameras made for Internet delivery), millions of people throughout the world are now even letting strangers into their daily lives. It would seem that a growing number of people simply find 'living in public' more exciting than living privately. Clearly, the boundaries between private and public have been eroded through the influence of TV. Everyone, from celebrities to housemakers, is airing personal laundry in public for everyone to see. Aware of the emerging 'culture of intrusion and humiliation', TV programmers have jumped on the 'reality bandwagon', coming up with an array of their own 'web-cammish' type shows which portray people in their daily habitats. Millions of TV watchers have access to the spectacle of human 'reality' at its most banal, venal, and doltish. Maybe at some deep unconscious level we are all trying to understand what human life is all about through such artificial people-watching. Who knows? But it certainly seems to be a bizarre way of doing so.

Today, TV genres have diversified significantly, as TV networks are forced to compete with smaller private channels that offer speciality programming. Still, the traditional genres seem to have much life left in them, despite their apparent inanity. *Seinfeld* (1990–98), for instance, was notable for being about 'nothing', unlike other sitcoms of the same era that focused on family issues (*Roseanne*, 1988–97), gender issues (*Home Improvement*, 1991–99), or social issues (*Third Rock from the Sun*, 1996–). Still, Seinfeld became the highest-rated and most profitable show on American television during its last years. It was TV's answer to cinematic postmodernism (chapter 5). But unlike the great postmodern movies, it offered little more than distraction, appealing to so-called 'Generation X-ers'. Seinfeld reflected, in fact, the many identity-less young adults of that era who felt they had nowhere to go and nothing to conquer. Living in a society without goals, and facing the constant threat of AIDS, child abuse, rape, cancer, divorce, unemployment, as well as being dissatisfied with the traditional workplace, Generation X-ers of the era saw *Seinfeld* as a mirror of their life.

The impact of TV

McLuhan was among the first to descry that TV had an impact far greater than that of the material it communicated, creating a global electronic village. And indeed, just as he predicted, with advances in satellite communications, TV now allows viewers even to see themselves as 'participants' in wars and conflicts going on in some other part of the world 'as they happen'.

There are three main psychosocial impacts that living in TV's global village have, arguably, had on people. These have been called various things by different social scientists. I will refer to them here as the *mythologizing effect*, the *history fabrication effect*, and the *cognitive compression effect*. Needless to say, all other electronic media produce similar effects. However, they do so to a much lesser degree than television.

Three main effects

The *mythologizing effect* refers to the phenomenon that television creates personages that are perceived as mythic figures, larger than life. Like any type of privileged space – a platform, a pulpit, etc. that is designed to impart focus and significance to someone – television creates mythic personages by simply 'containing' them in electronic space, where they are seen as suspended in real time and space, in a mythic world of their own. TV personages are infused with a deified quality by virtue of the fact that they are seen inside the mythical electronic space created by television. This is why meeting TV actors, sitcom stars, etc. causes great enthusiasm and excitement in many people. Such celebrities are the contemporary equivalents of the graven images of the Bible. The same effect applies, of course, to the personages in other media. An author of best-selling books, a radio personality, a recording artist, a movie actor, etc. are all perceived mythologically. But since TV reaches more people, the mythologizing effect in its case is more widespread.

The term *history fabrication effect* refers to the fact that TV literally fabricates history by inducing the impression in viewers that some ordinary event – an election campaign, an actor's love affair, a fashion trend, etc. – is a momentous happening. People make up their minds about the guilt or innocence of others by watching news and interview programmes; they see certain behaviours as laudable or damnable by tuning into talk shows or docudramas; and the list could go on and on. In a phrase, the events that are showcased on TV are felt as being more significant and historically meaningful to society than those that are not. A riot that gets airtime becomes a consequential event; one that does not is ignored. This is why terrorists are seemingly more interested in simply getting on the air, than in having their demands satisfied. TV imbues their cause with significance. Political and social protesters frequently inform the news media of their intentions, and then dramatically stage their demonstrations for the cameras. Sports events such as the *World Series*, the *Super Bowl*, the *Stanley Cup Playoffs* or the *World Cup* of soccer are transformed by television coverage into battles of Herculean proportion. Events such as the John Kennedy and Lee Harvey Oswald assassinations, the Vietnam War, the Watergate hearings, the Rodney King beating, the O.J. Simpson trial, the death of Lady Diana, the Bill Clinton sex scandal, and the like are perceived as portentous and prophetic historical events through the filter of TV coverage.

In a phrase, TV has become the maker of history and its documenter at the same time. People now experience history through TV, not just read about it in a book or study it at school. And, as a result, television is shaping history. Edward R. Murrow (1908–65) of *CBS News* became a cultural hero when he stood up to the fanatical senator Joseph McCarthy (1908–57), who led a campaign against a purported Communist subversion in the early 1950s on his *See It Now* documentary programme. In 1954, Murrow used footage of McCarthy's own press conferences to expose the excesses of his anticommunist campaign. This led to the Senate reprimanding McCarthy and paralysing him from taking further political action. The horrific images of the Vietnam War that were transmitted into people's homes daily in the late 1960s and early 1970s brought about an end to the war, mobilizing social protest. Significantly, an MTV flag was hoisted by East German youths over the Berlin Wall as they tore it down in 1989. More people watched the wedding of England's Prince Charles and Princess Diana, and later Diana's funeral, than had ever before in human history observed such events at the same time. The Bill Clinton–Monica Lewinsky sex scandal allowed common people to become part of the sexual flaws of a contemporary 'mythic figure'.

As mentioned, the history-making power of TV has led many to actually stage an historical event for the cameras. The social critic W.T. Anderson (1992: 125–30) calls these appropriately 'pseudoevents', because they are never spontaneous, but planned for the sole purpose of 'playing' to TV's huge audiences. Most pseudoevents are intended to be self-fulfilling prophecies. The American invasion of Grenada on 25 October 1983 and the Gulf War during January and February 1991 were concomitantly real events and pseudoevents. The actual military operations and conflicts were real events. But the reporting of those wars was orchestrated by a massive public-relations operation. Reporters were censored and kept away from the action so that the news coverage could be stylized and managed more effectively. The idea was to give the viewing public a military and social victory and, therefore, to allow Americans to 'feel good about themselves'. Pseudoevents constitute unscripted reality TV at its best, because they mesh reality (the real killing and terrorizing of people) with acting, drama, and social commentary. As Anderson (1992: 126–7) aptly puts it, the 'media take the raw material of experience and fashion it into stories; they retell the stories to us, and we call them reality'.

Of course, other media create (or have created) history as well. Books written about wars, historical eras, etc. have always shaped how we perceive certain events of the past. Before TV, newspapers and radio were primary fabricators of historical realities. But with the rise of TV in the 1950s, there is little doubt that most people started perceiving the making of history 'through the tube', so to speak, rather than through print or some other medium.

The *cognitive compression effect* refers to the fact that the TV medium presents its stories, information, and features in compacted form for time-constrained transmission. Consequently, viewers have little time to reflect on the topics, implications, and meanings contained in its messages. This leads, generally speaking, to a passive and cognitively effortless way of 'reading' the TV text. TV has thus made people habituated to large doses of 'meaning-suspended' information, cut up, packaged, and digested beforehand. TV viewing, in a phrase, is very easy to do, since the TV images themselves do the thinking for the viewer.

Take TV news programmes as a case-in-point. The amount of information presented in a short period of time on a news programme is torrential. We are able to take it all in because the various stories have been edited and stylized beforehand for effortless mass consumption. The camera moves in to select aspects of a situation, to show a face that cares, that is suffering, that is happy, that is angry, or whatever, and then shifts to the cool, handsome face of an anchorman or to the attractive one of an anchorwoman to tell us what it's all about. The news items, the film footage, and the commentaries are all fast-paced and brief. They are designed to present dramatic snippets of easily digestible information. 'Within such a stylistic environment', remarks Stuart Ewen (1988: 265), 'the news is beyond comprehension'. The facts of the news are subjected to the stylized signature of the specific news programme; and, indeed, the same story will be presented differently according to whoever is the television journalist. Thus it is that as 'nations and people are daily sorted out into boxes marked "good guys", "villains", "victims", and "lucky ones", style becomes the essence, reality becomes the appearance' (Ewen 1988: 265–6).

The device that intensified the cognitive compression effect is the remote control. It was invented in 1956 by a man named Robert Adler. But it wasn't until the 1980s that it became a standard prop of every television set. The remote control has had an enormous impact on how we view television. When we are bored with a programme on a specific channel, all we have to do from the comfort of our seats is to flick through the panoply of viewing options at our disposal rapidly and with very little deliberation or reflection.

TV as a social text

When looked at globally, programming differences in the overall TV text are matters of detail. As mentioned above, the various seemingly unrelated programmes coalesce into a syntext that, in the case of TV, can be called a social text. This is an overarching text from which the entire culture derives meaning for its daily life routines. To see what this means, it is useful to step back in time with one's imagination to some village in medieval Europe. What would daily life be like in that era? How would one organize one's daily life routines? What social text, in effect, would one be likely to be living by?

As history records, daily life schemes would be informed and guided by a Christian social text: i.e. they would be centred on a Christian way of doing things. Some of these are still around today. Religious dates such as Christmas and Easter, for instance, are still regularly planned yearly events around which many people in our society organize social activities. In medieval Europe, the Christian text probably regulated life on a daily basis. In that era, people probably went to church regularly, lived by strict moral codes derived from the Bible, and listened conscientiously to the admonitions and dictates of clergymen. The underlying subtext of the medieval Christian social text was that each day brought one closer and closer to one's true destiny – salvation and an afterlife with God. Living according to the text no doubt imparted a feeling of security, emotional shelter, and spiritual meaning to people's lives.

After the Renaissance, the Enlightenment, and the Industrial Revolution the Christian social text came gradually to be replaced by a more secular form of textuality. Today, unless someone has joined a religious community or has chosen to live by the dictates of the Bible or some other religious text, the social text by which people in general live is hardly a religious one. We organize our day around work commitments, social appointments, etc. that have hardly anything to do with salvation; and only at those traditional 'points' in the calendar (Christmas, Easter, etc.) do we synchronize our secular text with the more traditional religious one. The secular social text necessitates partitioning the day into 'time slots'. This is why we depend so heavily upon such devices as clocks, watches, agendas, appointment books, calendars, etc. We would be desperately lost without such things. In this regard, it is appropriate to note that in his great 1726 novel, *Gulliver's Travels*, Jonathan Swift (1667–1745) satirized the tendency of post-Renaissance people to rely on the watch to organize their daily routines – the Lilliputians were baffled to note that Gulliver did virtually nothing without consulting his watch! Like Gulliver, we need to know continually 'what time it is' in order to carry on with the normal conduct of our daily life.

Outside of special cases – such as in cloisters and monasteries – the textual organization of the day is hardly ever conscious. If we started to reflect upon the value of our daily routines, it is likely that we would soon start to question them and eventually to abandon them. This does indeed happen in the case of those individuals who have decided to 'drop out' of society, i.e. to live their lives outside of the dictates of social textuality.

Now, since the 1950s, when it entered the social scene, TV became almost instantly the medium through which our secular social text was delivered, and through which people gleaned information about life. If one peruses the daily TV listings and starts classifying the programmes into morning, noon, and evening slots, one will get an idea of what this means. With cable television and satellite dishes, the range of programming offered would, at first, appear to be a broad and random one. But a closer critical look at the listings will reveal a different story.

Consider morning programming. Virtually all the networks start off their daily fare of offerings with several stock types of shows. These are, invariably, information programmes (news, weather, sports), children's shows, exercise programmes, and (later in the morning) talk and quiz shows. There is very little digression from this menu. One may, of course, subscribe to a cable movie channel or to some special interest channel to suit one's fancy. But, as ratings research has shown, most people are inclined to watch the regular fare of morning programmes. The news and fitness programmes cater to working people; children's shows to young children; and the later talk, quiz, and information programmes to stay-at-home people in need of stimulation, recreation, or relaxation. The morning part of the TV text changes somewhat on weekends, reflecting the different kinds of social requirements associated with Saturdays and Sundays. But on weekday mornings 'Wake up people' is the underlying subtext. 'Here's what you need to know,' blurt out the newscasters. 'You're too fat and sluggish, so get into shape,' exclaim the fitness instructors. 'You're bored and need to gossip, so tune in to meet people with their weird or heart-wrenching stories,' bellow the talk show hosts. In the same way that the morning prayers reassured medieval people that their life was meaningful, so too does morning TV assure us that our busy lives have sense and purpose.

In the afternoon the primary viewing audience is made up of stay-at-home people. The soap opera continues to be the main type of programme. This started on radio as a drama, typically performed as a serial characterized by stock characters and sentimental situations. Rather than go out and chitchat or gossip, as did medieval people, we do virtually the same thing by peering daily into the complicated lives of soap opera personages. As the soaps change, so do social mores. One reflects the other. They are a fixed part of daily life, putting us on intimate terms with the private lives of make-believe lawyers, doctors, executives, etc.

The afternoon is also the time for TV's version of medieval morality plays and public confessions. Talk shows and interview programmes allow modern-day people to reveal and confess their 'sins' in public. A large viewing audience can thus participate cathartically in other people's acts of self-revelation and repentance. As Stern and Stern (1992: 123) write, talk shows 'are a relief in the sense that it is always nice to see people whose problems are worse than yours'. The afternoon is thus a time slot for moral issues, acted out upon a media stage that has replaced the pulpit as the platform from which they are discussed and where 'sin' is condemned publicly. TV hosts, like medieval priests, comment morally upon virtually every medical and psychological condition known to humanity.

The third part of the TV text has traditionally been called 'prime time', the period in the evenings, from about 7 p.m. to 10 p.m., when most people are home to watch TV. It is significant that the prelude to evening programming is, as it was for the morning time-slot, the 'news hour'. After this, quiz shows and gossip journalism maintain curiosity and interest, until family programming commences for a couple of hours, with sitcoms, adventure programmes, documentaries, movies, and the like. The 1980s also introduced soap operas into this time frame, but with only limited success. Prime-time programming meshes fictional narrative with moral and social messages for the entire family. Documentary programmes in particular showcase real-life events, often bolstered by dramatic portrayals of these events, so that appropriate moral lessons can be learned.

Prime time is followed by 'late night' programming – a kind of coda to the daily text. There was nothing for medieval people to do past the early evening hours. If they did not go to bed early, then they would talk in village gatherings or else pray. But in contemporary consumerist societies, when the kids are safely in bed, TV programmes allow viewers to indulge their more prurient interests. Under the cloak of darkness and with 'innocent eyes and ears' fast asleep, one can fantasize and talk about virtually anything under the sun on TV with social impunity.

Needless to say, there is now much choice, given the huge number of speciality channels that are available. But, as it turns out, these channels offer no more that the opportunity for focusing one's interest; they do not impugn the overall TV syntext in any way. For example, if one is a lover of cuisine, one will of course have the opportunity to satisfy this love by watching a food channel. However, this does not change the overall structure and cohesiveness of the TV textuality. Speciality channels provide the same kinds of options that specialized books in libraries do. One can immerse oneself in any hobby or subject area by taking out the appropriate books from a library. But this in no way impugns the general reading preferences in the culture. So too, the presence of speciality channels on TV in no way alters the basic structure of how TV delivers its social textuality.

TV mythologies

Given the increasing diversity of consumerist societies, it is little wonder that the TV social text has become similarly diverse. There are now speciality channels for sports, movies, and music enthusiasts, for instance. But one thing has remained constant, TV is the locus where mythologies are forged, developed, and eventually discarded. Consider, as a case-in-point, the mythology of fatherhood that TV constructed and changed from the 1950s to the late 1990s.

Sitcoms of the 1950s like *Father Knows Best, The Honeymooners,* and *The Adventures of Ozzie and Harriet* sculpted the father figure to fit the requirements of the traditional patriarchal family structure. Therefore, most of these early sitcoms painted the family in a rosy-coloured fashion. The father was in charge, with his wife working behind the scenes to maintain harmony through subservience. This mythology of fatherhood reflected the social mindset of the 1950s. TV reinforced it and gave it a narrative form for people to take in on a weekly basis, allowing them to evaluate their own family situations in terms of plot, character, and setting. There were two notable exceptions to this: *The Honeymooners* and *I Love Lucy,* both of which revolved around strong-willed wives who were, in effect, precursors of later TV feminist characters. But, in general, the subtext to the 1950s' TV sitcom was: *father = know-all and be-all.* This was the metaphorical signification system that was created for weekly consumption and against which people monitored their own family lives.

In the 1960s and early 1970s the signification system was changed drastically, and the mythology was changed to reflect new times. New kinds of narratives and connotative systems were developed. The TV father was becoming an increasingly ludicrous character. The sitcom that reflected this new subtext brilliantly was *All in the Family.* The North American continent was divided, ideologically and emotionally, into two camps – those who supported the views and attitudes of the TV father, Archie Bunker, a staunch defender of the Vietnam War, and those who despised the War and thus the persona of Archie Bunker. What was happening inside the TV Bunker family was apparently happening in families across the continent. North American society had entered into a period of emotional turmoil and bitter debate over such controversial issues as war, racism, the role of women in society, and the hegemony of the patriarchal family. The new metaphorical subtext that was informing the sitcoms of the late 1960s and early 1970s was: *father = opinionated, ludicrous character.* Its symbolic characterization was Archie Bunker.

The total 'deconstruction' of the 1950s mythology of fatherhood took place in sitcoms from the 1980s and 1990s. A typical example was *Married, with Children,* a morbid parody of fatherhood and of the nuclear family. The father on this programme, Al Bundy, was little more than a physical brute, a reprehensible character who was hardly deserving of the title of 'father'. Indeed, as the name of the sitcom suggested, he was merely 'married' and just happened to have 'children', just as shallow and despicable as he was – Bud, his boorish, sex-crazed son, and Kelly, his empty-headed and over-sexed daughter. There was no sugar-coating in that sitcom. *Married, with Children* was implanted on a new parodic subtext: *the father = moron.*

The television programmes of the 1950s and 1960s had built up a patriarchal mythology of fatherhood. That mythology was challenged not only by *All in the Family*, but also throughout the 1970s by programmes such as *The Mary Tyler Moore Show*, *Wonder Woman*, *Rhoda*, *Maude*, *The Days and Nights of Molly Dodd*, *Cagney and Lacey*, and others that portrayed strong, independent women who were attempting to survive, socially and professionally, in a world that was disassembling patriarchal structures. By the late 1980s the deconstruction of patriarchy was complete. *Married, with Children*, and other sitcoms similar to it (e.g. the cartoon sitcom *The Simpsons*), constituted a scathing indictment of traditional family values. The fathers on those sitcoms were anti-heroes, who had all the wrong answers to family problems.

It is interesting to note that in the midst of that mythological reconfiguration, the *Bill Cosby* show – a throwback to the 1950s – achieved unexpected success throughout the 1980s. In hindsight, there were a number of reasons for its success. First and foremost was the fact the Bill Cosby himself was a great comedian who could easily endear himself to a large audience. But, more importantly, the *Bill Cosby Show* was appropriate for the 1980s. Throughout the 1970s, programmes like *All in the Family* and *The Jeffersons* were reflexes of an iconoclastic movement to tear down authority models and figures. But during the 1980s, with the ascendancy of a new right-wing moralism, as evidenced by the election of Ronald Reagan in the United States, the mythology of patriarchal authority was attempting to make a comeback. Once more, certain kinds of audiences were searching for TV father figures who were gentle and understanding at the same time. Bill Cosby fitted this image perfectly. But there was a difference. Unlike the wife in *Father Knows Best*, Cosby's wife had a more assertive role to play in the family. This 'new-look' patriarchal family provided a symbolism of reassurance in traditional values in a world that was, and continues to be, in constant moral doubt and flux.

Today's 'sitcom fathers' reflect the diversity that characterizes society at large. Some are cast in the traditional mould; but many others convey a panoply of fatherhood images.

TV and social change

The above discussion is not meant to imply that TV has not been used as an artistic medium or as an agent for social change. Indeed, because TV has showcased racial protests, riots, and other significant social events, it has forced the hand of change several times. Without it, there probably would have been no civil rights legislation, no Vietnam War protests, and no 'accountability' politics after Watergate. Moreover, many TV programmes were pivotal in bringing about a change in social mindset vis-à-vis certain issues. Here's just a sampling from the late 1960s to the early 1990s:

- In 1968, *Star Trek* featured the first interracial kiss in an episode titled *Plato's Stepchildren*.
- In 1970, the first divorced couple appeared on the *Odd Couple*.
- In 1971, *All in the Family* cast the first homosexual characters in prime time.
- In 1973, the same programme dealt with the topic of rape.
- In 1977, the mini-series *Roots* was among the first to deal forcefully with the enduring problem of racism.
- In 1991, the first scene of a woman kissing another woman was aired on an episode of *L.A. Law*.
- In 1992, an episode of *Seinfeld* dealt with one of the more taboo subjects of our society, masturbation.

With the advent of satellite transmission, television has also become a powerful medium for inducing radical social, moral, and political changes in cultures across the world. When asked about the stunning defeat of communism in Eastern Europe in the late 1980s, the Polish leader Lech Walesa was reported by the newspapers as having said that it 'all came from the television set', implying that television had undermined the stability of the communist world's relatively poor and largely sheltered lifestyle with images of consumer delights seen on Western programmes and commercials. As McLuhan often commented, TV has indeed shrunk the world into a global village.

Most people in the west born after 1960 cannot remember a time without a television set in their homes. There are now more than 1 billion TV sets around the globe. As the automobile did at the turn of the century, television has changed the general shape of world culture. Demographic surveys show consistently that people spend more time in front of television sets than they do working. As a consequence, it is claimed that watching TV is bringing about a gradual decline in reading, that television's popularity is leading to the demise of the nation state concept as ideas and images cross national boundaries daily through the same television programmes, and that TV is responsible for inducing an insatiable appetite for entertainment. But, even though people might mindlessly absorb the messages promulgated constantly by television, and although these may have some effects on their behaviour, people today are affected by media images mainly if they reflect or reinforce already-established trends within the culture. It is more accurate to say, in my opinion, that television produces programmes and images that reinforce current lifestyles, not engender them.

It is also interesting to note that some programmes, with their 'satirical thrust', have now taken over from the traditional philosophical writing in promulgating ideas, ideologies, and epistemologies. This is the basic theme of the fascinating studies collected by Irwin *et al.* (2001) on *The Simpsons and Philosophy*. The gist of the studies is that *The Simpsons* uses irony in order to probe the meaning of life and the politics of the nuclear family.

Current trends

Juvenilization now largely shapes the TV syntext. Many of the sitcoms now on television are designed specifically for adolescent and young adult audiences. The preoccupations and speech habits of a constantly changing horde of sitcom actors are indistinguishable from those of teenagers generally. Some programmes, in fact, can only be deciphered by teens. In the mid-1990s *Beavis and Butthead*, for example, was designed to cater primarily to male teens. *Beavis and Butthead* was one of MTV's top-rated shows in the mid- to late 1990s, hated by parents, loved by teens. Beavis had reddish brown hair, Butthead brown hair and braces. They sat together at the back of a high school classroom, picking their noses. Typical verbal exchanges between them included: 'Cool', 'Sucks (school sucks, life sucks)', 'Nachos rule', 'Burn it', 'Dude', 'Chicks', 'Ass', 'Asswipe'. They spent a lot of their time watching music videos and TV commercials. In a phrase, they were adolescent boors.

Discovering the popularity of these two characters, it was inevitable that the TV programmers would come up with a female counterpart in 1997. Her name was Daria Morgendorffer, who symbolized a new type of 'female dork'. She was an expressionless high schooler with black glasses, dispensing wry witticisms. She stood in contrast to more combative female characters, such as those showcased on programmes such as the *Powerpuff Girls*.

The promulgation of adolescent humour as basically 'disgusting child's play' is not restricted to such teen-directed programmes. It is noticeable everywhere on TV. Take, for instance, *South Park*, a highly popular programme in the late 1990s. This cartoon programme for adults can perhaps be characterized as a 'comedy of vulgarity', based on such themes as digestion, defecation, flatulence, and copulation. Although the satirical thrust of the programme was rather transparent, its vulgar style made it little more than an outlet for a 'male-type adolescent' humour. The general principle guiding its form of satire can be expressed as: the more vulgar and disgusting, the funnier. There have, of course, been other adult programmes of this type, such as the great British *Monty Python* shows. But these never degenerated into buffoonery that could only be really fully appreciated by a particular age and gender group (male teens). In a way, a programme such as *South Park* is preferable to many soppy sitcoms and adult crime, lawyer, and adventure shows that are populated with self-centred characters, totally wrapped up in their personal problems. At least *South Park* is not so sanctimonious and empty.

Why do major networks or channels promote such vulgar shows? The answer is the same as it was during the hippie era. Youth sells! And, today if it is disgusting, young people will probably love it. What teen does not think that burping, vomiting, mucous discharge, and flatulence are hilarious? Sophomoric humour is the hallmark of adolescence, and it has become the hallmark of the entertainment industry as well. Words and behaviours not long ago considered private have invaded mass culture. Blatant or suggested flatulence, for example, has been used in such mainstream movies as the *Mighty Ducks*, *Lion King*, and *Little Giants*, all made for young audiences. Irreverent logos and phrases now appear regularly on T-shirts and caps – 'Snot candy', 'Gummy Boogers', 'Monster Warts', etc. Wholesomeness simply does not sell in a market that is driven by juvenilized aesthetics.

Future trends

The analysis of TV genres and programming up to the last few years has been based on the presupposition that the audience for such shows was fairly homogeneous in its tastes and expectations. But this is rapidly changing with media convergence and the rise of interactive technologies. The advent of cable and satellite TV, along with the use of digital technologies, is starting to change the nature of the hegemonic TV social text that has prevailed for over 50 years. The new kind of social text is much more individualized and based on a diversity of lifestyles.

Before cable and satellites, it was syndicated programming that made inroads into the hegemony that the main networks enjoyed. Syndicated programmes are programmes rented or licensed by their producers to other companies for broadcast, distribution, or exhibition. Programmes such as *The Wheel of Fortune* (1983–) came forward in the mid-1980s to challenge the dominion over audiences that the networks had. It continues to be a popular prime time quiz programme.

Cable television was first developed in the late 1940s to serve shadow areas – i.e. areas that are blocked from receiving signals from a station's transmitting antenna. Today, cable and satellite TV have become the norm. Digital data-compression techniques, which convert television signals to digital code in an efficient way, are starting to increase cable's capacity to 500 or more channels.

Cable television has introduced narrowcasting into the TV medium. Currently, genre channels such as those listed in Table 6.2 are available with most basic cable services in the United States.

Table 6.2

Genre	Examples
Educational	Knowledge TV, Discovery Channel, Arts & Entertainment Channel, The Learning Channel
Movie	Home Box Office, Showtime, The Movie Network, Cinemax
Music	Music Television, Country Music Television, VH-1
News	CNN, CNN Headline News, The Weather Channel, Fox News
Religious	The Inspirational Network, The Christian Network
Government	C-SPAN, S-SPAN II
Sports	ESPN, Fox Sports Channel
Shopping	Home Shopping Network, QVC Network
Animation	The Cartoon Network
Science fiction	The Sci-Fi Channel
Comedy and sitcom	The Comedy Channel
Courtroom coverage	Court-TV
Women	Lifetime, The Women's Channel
Children	Nickelodeon, The Disney Channel
Families	The Family Channel
African Americans	Black Entertainment Television
Hispanics	Galavision
Country	The Nashville Network

In addition to basic service channels, some of the above are part of a pay-per-view system, which allows individuals access to many other kinds of specialized programmes, from adult erotic movies to wrestling and boxing tournaments, video game channels, such as *The Nintendo Channel*, musical channels for highly specialized tastes, and print-based services specializing in news headlines, programme listings, weather updates, and the like. Cable companies now also offer computer and Internet services; @Home is the leading Internet cable service currently available in the US.

Direct-broadcast satellite (DBS) companies pick up satellite feeds from cable networks, and originate their own programming that is not available on cable. Communications satellites receive television signals from a ground station, amplify them, and relay them back to Earth over an antenna that covers a specified terrestrial area. Instead of a normal aerial antenna, receiving dishes are used to capture the signal and deliver it to the television station or set. The dishes can be fairly small for home use, or large and powerful, such as those used by cable and network television stations. Programmes intended for specific subscribers are scrambled so that only the intended recipients, with appropriate decoders, can receive them.

Although there appears to be much more choice for viewers in the Digital Galaxy, narrowcasting has in fact produced 'more of the same thing', as media conglomerates gain control of both the content and the channels of transmission (TV stations, cable franchises, etc.). With every merger, 'homogenizing formulas' are established. There may be a hundred channels, but, as many subscribers quip, 'there's nothing on'. Indeed, the explosion in the number of channels has simply resulted in a multiplicity of mediocrities that all have the same pre-packaged contents. Every new television station looks like every other one.

Online programming has also become routine in the Digital Galaxy. Currently, services such as *TiVo, Replay TV,* and *America Online TV* offer interactive formats permitting viewers to have more of a choice in what they desire to watch at a certain time. But 'interactive TV' is not new. In the winter of 1953, in the infancy of television broadcasting, a kid's show called *Winky Dink* was the first programme to feature an interactive component. To interact with the show, viewers bought a kit that included a piece of plastic to cover the TV screen and a Magic Crayon. Kids could then help the hapless Winky character out of jams. Prompted by the show's announcer, they could draw a bridge for him, for example, so that he could cross over a ravine and then erase the bridge, as instructed by the announcer, so that the bad guys would plunge into the ravine. The show ran for four years, and was revived in 1970.

The next step in interactive TV was taken in Columbus, Ohio on 1 December 1977, where cable companies made a 'relay box' available to customers so that they could order movies whenever they wished. The system also showed city council meetings during which viewers got to express their opinion through the box. There was also a 'Your Call Football' service whereby viewers could anticipate the plays in semi-professional football games. Such 'boxes' are still around today, but with many more interactive functions and sophisticated new features added to them. By the early 1990s, Interactive TV was very much in the air. Some speciality channels provided by cable companies devised schemes that would allow viewers to watch shows whenever they chose to do so. In the mid-1990s, interactivity exploded on the World Wide Web. Not only do virtually all channels and programmes have websites today, which viewers can visit during, before, or after broadcasts of shows, but features such as interactive games and e-mail are now becoming available to larger and larger audiences. In this area Europe has taken the lead, with America, however, not far behind. *TiVo* and *Replay TV*, for instance, allow viewers in America to record shows onto low-cost hard drives with the click of a button. Microsoft's *WebTV* and *AOLTV* (America Online TV) allow users to pull up detailed information while they are watching a news or documentary broadcast. As Swann (2000: 22) observes, it is apparent that Interactive TV is the wave of the future. It will become ubiquitous by the end of the first decade of the twenty-first century, and greatly augment the functions of TV generally: 'The television will become a home networking center, enabling consumers to control all their electronic products and household appliances with the remote control'.

Perhaps the most interactive format of all is that of *virtual reality* (VR) television. This consists of a system of devices that enables users to move and react in a computer-simulated environment, sensing and manipulating virtual objects (objects in computer or cyberspace) much as they would real objects. This style of interaction gives participants the feeling of being immersed in the simulated world. Virtual worlds are created by computer programmes. But VR simulations differ from other computer simulations in that they require special interface devices that transmit the sights, sounds, and sensations of the simulated world to the user. These devices also record and send the speech and movements of the participant to the simulation programme. In effect, the human subject is interacting with a world totally made-up, a kind of representational space where the user is interacting with the representation.

To see in the virtual world, the user wears a head-mounted display (HMD) with screens directed at each eye. The HMD contains a position tracker to monitor the location of the user's head and the direction in which the user is looking. Using this information, a computer recalculates images of the virtual world to match the direction in which the user is looking and displays these images on the HMD. Users hear sounds in the virtual world through earphones in the HMD. This interface feature, which relays the sense of touch and other physical sensations in the virtual world is, as I write, the least developed one. Currently, with the use of a glove and position tracker, the user can reach into the virtual world and handle objects but cannot actually feel them.

Regardless of the meaning that the TV syntext may acquire in the future, the years in which it dominated mass communications will be remembered as a period when vast national populations shared political and cultural events, such as the address of a leader, a singer's performance, a comedian's monologue, a tear-jerking drama, or a sports event. Although still possible, assembling so large an audience for any single event is becoming increasingly rare as the number of viewing alternatives available to society continues to increase.

7 The computer and the Internet

The greatest difference between the cross-references in the Bible and the links on the World Wide Web is the difference between words written on parchment or paper in books that were meant to last forever and words written on the transient phosphorescence of a computer screen, where they will soon be effaced by others. This may or may not be the same contrast, written down 1900 years ago, between the wise man who built his house upon rock and the foolish man who built his house upon sand.

Edward Mendelson (1946–)

As we saw in the opening chapter, by the middle part of the twentieth century, the great advances made in the field of computer technology had started to radically transform systems and modes of mass communications and thus to shape cultural signifying orders throughout most of the world. By century's end, the computer had become interconnected with all aspects of daily life, giving rise to the Digital Galaxy, as it has been called in this book – although it could easily have been called 'Babbage's Galaxy' after the person who invented the first true computer, Charles Babbage (1792–1871). Today's personal computers can store the equivalent of thousands of books. Within seconds, anyone with a modem can gain access to an enormous store of human information. Almost every text we consider meaningful or functional has been transferred to computer memory systems. Print technology opened up the possibility of founding a world civilization; computer technology has brought that possibility closer and closer to realization.

However, nothing is new, so to speak, under the new digital sun. In the Digital Galaxy, the same signification systems are employed in the delivery of messages by the mass media. Moreover, the written word continues to be the cornerstone of modern culture – the medium through which knowledge is encoded and transmitted. From this perspective, it is more accurate to say that the Digital Galaxy is an extension, or outgrowth, of the Gutenberg Galaxy.

Indeed, it could never have been brought into existence without the printed book, for the science behind the computer was made possible by scientific knowledge recorded and preserved in books.

Mass communication systems have indeed entered the Digital Galaxy, transforming signifying orders in at least one fundamental way – in the access to information of all kinds that the computer has now made possible and the facility and speed with which it can be accessed. In this Galaxy the reception and decipherment of mediated messages are coming more and more under the direct control of receivers, who have before them an infinite array of options. But all this comes with a caveat. The senders of messages have never had so many media tools at their disposal to persuade receivers. As we shall see in the next chapter, advertisers, for instance, have at their fingertips a host of new technological gadgets that they can use to strengthen their goal of 'getting the message out'.

On this leg of our journey through our mediated world, we stop to look at computer media. The goal of media semiotics in this domain is not so much to look at the signification systems that have been transferred to digital form, since these are the same ones discussed in previous chapters. Rather, the goal is to focus on the new 'digital signifiers', i.e. on the new modes of encoding, storing, and retrieving texts of all kinds. A second topic of concern is the emerging metaphorical concept of 'the mind equals the machine' which has surreptitiously started to gain unconscious acceptance by society at large.

Computer media

The first general-purpose all-electronic computer was built in 1946 at the University of Pennsylvania by the American engineer John Presper Eckert, Jr (1919–95) and the American physicist John William Mauchly (1908–80). Called ENIAC, for Electronic Numerical Integrator and Computer, the machine could perform several hundred multiplications per minute. Its overall design constituted the blueprint for modern-day computers. The development of transistor technology and its use in computers in the late 1950s made it possible to manufacture smaller, faster, and more versatile computing machines. Late in the 1960s the integrated circuit was introduced which, by the mid-1980s, made the ownership of a computer affordable for virtually everyone.

Modern computers are all conceptually similar to the ENIAC blueprint, regardless of size. Since features of their design and operation have become modern-day analogues of human mental design and operation in many fields of psychology and behavioural science, it is worthwhile here to cast a schematic glance at them.

The physical and operational system of the computer is known as its *hardware*. This is composed of five distinct components:

- a *central processing unit* made up of a series of chips that perform calculations and that time and control the operations of the other elements of the system;
- *input devices*, such as a keyboard, that enable a computer user to enter data, commands, and programs into the central processing unit;
- *memory storage devices* that can store data internally (RAM) and externally (tapes, disks, etc.);
- *output devices*, such as the video display screen, that enable the user to see the results of the computer's calculations or data manipulations;
- a *communications network*, called a 'bus', that links all the elements of the system and connects the system to the external world.

A program directs the computer's hardware system. This is a sequence of instructions that tells the hardware what operations to perform on data. Programs can be built into the hardware itself, or they may exist independently in a form known as *software*. A general-purpose computer contains some built-in programs or instructions, but it depends on external programs to perform useful tasks. Once a computer has been programmed, it can do only as much or as little as the software controlling it at any given moment enables it to do. A wide range of applications programs are in use, written in special machine, computer or programming languages.

Software can be divided into a number of categories. The two primary ones are: operating or system software, which controls the workings of the computer, and application software, which makes it possible to carry out the multitude of tasks for which people use computers. System software handles such essential, but often invisible, chores as maintaining disk files and managing the screen, whereas application software performs word processing, database management, and the like. Two additional categories are: network software, which enables networks of computers to communicate with each other, and language software, which provides programmers with the tools they need to write programs.

In addition to these task-based categories, there are several types of software that are labelled in such a way as to inform consumers about what they are capable of carrying out. These include: packaged software, developed and sold primarily through retail outlets; freeware and public-domain software, which is made available without cost by its developer; shareware, which is similar to freeware but usually carries a small fee; and the infamous 'vapourware', which is software that either does not reach the market or appears much later than promised.

A technological background

The history of computing began, actually, in 1623 when a relatively unknown German scientist named Wilhelm Schikard invented a machine that could add, multiply and divide. In 1642, the great French philosopher and mathematician Blaise Pascal (1623–62) invented a machine that was capable of carrying out many more arithmetical operations. Pascal created fifty copies of his machine, most of which were intended to serve as curiosities in parlours of the wealthy and, thus, gain Pascal fame and perhaps a little wealth. Shortly thereafter, the German mathematician Gottfried Leibniz (1646–1716) refined Pascal's machine, thus establishing the basic operational principles of 'computing' machines, or simply 'computers', as these raw forerunners of modern-day electronic machines were named.

In the early nineteenth century French inventor Joseph Marie Jacquard (1752–1834) established the basic principles of computer programming with his invention of the loom, a device that was designed to run automatically by means of punched cards which programmed patterns into it that were then converted into woven fabrics by the machine. Incidentally, Jacquard's technological invention nearly cost him his life. He was forced to flee from the city of Lyon, pursued by hostile and belligerent weavers who feared their jobs were in jeopardy because of his despised invention. Jacquard's loom nevertheless survived the assault, and is still used today, especially in the manufacturing of furniture fabrics. It had all the basic features of the modern-day computer:

- a program (or set of instructions) that could be *inputted* into the machine;
- punched cards which functioned as a primitive memory system;
- the set of operations that the cards activated to bring about a required *output*.

Another early mechanical computer was the Difference Engine, designed in the early 1820s by British mathematician and scientist Charles Babbage. The machine had the potential to solve mathematical problems involving numbers with up to 20 decimal places. Babbage also made plans for another machine, the Analytical Engine, which he claimed would perform many complex arithmetical operations automatically. However, Babbage's lack of political skills kept him from obtaining the approval and funds that he required to build it. It was Augusta Ada Byron (1815–52), daughter of the famous poet Lord Byron and a personal friend and student of Babbage, who developed the appropriate programs to run Babbage's Analytical Engine. This led to the naming of its programming language as 'Ada', in her honour. Although the Analytical Engine was never finished, its key concepts, such as the capacity to store instructions, the use of punched cards, and the ability to print, established the basic blueprint for building modern-day computers.

American inventor Herman Hollerith (1860–1929) took the first true step towards building the modern-day electronic computer when he combined the use of Jacquard's punched cards with devices that created and electronically read them. Hollerith's 'electronic computer' was used for the 1890 US census, making the computational time needed to process data much shorter than the time previously needed for hand counts. Hollerith's Company eventually merged with other companies in 1924 to become International Business Machines, or IBM.

The next major step came in 1936, when British mathematician Alan Turing (1912–54) built a machine that could process equations without human direction. The machine (now known as a *Turing machine*) resembled an automatic typewriter that used symbols instead of letters. Turing intended the device to be used as a 'universal machine' that could be programmed to duplicate the function of any other existing machine.

In the 1930s, American mathematician Howard Aiken (1900–73) developed the Mark I calculating machine, which was built by IBM. Aiken's computer used relays and electromagnetic components to replace mechanical components, and later vacuum tubes and solid state transistors (tiny electrical switches) to manipulate the binary numbers in its program. Aiken subsequently introduced his computer device to the university community, establishing the first computer science programme at Harvard University. And it was in a university setting that the final touches on the blueprint for the construction of a true multi-purpose electronic digital computer were put. At the Institute for Advanced Study in Princeton, it was the Hungarian-American mathematician John von Neumann (1903–57) who finally built a computer with the capacity to solve problems in mathematics, meteorology, economics, and hydrodynamics. Von Neumann's 1945 Electronic Discrete Variable Computer (EDVAC) was the first electronic device to use a program stored entirely within its memory.

In the same year, Mauchly and Eckert (mentioned above) built ENIAC at the Moore School of Engineering at the University of Pennsylvania in Philadelphia. ENIAC was used initially for military purposes, such as calculating ballistic firing tables and designing atomic weapons. Eckert and Mauchly eventually formed their own company, which was subsequently bought by the Rand Corporation. Rand produced the Universal Automatic Computer (UNIVAC), which was used for a broader array of commercial computing tasks.

In the late 1960s and throughout the 1970s refinements in integrated circuitry technology and in the manufacturing of tiny transistors led to the development of the modern microprocessor, a smaller and cheaper computer that could be built even for personal uses. The invention was revolutionary and led to a true paradigm shift in society. The first of the so-called personal computers (PCs) was sold by Instrumentation Telemetry Systems. Their Altair 8800 appeared in 1975. It had 256 bytes of RAM. Refinements in the PC continued throughout the early 1980s. Graphical user interfaces were first developed by the Xerox Corporation, then later used successfully by the Apple Computer Corporation with its Macintosh computer. The first operating systems were not unlike the sophisticated operating systems in use today, such as Windows and Unix. They enabled computer users, unskilled in technology, to run programs and manipulate data in easy ways. The term 'user-friendly' emerged to characterize the new computers.

In the Digital Galaxy, the rapidity of technological change is the norm, not the exception. In 1965, semiconductor pioneer Gordon Moore predicted that the number of transistors contained on a computer chip would double every year. This is now known as 'Moore's Law'; and it has proven to be accurate. The number of transistors and the computational speed of microprocessors currently doubles approximately every 18 months. Components continue to shrink in size and are becoming faster, cheaper, and more versatile.

Computers have made the dream of easy and efficient long-distance communication and information storage concrete realities. Unfortunately, as computer use becomes more widespread, so do the opportunities for misuse. Computer hackers – people who illegally gain access to computer systems – often violate privacy and can tamper with or destroy records. Programs called viruses or worms can replicate and spread from computer to computer, erasing information or causing computer malfunctions. New ethical issues also have arisen, such as how to regulate material on the Internet and the World Wide Web.

The personal computer

American computer designers Steven Jobs and Stephen Wozniak, working out of their garage, created the Apple II in 1977. This was one of the first PCs to incorporate a colour video display and a keyboard that made the computer easy to use. Jobs and Wozniak later founded Apple Computer Corporation. Its first uses were to run games software for people to pit their logical skills against those of the software programmer. In 1984 the first Apple Macintosh was manufactured. That machine featured a graphical user interface (GUI), a visually-based system for representing computer commands and data on the screen. The Macintosh GUI combined icons (pictures that represent files or programs) with windows (boxes that contain an open file or program). A pointing device known as a mouse controlled information on the screen. The

Macintosh user interface made computers easy and fun to use and eliminated the need to type in complex commands.

PCs have since become as intrinsic to the system of everyday life as automobiles and TV sets. PCs now enable artists to create images. Musicians use them for composing and recording music. Businesses keep track of their finances and forecast performance using PCs. Journalists, students, instructors, and many more 'print-based' professionals can now compose their verbal texts on portable PCs and electronically communicate them to others from remote locations. Many people work at home and communicate with fellow workers with their PCs – a practice known as telecommuting. PCs can also be used to interface with worldwide communication networks in order to find information on any subject.

Hypertextuality

As discussed briefly in chapter 3, the computer has introduced a new form of textuality known as hypertextuality. Reading a printed page is, at the level of the signifier (i.e. of deciphering the actual signs on the page), a one-dimensional process, since it consists of decoding the individual words and their combinations in sentences in the framework of a specific signification system (a novel, a dictionary, etc.). Information of any specific sign in the text must be sought out physically: e.g. if one wants to follow up on a reference in the text, one has to do it physically by consulting other printed texts. This is of course what must be done when, for instance, one wants to look up the meaning in a dictionary of a word found in a text.

The computer screen has greatly facilitated such tasks, as we saw in chapter 3, by introducing a hypertextual dimension in computer textuality. The term hypertext was coined in 1965 to describe an interlinked system of texts in which a user can jump from one to another. This was made possible with the invention of hyperlinks – portions of a document that can be linked to other related documents. By clicking on the hyperlink, the user is immediately connected to the document specified by the link. Web pages are written in a simple computer language called HTML (Hypertext Markup Language). A series of instruction 'tags' are inserted into pieces of ordinary text to control the way the page looks and can be manipulated when viewed with a Web browser. Tags determine the typeface or act as instructions to display images, and they can be used to link up with other Web pages.

As opposed to the linear textuality of paper books, hypertextuality permits the user to browse through related topics, regardless of the presented order of the topics. The links are often established both by the author of a hypertext document and by the user, depending on the intent of the document. For example, 'navigating' among the links to the word 'language' in an article contained on a CD-ROM might lead the user to the International Phonetic Alphabet, the science of linguistics, samples of languages, etc.

Hypertextuality was introduced as a regular feature of computer systems in 1987 when Apple began distributing a new program called 'Hypercard' with its new PCs. This was the first program to provide a linking function permitting navigation among files of computer print text and graphics by clicking keywords or icons. By 1988 compact disc players were built into computers, introducing CD-ROMs onto the computer market. But hypertextuality has not changed the basic 'print code' for making written texts. It has simply amplified it by introducing an information-facilitating element into it. Hypertextuality in no way impugns the basic linearity of printed texts. In writing a computer hypertext, the author must still lay out his or her ideas in linear fashion and then choose which ones can be highlighted for clicking.

Interpreting a text involves three types of processes. First, it entails the ability to access the actual contents of the text at the level of the signifier, i.e. the ability to decode its words, images, etc. Only someone possessing knowledge of the codes (verbal and non-verbal) with which the text has been assembled can accomplish this. If it is in Finnish, then in order to derive an interpretant (a specific kind of meaning) from it, the decoder must know the Finnish language, the conceptual metaphors that characterize Finnish modes of speaking, and so on and so forth. The second referential capacity entails knowledge of how the $X = Y$ relation unfolds in the specific text, i.e. how the text (X) generates its meanings (Y) through a series of internal and external signification processes. This requires some knowledge on the part of the decoder of cultural codes other than the strictly verbal and non-verbal ones used to physically create the text. This is, in fact, the level of the signified that can be encapsulated in the question: what does it mean? Finally, various contextual factors enter into the entire process to constrain the interpretant, such as what the individual decoder will get from it, what the intent of the author was, etc. The integration of these referential dimensions makes possible the extraction of a meaning from the text. Clearly, this is hypertextual in nature because the decoder of the text must possess not only the ability to understand its 'surface language', but also to navigate through the various codes that it harbours within it. The type of 'mental navigation' that this entails is analogous to what is done on a computer screen by clicking keywords and icons. In effect, the physical structure of hypertextuality on the computer screen may constitute a kind of 'mirror model' of how people attempt, in effect, to derive an interpretant (specific meaning) from a text.

The Internet

As discussed briefly in the opening chapter, in the late 1960s the US Department of Defense created ARPANET to keep its computers secure in the event of war or natural disaster. Soon after, universities and other knowledge-based institutions created their own networks. These eventually merged with ARPANET to form the Internet in 1969. ARPANET was abandoned in 1982.

During the 1980s, large numbers of people and groups connected their computers to the Internet. On the Internet, one can find sites containing information on virtually every branch of human knowledge and enterprise – from the most serious scientific topics to catalogues of jokes and erotic pictures. Due to advances in worldwide telecommunications technologies, the Internet has also become a truly global network.

Features

Each connected individual can communicate with anyone else anywhere in the world on the Internet, publish ideas, and sell products with a minimum overhead cost. The Internet is also having a dramatic impact on higher education and business as more universities offer courses and more companies offer goods and services online. There are also other types of computer networks in use today, called 'intranets', that are closed to public use. Intranets are the most common types of networks used, for instance, by companies and organizations where it is important to restrict access to the information contained on the network.

The transfer of large databases onto the Internet has created a new way of viewing and organizing the classification of information. In the Gutenberg Galaxy, the basic system of classification – based on the physical nature of books – is alphabetic, for the simple reason that books can be organized on shelves in libraries (or referred to in, say, bibliographies) according to the first letter of the surname of the author or title of the book. Subdivision systems were also developed for further organizing 'book-contained' knowledge: e.g. classification according to subject area, according to the nature of the information, etc. One such system of cataloguing books is the so-called 'Dewey Decimal Classification' system, according to which all knowledge is divided into ten main classes, each of which is designated by a 100 number-span. The first class, 000–099, includes general works, such as encyclopedias, newspapers, and periodicals; 100–199 is used for philosophy and psychology; 200–299 for religion and mythology; 300–399 for the social sciences; 400–499 for language; 500–599 for pure science; 600–699 for technology; 700–799 for the arts (including sports and recreations); 800–899 for literature; and 900–999 for history, geography, biography, and travel. Each main class is then subdivided into ten subclasses; e.g. in the 800s, 810 is used for American literature, 820 for English literature, 830 for German, etc. Each of these in turn is subdivided further: e.g. in the 810s, 811 indicates American poetry and 813 fiction. Even more specific breakdowns, to indicate geographic location, chronological period, or the form of the material, are designated by numbers after a decimal point following the third digit. For example, 813.4 is used for American fiction from 1861 to 1900, and 813.46 indicates a work by or about the novelist Henry James.

On the Internet, such an 'orderly' framework cannot be adopted, given the kinds of information that are posted on websites. For instance, through computerized 'bulletin boards' people can post their own messages, opinions, commentaries, and ideas on any subject imaginable, making any overarching framework for organizing such boards *à la* Dewey impracticable. There are also 'newsgroups' on a host of topics. Participants in these groups can share information quickly, despite geographical separation. But access to specific items is difficult because they are not classified in any specific way.

In addition to problems of classification, an increasingly important area of concern related to the Internet is the authorship and/or ownership of texts. Documents and programs can be downloaded so easily that with some manipulation any text can easily be appropriated and used as if it were one's own. The Internet is leading, therefore, to a fundamental re-evaluation of the notions of authorship and plagiarism.

Problems of organizing, storing, and classifying information have become even more noticeable since the introduction of the World Wide Web (WWW) in 1989. The WWW was devised by English computer scientist Timothy Berners-Lee to aid communication between physicists working in different parts of the world for the European Laboratory for Particle Physics. As it grew, however, the WWW revolutionized the use of the Internet because, during the early 1990s, increasingly large numbers of users who were not part of the scientific or academic communities began to use the Internet, due in large part to the WWW.

Until the early 1990s, most information on the Internet consisted only of printed text. The introduction of the WWW made it possible to include graphics, animation, video, and sound. The WWW contains tens of millions of documents, databases, bulletin boards, and electronic publications, such as newspapers, books, and magazines in all media forms (print, visual, etc.). The miasma of information it contains made it immediately obvious to Internet users, shortly after its introduction, that appropriate technology was needed for them to be able to locate specific types of information. This led to the development of uniform resource locator (URL) technology. Using software that connects to the Internet – called navigation or browser software – a computer operator can select a URL that contains information he or she wishes to access. The computer then contacts that address, making the information available to the operator. With millions of separate URLs, classification and indexing have clearly become critical Internet functions. Indexing services – located on the Internet itself – enable users to search for specific information by entering the topic that interests them. The URL of the main Web page for the American White House, for instance, is http://www2.whitehouse.gov/WH/Welcome.html. The http indicates that the document is on the WWW. The next part, www2.whitehouse.gov, is the hostname and identifies the computer, www2. The .gov extension identifies the computer as belonging to the United States government. Next comes the path, or chain of directories; in this case, the only directory is WH. Last is the document name.

Other common extensions (also known as domains) are as follows:

.edu is reserved for educational users, including colleges, and universities. Sites contain electronic copies of paper documents that the institution publishes, including library catalogues, course schedules, and even virtual courses.

.gov is reserved for government agencies. Sites contain electronic versions of print documents that the institution publishes, including application forms, tax return forms, etc.

.org is set aside for nongovernment, nonprofit agencies, such as PBS. Sites contain electronic versions of their products and services.

.mil is reserved for military organizations, a reminder that the Internet originally evolved from a military weapons project.

.net is reserved for service providers such as Usenet. Sites in this domain contain descriptions of network availability, rates, special services, among others.

.com is set aside for businesses, corporations, etc. and their products. Sites contain everything from computer games and advertisements to sites that allow users to purchase products.

There are many other domains, encompassing a virtual world which, as the saying goes, can be 'surfed' without moving from a computer screen. Domains such as .firm, .store, .arts, .rec, and .info make it obvious that the convergence of media and diverse types of information is much more than a dream in the cyberworld. It is its primary characteristic.

There is no question that the Internet has already changed the way we live. A new breed of worker, called the 'teleworker', has already emerged. He or she works at his screen anywhere he or she desires to – not in any specific location, such as an office room in a building. It has also become a primary reference tool, a source of news, a shopping venue, and so on. Unlike the newspaper, the news on the Internet can be updated throughout the day. All the major newspapers now have an online version of their text. All kinds of music genres now also have their sites to which access will guarantee music content. And the list could go on and on. Cyberspace is fast becoming the only kind of space to which people will resort to interact socially and intellectually.

Digital communication systems

Most online services provide news, bulletin boards, databases, games, software libraries, and many other such things. Of these, electronic mail (e-mail) is one of the most-used digital communication systems in the world. Just as every website or Internet location has an electronic address, so too does every individual computer connected to a local access provider or online service. The user can write an e-mail message in a word-processing program, then transfer it to a communications program. The user can also write the message in an e-mail form – a box displayed on the monitor. Most communications software and online services provide such forms. After completing the message, the user can attach non-verbal material, such as graphics files, to it. He or she then addresses the message, and can send it to several addresses without rewriting it, by merely entering all the addresses as prompted by the computer. An 'electronic mailbox' at each computer address stores the mail.

E-mail has made regular mail appear cumbersome and inefficient. And because of listservs – electronic mailing lists that make it possible to send e-mail to special-interest groups – it has truly created a worldwide system of time-efficient communications. And with the advent of Instant Messaging (IM), this is being enhanced further. IM is instantaneous, thus bypassing the lag time inherent in sending and receiving e-mail. With IM a line typed on one PC is seen almost instantly on the screen of the receiving PC. IM is a 'visual walkie-talkie' system that is leading to the employment of a new 'language code' online that is becoming increasingly compressed to meet the needs of instant messaging.

An interesting trend that is taking place in this domain of communications regards the nature of the 'personal imprint' bestowed upon a written message (such as a letter) that comes from signatures. A signature is, of course, a person's name written by that person. But more significantly, it is an identifying characteristic or mark of that person – an index of the Self. This view is implicit, of course, in such practices as handwriting analysis which claims to be able to detect personality characteristics in the form of the signature. Clearly, on an e-mail the handwritten signature cannot be relayed directly. But the need to provide personal imprinting to messages has not disappeared. A kind of 'e-signature' practice has emerged which identifies the subject of the e-mail in the style and idiosyncrasies of the language used. In effect, one can tell who the sender of an e-mail is by the type of titles of the e-mail message and by the nature of the message. The digital medium has hardly eliminated the need to convey the Self in the communication text. It has simply forced people to come up with different kinds of signifiers to do so.

Another digital mode of communication, called 'chat', is also changing the nature of language. It is analogous to a conversation among several people, but it unfolds, of course, in 'disembodied' form. Computer users connect their PCs over the Internet or through an online service and type messages to one another. The individual networks are known as chat rooms. In the daily face-to-face form of verbal interaction, the body is as crucial a contributor to meaning as is the language used. Facial expressions, interjections, glances, etc. are all critical non-verbal components of dialogue. These are not possible in chat rooms. The question thus becomes: will the chat room form of dialogue change the fundamental nature of how we communicate in face-to-face situations over the course of time, conditioning people to communicate in a more disembodied fashion? This remains to be seen.

Actually, digital forms of communication have had more of an impact on the written word than they have on the spoken word. In carrying out writing tasks, people are becoming more and more accustomed to formatting their texts in accordance with the particular features of various word-processing software programs that are currently available. A digitally-produced text, moreover, can include features that the traditional print format cannot, such as animations and sounds. Moreover, in electronic publishing, space is much less limited than it is in print publishing. Printed material must often be edited to fit the number of pages available. But a standard CD-ROM, for example, can hold the equivalent of more than 250 000 pages of text. With Internet distribution, text length is a relatively minor concern. Much more important is the size of sound and visual files, which can take a long time to transmit to a computer.

Clearly, the advent of digital communication has enormous implications for how we carry out communication and how we will be creating our representations, especially as companies start to carry out increasingly larger portions of commerce online, including advertising, selling, buying, distributing products, and so on. The Internet is also being used more and more for voice and video conferencing and other forms of communication that allow people to telecommute, or work from a distance. E-mail has greatly accelerated communication between individuals and institutions. Media and entertainment companies use the Internet to broadcast audio and video, including live radio and television programmes; to offer online chat rooms, in which people carry on discussions using written text; and to provide online news and weather programmes. Scientists and scholars use the Internet to communicate with colleagues, to conduct research, to distribute lecture notes and course materials to students, and to publish papers and articles. The Digital Galaxy is expanding literally at the speed of light.

Convergence

Everything, from advertising messages to sound recordings, is now available through the computer. Television and print media are now fully integrated with websites so that audiences of such media can continue to engross themselves in the complementary websites that they provide.

The Internet has become, above all else, a highly effective medium of advertising, making it possible for all kinds of businesses the world over to communicate effectively and inexpensively with the entire globe. The feature of the Internet that makes it attractive to the advertiser is the fact that the product or service can be ordered directly from the ad. Not only does an online ad about a specific product or service reach millions of potential customers through the WWW, but its users can acquire or request it 'on the spot', by simply clicking the appropriate icons.

The convergence of the computer with all other media technologies is the defining characteristic of mass communications today. Computers can now be put on top of TV sets so that people can interface with the Internet as well as the new digital TV services. More and more computer boxes are being built into digital sets. Personal data assistants (PDAs), pocket-sized information devices that accept handwriting, keep people in contact with the Internet and other media as well. In the near future, computers will be in charge of most communication channels, turning the world into a true digital global village.

But all this has its setbacks. Over-reliance on computers has induced a mindset that sees computers as intrinsic components of human processes. This became apparent on the threshold of the year 2000 when the 'millennium bug' was thought to be a harbinger of doom. So reliant had people become on the computer that a mere technological problem – making sure that computers could read the new '00' date as '2000, and not '1900' or some other '...00' date – was interpreted in moral and apocalyptic terms. That was striking evidence that computers had acquired connotative signification that far exceeded their original function as 'computing machines'. Constant exposure to 'virtual realities' in cyberspace, moreover, is leading surreptitiously and gradually to an entrenchment of a bizarre modern form of Cartesian 'dualism', the view that the body and the mind are separate entities. Computers allow users to move and react in a computer-simulated environment, manipulating virtual objects in place of real objects. Constant engagement in such environments is conditioning people more and more to perceive the body as separable from the mind.

Contributing to this 'disembodiment process' are virtual reality devices, mentioned briefly in chapter 6 and above. Virtual worlds differ from other computer simulations in that they require, at present, special interface devices that transmit the sights, sounds, and sensations of the simulated world to the user. These devices also record and send the speech and movements of the participants to the simulation program. In effect, the human subject is interacting with a world totally made up, a kind of representational space where the user is interacting with representation in itself.

As VR becomes more and more widespread, and less dependent on external devices, it will perhaps further entrench the process of disembodiment. So too will the continuing process of creating cyberplaces and cyberevents in cyberspace. Incidentally, the term 'cyberspace' was coined by American writer William Gibson in his 1984 science fiction novel *Neuromancer*, in which he described cyberspace as a place of 'unthinkable complexity'. The term has given rise to a vocabulary of 'cyberterms', such as 'cybercafes' (cafes that sell coffee and computer time), 'cybermalls' (online shopping services), and 'cyberjunkies' (people addicted to being online).

Semiotically speaking, the convergence of media and the constant exposure to cyberspace mediation will eventually reshape the world's signifying orders, by turning upside down traditional ideas of human interaction, communication, representation, physical place, textuality, and even reality. In cyberspace, signifieds float around, so to speak, with no material world in which to exist. They are 'virtual signifieds' transmitted by a host of multimedia signifiers. What is emerging is a 'cybersystem' without the usual constraints that traditional print systems impose on representation and communication.

According to Baudrillard (1998), digital media have put people in the position of having to rebuild signifying orders from the ashes of the 'dead signs' of the 'real' world. But, as it turns out, these new signs are not that much different from the old ones. So, Baudrillard predicts, in a short time 'virtual communication' will become 'real communication' again, as people begin to realize that their bodies are as much a part of creating signs as are their minds. Paradoxically, Baudrillard goes on to quip, the computer will engender a desire to 're-embody' communication and representation.

The computer and the mind

In movies, TV programmes, comic books, and other media, it is now a common thing to find robots, cyborgs, and other 'intelligent' machines featured as heroes or villains, and possessing qualities that only the heroes and villains of myth and legend were once portrayed as embodying. The representation of machines as having human qualities and, vice versa, of humans being little more than biological machines has been a popular one in all media for some time. But the interest in intelligent machines is not limited to the media. In certain sciences of the mind, such as artificial intelligence, the question is now raised with all sincerity if truly intelligent computers can be built to live alongside humans. This is why specific kinds of computers are being constructed with the sole purpose of duplicating the complex functions of human thought. But, amid all this 'cyber excitement', it is misguided, in my view, to assume a similarity between human and machine intelligence. The former grew out of lived experiences and developed through historical forces; the latter has been literally invented by humans themselves.

The idea that computers can think autonomously is really no more than a modern-day version of the philosophy known as 'animism' – the view that there is a spirit in all things, animate and inanimate. The modern version can be called 'machinism'. Given the importance of the computer in the Digital Galaxy, the belief in machinism will only expand, especially since media representations are constantly transmitting images of robots and cyborgs embodying all the qualities that were once considered uniquely human – altruism, spirituality, artistry, etc. It is therefore relevant to discuss machinism in the context of the theme of the present chapter.

In part, the idea of intelligent machines has been energized by the remarkable advances in the technology of computer hardware, software, and networks. In the Digital Galaxy, such technology reinforces the illusion that knowledge and information exist independently of their makers – a belief that, as we saw in chapter 3, was forged in the Gutenberg Galaxy. But human signs are not equivalent to computational data that can be neatly classified as true or false. Rather, human signs are designed not only to convey information, but also to provide perspective, emotion, and other impenetrable aspects of human consciousness that machines will never be able to fathom.

Machinism

The science of artificial intelligence (AI) is an offshoot of the technology of computers. It emerged in the middle part of the twentieth century to provide a highly technical theoretical apparatus for modelling certain aspects of human cognition in computer software. One of its primary objectives is attempting to answer the question of what the human mind is and if it is possible to recreate it in the form of computer software.

This whole line of inquiry, however, leads on to the thorny question of what the word 'mind' designates in the first place. What is its signified? As a noun, it is used commonly to denote the faculty of thinking, reasoning, and acquiring and applying knowledge. As such, it is opposed commonly to 'heart', 'soul', or 'spirit'. But then, words such as 'thinking', 'reasoning', and 'learning' are really no more than synonyms of the word 'mind'. As we saw in chapter 1, the problem is that the denotative meanings of words can only be determined in reference to other meanings. The meaning of 'mind' simply cannot be established in the absolute, but only in relation to other signs: e.g. mind vs. heart; mind vs. body; etc. From such oppositions we can see, one or two features at a time, what makes the mind unique. AI theorists avoid, however, this whole line of questioning by simply characterizing the mind as a 'machine' – obviously unaware of the conceptual pitfalls this entails. In line with this view, the psychologist P.N. Johnson-Laird has identified three types of 'machines', in his book *Mental Models* (1983: 24). These are designations that have entered the lexicon of AI theory:

1 'Cartesian machines' that do not use symbols and lack awareness of themselves;
2 'Craikian machines' (after Craik 1943) that construct models of reality, but lack self-awareness;
3 self-reflective machines that construct models of reality and are aware of their ability to construct such models.

The computer software designed by AI engineers to simulate human mentality produces types (1) and (2) forms of intelligence. But, at present, only human beings are capable of the type (3) form. Unlike a Cartesian or a Craikian machine, a human being is not only capable of constructing models of his or her mind, but is aware of doing so. AI theorists claim that type (3) awareness is definitely within the realm of the computers of the not-too-distant future. Are they right?

The computer is one of *Homo sapiens'* greatest intellectual achievements. It is an extension of rational intellect. As a maker of objects and artefacts, *Homo sapiens* has finally come up with a machine that will eventually take over most of the arduous work of ratiocination. In this regard, the caveat with regard to viewing the computer as a competitor issued eloquently by the psychologist Arnheim (1969: 73) is still valid today: 'There is no need to stress the immense practical usefulness of computers. But to credit the machine with intelligence is to defeat it in a competition it need not pretend to enter.'

The belief of AI researchers that computers can become truly intelligent is not something that has crystallized in the Digital Galaxy. It is, as a matter of fact, an ancient one. In some Sumerian and Babylonian myths, for instance, there are descriptions of inanimate matter being brought to life. The modern form of animism, however, traces its origin to the publication of Mary Shelley's grotesque and macabre 1818 novel *Frankenstein* (chapter 3). Since then, the idea that robots could become intelligent has been a target of fascination for creative artists, philosophers, media moguls, and scientists of the mind. Machinism has, in effect, become a modern-day mythology. This is why we talk of computers as if they were human – as being 'infected' with 'viruses' – and why so many robot characters are found in media narratives today.

AI and the media have, in a fundamental sense, joined forces. Both have contributed in inculcating the popular view of computers as extensions of human mentality. Computer terms such as 'storage', 'retrieval', 'processing', etc. have, in fact, become signifiers of how we perceive ourselves. As Howard Gardner (1985: 6) has aptly pointed out, from its very outset AI has been shaped by the view that there exists a level of mind wholly separate from the biological or neurological, on the one hand, and the sociological or cultural, on the other, that works like an electronic computer. Even though not all AI scientists think in this way, this 'machinist bias' is, as Gardner (1985: 6) phrases it, 'symptomatic' of the whole enterprise. By developing computer programming theory, AI scientists insist that everything from problem-solving to emotions and creativity will eventually become intrinsic features of machine intelligence.

The basis for this view is, clearly, the concept of 'machine', which is a mathematical abstraction tracing its roots to the work of the mathematician Alan Turing (chapter 5). Turing showed that four simple operations on a tape – move to the right, move to the left, erase the slash, print the slash – allowed a computer to execute any kind of program that could be expressed in a binary code (as, for example, a code of blanks and slashes). So long as one could specify the steps involved in carrying out a task and translating them into the binary code, the Turing machine – now called a computer program – would be able to scan the tape containing the code and carry out the instructions.

Although Turing himself was well aware of the limitations of his notion, openly admitting that it could never come close to emulating the more spiritual aspects of human consciousness, to many AI theorists his clever insights suggested that humans too were, in effect, special kinds of protoplasmic machines, whose cognitive states, emotions, and social behaviours were not only representable in the form of computer-like programs, but that mechanical machines themselves could eventually be built to think, feel, and socialize like human beings. As Minsky (1986), Konner (1991), and other radical computer scientists have insisted, even concepts such as the soul or the spirit are really no more than fanciful notions for referring to the intelligence of an advanced Turing machine in the mortal brain and body of an animal. For such scientists, therefore, consciousness is really no more than a consequence of the workings of a biological programme that allows individual human machines to express and modify the emotions of their brains and the impulses of their bodies.

The AI movement is really a contemporary outgrowth of the 'Cartesian project' that ushered in the modern era of science. According to Descartes, all human problems, whether of science, law, morality, or politics could eventually be solved by developing a universal method of philosophy based on logical computation. This project seemed realizable when the engineer Claude Shannon demonstrated that information of any kind, in both animal and mechanical systems of communication, could be described in terms of binary choices between equally probable alternatives – as we saw in the opening chapter. By the 1950s, enthusiasm was growing over the possibility that computers could eventually carry out human thinking processes, since the brain was thought to be really no more than a Turing machine operating on the basis of its own kind of biological binary code. By the 1960s, phenomenal advances in computer technology seemed to make Descartes' dream a reality.

But true intelligence by machines has never been realized, nor will it be realized in the future, because it is beyond the capacities of machines to feel, imagine, invent, dream, construct rituals, art works, and the like. These are derivatives of bodily and psychic experiences. AI theories and models of consciousness can perhaps give us precise information about the nature of the formal properties of mental states; but they tell us nothing about how these states were brought about in the first place.

In a fundamental sense, machinism is a product of metaphorical thinking: the mind equals a machine (chapter 2). This is not to imply that technological discoveries are purely metaphorical and thus imaginary. On the contrary, technology is a product of human ingenuity; metaphor is a cognitive strategy for understanding the products of that ingenuity. Bicycles and cars extend the human foot, weapons the hands, nails, and teeth, clocks the body's internal rhythms, houses the body's heat-control system, clothing the skin, the computer the central nervous system, and so on. These extensions are real and tangible. Many historians of science argue correctly that technology has not only become an essential condition of advanced industrial civilizations, but also that we now evolve and survive through it. Technological innovations seem to appear at a rate that increases geometrically, without respect to geographical limits or social systems. These innovations tend to transform traditional cultural systems, frequently with unexpected social consequences. The steam engine, for example, was commonplace before the science of thermodynamics elucidated the physical principles underlying its operations. Its use and development spread to societies all over the world, changing them radically. From this process institutions and professional goals emerged in different cultures with, however, identical points of reference and codes (e.g. theoretical notions, scientific procedures, manufacturing processes, transportation infrastructures, etc.). No wonder, then, that the metaphor that the mind is a machine is so believable.

The above discussion in no way implies that other conceptual metaphors for the mind do not exist. On the contrary, the following show how conditioned we have been by our own media technologies to conceptualize the world through them:

From print media

- He has a great *character*.
- I cannot *read* your mind.
- Make a mental *note* of what I just said.
- It is time to turn over a new *leaf*.
- His life is an open *book*.
- You must start over *tabula rasa*.
- Her story is *written* in my heart.

etc.

From electronic, photographic, and filmic media

- I just had a *flashback*.
- What mental *picture* do these words evoke?
- My mind is out of *focus*.
- He has a *photographic memory*.
- I am going over what you said in *slow motion*.

etc.

From the computer medium

- He is *hard-wired* for action.
- My mental *software* no longer works.
- I can't quite *retrieve* that memory.
- I haven't yet *processed* what he said.
- Did you *store* away what I told you?

etc.

Such expressions overlap constantly in discourse, suggesting that we see our media as extensions of our mental selves. More importantly, they reveal that we know virtually nothing about the mind and, therefore, resort to metaphor in order to fill the signification gap that the mind signifier leaves. That is something, obviously, that AI scientists have yet to realize.

Re-embodiment

Rather than take the mind out of the human body and transfer it to cybersystems or humanoid machines, the whole technology that undergirds the Digital Galaxy will, in my view, bring about a reintegration of the body and the mind, as suggested above. This process of re-embodiment is a result of what McLuhan (1964) called 're-tribalization'. As digital technologies continue to advance the possibility of global communication 'on the spot', so to speak, people want the protection and emotional shelter of the 'tribe' more and more. This is because, like most other species, humans have always lived in groups. The tribe remains the type of collectivity to which human beings instinctively relate even in modern times. In complex city-societies, where various cultures, subcultures, countercultures, and parallel cultures exist in constant competition with each other, where the shared territory is so large that it becomes an abstraction or figment of mind, the tendency for individuals to relate to tribal-type groupings or arrangements that exist within the larger societal context manifests itself regularly and predictably. People continue to perceive their membership in smaller groups as more directly meaningful to their lives than allegiance to the larger society or nation. This inclination towards re-tribalization reverberates constantly within modern-day humans, and may be the source of the angst and sense of alienation that many city-dwelling individuals feel, living in large, impersonal social systems.

Re-tribalization involves re-embodiment, since it engages people in face-to-face contact. The manifestations of this process are everywhere. Even though people today see themselves as interconnected to world events (especially through TV and the Internet), they still have a strong desire to live in the 'real' world. So, rather than having resolved conflicts among people by allowing them to get into contact, digital technology has brought out the 'tribal animal' within us even more. Not only across the globe, but also within nations, there are more and more subcultures (such as teenage gangs) which have developed their own peculiar forms of tribalism. Indeed, the more the computer is used to conduct everyday affairs, the more people seem to resort to traditional forms of discourse and interaction. The paradox of everyday life in the Digital Galaxy is that it engenders both 'globalism' and 'tribalism' at once.

8   Advertising

I have discovered the most exciting, the most arduous literary form of all, the most difficult to master, the most pregnant in curious possibilities. I mean the advertisement. It is far easier to write ten passably effective Sonnets, good enough to take in the not too inquiring critic, than one effective advertisement that will take in a few thousand of the uncritical buying public.

Aldous Huxley (1894–1963)

The messages of advertisers are everywhere. They are on billboards, on the radio, on television, on buses and subways, in magazines and newspapers, on posters, on clothes, shoes, hats, pens – and the list could go on and on. To say that advertising has become a ubiquitous form of textuality in today's 'global culture' is an understatement – it is estimated that the average American is exposed to over 3000 advertisements a day and watches three years' worth of television commercials over the course of a lifetime (Kilbourne 1999). Using both verbal and non-verbal techniques to make its messages as persuasive as possible, advertising has become an integral category of modern-day signifying orders designed to influence attitudes and lifestyle behaviours by covertly suggesting how we can best satisfy our innermost urges and aspirations through consumption. As the American author E.B. White (1899–1985) aptly observed in 1936, in a *New Yorker* article (11 July):

Advertisers are the interpreters of our dreams – Joseph interpreting for Pharaoh. Like the movies, they infect the routine futility of our days with purposeful adventure. Their weapons are our weaknesses: fear, ambition, illness, pride, selfishness, desire, ignorance. And these weapons must be kept as bright as a sword.

Given its obvious importance to understanding modern signifying orders, it is little wonder that advertising has become a target of great interest to semioticians. The two questions that media semiotics attempts to answer in this domain are: (1) How does advertising textuality encode meanings? (2) How do advertisers create signification systems that are perceived by hordes of people as so meaningful? Those will be the questions that will guide the discussion in this chapter.

What is advertising?

After the publication of Vance Packard's 1957 work on the psychosocial effects of advertising, *The Hidden Persuaders*, an outpouring of studies in the 1970s, 1980s, and 1990s started examining the impact of advertising on individuals and on society at large. The implicit question that most of the studies entertained, without answering it in any definitive fashion, was whether advertising had become an ideological force moulding cultural mores and individual behaviours, or whether it constituted no more than a 'mirror' of deeper cultural tendencies within urbanized contemporary societies. Without going into the debate here, suffice it to say that there is one thing with which virtually everyone agrees – advertising has become one of the most recognizable and appealing forms of mass communications to which virtually everyone in society is exposed. The images and messages that advertisers promulgate on a daily basis delineate the contemporary social landscape. In themselves, they are not disruptive of the value systems of the cultural mainstream. Rather, they are effective because they reflect 'shifts' already present in popular culture.

Moreover, advertising is no longer just the servant of commercial interests. It has become a common strategy adopted by anyone in society who wants to persuade people to do something: e.g. to endorse a political candidate, to support a cause, and so on and so forth. Business firms, political parties and candidates, social organizations, special-interest groups, and governments alike advertise routinely in various media to create favourable 'images' of themselves in the minds of people. Since the 1960s advertising campaigns have also been mounted and directed toward issues of social concern (cancer, AIDS, human rights, poverty, etc.).

The term 'advertising' derives from the medieval Latin verb *advertere* 'to direct one's attention to'. It designates any type or form of public announcement or representation intended to promote the sale of specific commodities or services. Advertising is to be distinguished from other kinds of representations and activities aimed at swaying and influencing opinions, attitudes, and behaviours such as propaganda, publicity, and public relations. In the twentieth century, advertising evolved into a form of persuasive social discourse intended primarily to influence how we perceive the buying and consumption of goods. Advertising discourse ranges from simple notices in the classified sections of newspapers and magazines to sophisticated magazine lifestyle ads and television and Internet commercials. Advertising has, therefore, become a kind of privileged discourse that has replaced, by and large, more traditional forms of discourse – sermons, political oratory, proverbs, wise sayings, etc. – which in previous centuries had rhetorical force and moral authority. But advertising exalts and inculcates Epicurean, not moralistic, values. It envisions human beings as 'recurrent units' that can be classified into 'taste groups', 'lifestyle groups', or 'market segments', which can be managed and manipulated according to the laws of statistics. As the psychoanalyst Carl Jung (1957: 19–20) warned several decades ago, we live indeed in an age that views a human being dangerously as a cog in an assemblage, rather than as 'something unique and singular which in the last analysis can neither be known nor compared with anything else'.

Advertising falls into two main categories: (1) consumer advertising, which is directed towards the promotion of some product, and (2) trade advertising, in which a sales pitch is made to dealers and professionals through appropriate trade publications and media. The focus of this chapter is on the former, which can be defined more specifically as a form of discourse designed to promote the sale of marketable goods and services.

Consumer advertising, incidentally, gave birth to the first agency for recording and analysing data on advertising effectiveness in 1914 with the establishment of the Audit Bureau of Circulations in the United States, an independent organization founded and supported by newspaper and magazine publishers wishing to obtain circulation statistics and to standardize the ways of presenting them. Then, in 1936 the Advertising Research Foundation was established to conduct research on, and to develop, advertising techniques with the capacity to enhance the authenticity, reliability, efficiency, and usefulness of all advertising and marketing research. Today, the increasing sophistication with statistical information-gathering techniques makes it possible for advertisers to target audiences on the basis of where people live, what income they make, what educational background they have, etc. in order to determine their susceptibility to, or inclination towards, certain products.

Advertising is thus closely linked to marketing science. Advertisers and marketing agencies conduct extensive and expensive surveys to determine the potential acceptance of products or services before they are advertised at costs that may add up to millions of dollars. If the survey convinces the manufacturer that one of the versions exhibited will attract enough purchasers, a research crew then pre-tests various sales appeals by showing provisional advertisements to consumers and asking them to indicate their preference. After the one or two best-liked advertisements are identified, the advertiser produces a limited quantity of the new product and introduces it in a test market. On the basis of this market test the advertiser/manufacturer can make a decision as to whether a national campaign should be launched.

By spreading advertising messages constantly through numerous and varied media – newspapers, television, direct mail, radio, magazines, business publications, calendars, Internet sites, etc. – the aim of campaigns is to saturate the signifying order with advertising messages. This creates the illusion that there is a correlation between the products advertised and social processes and trends. As Barthes often claimed in his writings, for this reason advertising is identifiable as the root cause of neomania. Through adaptive change, advertisers are constantly trying to ensure that any shifts in social or entertainment trends (fashion, music, values, popularity of media personalities, etc.) are reflected in their advertising texts as well. Indeed, the contemporary mediated world is distinguished above all else by a dynamic interplay between advertising, pop culture trends, and general social tendencies, whereby one influences the other through a constant synergy.

A brief history

The first advertising texts of human civilization were the many outdoor signs displayed above the shop doors of ancient cities of the Middle East. As early as 3000 BC, the Babylonians used such signs to advertise the stores themselves. The ancient Greeks and Romans also hung signs outside their shops. Since few people could read, the merchants of the era used recognizable visual symbols carved in stone, clay, or wood for their signs. Throughout history, poster and picture ads in marketplaces and temples have, in fact, constituted popular media for disseminating information and for promoting the barter and sale of goods and services.

The use of shop signs and posters continued uninterrupted right into medieval times. With the invention of the printing press in the fifteenth century, fliers and posters could be printed quickly and cheaply, and posted in public places or inserted in books, pamphlets, newspapers, etc. The printing press also spawned a new form of advertising, known as the handbill. This had an advantage over a poster or sign because it could be reproduced and distributed to many people living near and far apart.

The growing use and influence of advertising in the nineteenth century led to the establishment of the first advertising agency by Philadelphia entrepreneur Volney B. Palmer in 1842. By 1849, Palmer had offices in New York, Boston, and Baltimore in addition to his Philadelphia office. In 1865, George P. Rowell began contracting with local newspapers as a go-between with clients. Ten years later, in 1875, N.W. Ayer and Son, another Philadelphia advertising agency, became a rival of Rowell and Palmer. In time, the firm hired writers and artists to create print ads and carried out complete advertising campaigns for clients. It thus became the first ad agency in the modern sense of the word. By 1900, most agencies in the United States were writing ads for clients, and were starting to assume responsibility for complete advertising campaigns. By the 1920s, such agencies had themselves become large business enterprises, constantly developing new techniques and methods that would be capable of influencing the so-called 'typical consumer'. It was at that point in time that advertising came to be perceived primarily as an instrument of persuasion by corporate executives. Business and psychology had joined forces by the first decades of the twentieth century, broadening the attempts of their predecessors to build a textual bridge between the product and the consumer's consciousness.

In the 1920s, the increased use of electricity led to the possibility of further entrenching advertising into the social landscape through the use of new electronic media. Electricity made possible the illuminated outdoor poster; and photo-engraving and other printing inventions helped both the editorial and advertising departments of magazines create truly effective illustrative material that could be incorporated into ad texts. The advent of radio, also in the 1920s, led to the invention and widespread use of a new form of advertising, known as the commercial – a mini-narrative or musical jingle revolving around a product or service and its uses (chapter 4). The commercial became immediately a highly persuasive form of advertising, since it could reach masses of potential customers, print literate or not, instantaneously. The commercial became even more influential as a vehicle for disseminating advertising messages throughout society with the advent of television in the early 1950s. TV commercials of the day became instantly familiar creating a perception of the product as being inextricably intertwined with the style and content of the commercials created to promote it. Recently, the Internet has come forward to complement and supplement both the print and commercial (radio and TV) forms of advertising. However, advertising textuality has not changed drastically from the way it was fashioned by the traditional media. As in TV commercials, Internet advertisers use graphics, audio, and various visual techniques to enhance the effectiveness of their messages.

The 'language' of advertising has become the language of virtually everyone – even of those who are critical of it. As Twitchell (2000: 1) aptly puts it, 'language about products and services has pretty much replaced language about all other subjects'. We assimilate and react to advertising texts unwittingly and, in ways that parallel how individuals and groups have responded in the past to religious texts, we utilize such texts unconsciously as templates for planning, interpreting, and structuring social actions and behaviours. Advertising has become one of the most ubiquitous, all-encompassing forms of social discourse ever devised by humans. As McLuhan (1964) quipped, the medium in this case has indeed become the message. There are now even websites, such as AdCritic.com, that feature ads for their

own sake, so that audiences can view them for their aesthetic qualities
alone.

Spreading the message

The two main techniques used by advertisers to embed advertising into the
social mindset are called *positioning* and 'image-creation'. *Positioning* is the
placing or targeting of a product for the right people. For example, ads for
Budweiser beer are normally positioned for a male audience, whereas ads for
Chanel perfume are positioned, by and large, for a female audience. The
advertising of the Mercedes Benz automobile is aimed at socially upscale car
buyers; the advertising of Dodge vans is aimed, instead, at middle-class
suburban dwellers. Creating an image for a product involves fashioning a
'personality' for it with which a particular type of consumer can identify. The
product's name, packaging, logo, price, and overall presentation create a
recognizable character for it that is meant to appeal to specific consumer types.
Take beer as an example. What kinds of people drink Budweiser? And what
kinds drink Heineken instead? Answers to these questions would typically
include remarks about the educational level, class, social attitudes, etc. of the
consumer. The one who drinks Budweiser is perceived by people as vastly
different from the one who drinks Heineken. The former is imagined to be a
down-to-earth (male) character who simply wants to 'hang out with the guys';
the latter a smooth sophisticated type (male or female) who appreciates the
'finer things' of life. This personification of the product is reinforced further by
the fact that Budweiser commercials are positioned next to sports events on
television, whereas Heineken ads are found next to current affairs
programmes, and certain types of sitcoms. The idea behind creating an *image*
for the product is, clearly, to speak directly to particular *types* of individuals,
not to everyone, so that these individuals can see their own personalities
represented in the lifestyle images created by advertisements for certain
products.

Brand image is further entrenched by the technique of mythologization. This
is the strategy of imbuing brand names, logos, product design, ads, and
commercials intentionally with some mythic meaning. For instance, the quest
for beauty, the conquest of death, among other mythic themes, are constantly
being woven into the specific images that advertisers create for certain products.
In the case of beauty products, this strategy often can be literally seen in the
people who appear in ads and commercials. These are, typically, attractive
people, with an 'unreal', almost deified, quality about the way they look.

Another way in which advertisers entrench product mythology is through
logo design. Take, as an example, the McDonald's golden arches logo. Most
people today go to fast-food restaurants to be with family or with friends, so

as to get a meal quickly and because the atmosphere is congenial. Most people would also admit that the food at a McDonald's restaurant is affordable and that the service is fast and polite. Indeed, many today probably feel quite 'at home' at a McDonald's restaurant. This is, in fact, the semiotic key to unlocking the meaning that the McDonald's logo is designed to create. The arches reverberate with mythic symbolism, beckoning good people to march through them triumphantly into a paradise of order, cleanliness, friendliness, hospitality, hard work, self-discipline, and family values. In a sense, McDonald's is comparable to an organized religion. From the menu to the uniforms, McDonald's exacts and imposes standardization, in the same way that the world's organized religions impose standardized interpretations of their sacred texts and uniformity in the appearance and behaviour of their clergy. The message created unconsciously by the golden arches logo is therefore that, like paradise, McDonald's is a place that will 'do it all for you', as one of the company's past slogans so aptly phrases it.

Advertisers create brand names, logos, package designs, bottle shapes, print ads, and commercials that, below their surface appearance, tap into unconscious desires, urges, and mythic motifs. Ads and commercials now offer the same kinds of promise and hope to which religions and social philosophies once held exclusive rights – security against the hazards of old age, better positions in life, popularity and personal prestige, social advancement, better health, happiness, etc. In a phrase, the modern advertiser stresses not the product, but the benefits that may be expected to ensue from its purchase. The advertiser is, clearly, quite adept at setting foot into the same subconscious regions of psychic experience that were once explored only by philosophers, artists, and religious thinkers.

Creating a signification system

To create a personality for a product, advertisers construct a signification system for it. This is achieved, first and foremost, by giving it a *brand name* and, whenever possible, creating a visual symbol for it known as a *logo*. By assigning it a name, the product, like a person, can be recognized in terms of its name. No wonder, then, that trademarks – which is the legal term for brand names – are so fiercely protected by corporations and manufacturers. So important is the brand name as an identifier of the product that, on several occasions, it has become the general term to refer to the product type. Examples include aspirin, cellophane, and escalator.

Brand names

As was discussed in chapter 2, the name *Acura* was designed to be imitative of the phonology of both Japanese and Italian words. By metaphorical extension, it is designed to evoke, arguably, the perceived qualities of both the Japanese and Italian cultures. In effect, the name on its own generates a signification system for the product. Here are other examples of how some brand names are constructed to generate specific kinds of metaphorical connotation systems:

- Names referring to the actual manufacturer evoke connotations of 'tradition', 'reliability', 'artistry', 'sophistication', etc.: e.g. *Armani, Benetton, Folger's,* etc.
- Names referring to a fictitious personality elicit specific kinds of images: e.g. *Wendy's* evokes the image a 'friendly young girl', *Mr Clean* of a 'strong toiler', etc.
- Names referring to some aspect of Nature bestow upon the product the qualities associated with Nature such as 'water', 'health', 'cleanliness', etc.: e.g. *Tide, Surf, Cascade, Aqua Velva, Mountain Dew,* etc.
- Names constructed as hyperboles emphasize product 'superiority', 'excellence', etc.: e.g. *MaxiLight, SuperFresh, UltraLite,* etc.
- Names constructed as combinations of words elicit composite meanings: e.g. *Fruitopia* ('fruit + Utopia'), *Yogourt* ('yogurt + gourmet'), etc.
- Some names are designed simply to tell what the product can do: e.g. *Easy Off, Lestoil, One Wipe, Quick Flow, Easy Wipe,* etc.
- Some names are designed to show what can be accomplished with the product: e.g. *Close-Up Toothpaste, No Sweat Deodorant,* etc.

To be effective, however, brand-naming must keep in step with the times. In early 2000, car makers, for instance, started looking at newer naming trends that appeal to a generation of Internet users who have become accustomed to a different style of communication. Cadillac, for instance, announced a new model with the monogram name CTS in 2001. Names using just letters and numbers have, in fact, become widespread. Acura itself has transformed its line of models with names such as: TL, RL, MDX, RSX. Such names are consistent with 'Internet discourse', which can be called simply 'Internetese', a type of highly telegraphic form of communication that is centred on monogrammatic and alpha-numeric signifiers. Hyundai's XG300 model, for instance, sounds perfect for the times. On the other side of the naming equation, such abbreviations are hard to remember, especially for older customers who have not yet tapped into Internetese.

Brand names, clearly, do much more than just identify a product. As the above examples show, they are constructed to create connotative signification systems for the product. At a practical informational level, naming a product has, of course, a denotative function; i.e. it allows consumers to identify what product they desire to purchase (or not). But at a connotative level, the product's name generates images that go well beyond this simple identifier function. Consider Armani shoes as a specific case-in-point. Denotatively, the name allows us to identify the shoes, should we desire to buy them rather than, say, Russell & Bromley shoes. However, this is not all it does. The use of the manufacturer's name, rather than some invented name or expression, assigns an aura of craftsmanship and superior quality to the product. The shoes are thus perceived to be the 'work' of an artist (the manufacturer). They constitute, in effect, a 'work of shoe art', so to speak, not just an assembly-line product for everyone to wear.

Clearly, in the fashion industry, designer names such as Gucci, Armani, and Calvin Klein evoke images of *objets d'art*, rather than images of mere clothes, shoes, or jewellery; so too do names such as Ferrari, Lamborghini, and Maserati in the domain of automobiles. The manufacturer's name, in such cases, *extends* the denotative meaning of the product considerably. This extensional process is known, of course, as connotation. The signification system created to ensconce product image into the social mindset is a *de facto* connotative one. When people buy an Armani or a Gucci product, for instance, they feel that they are buying a work of art to be displayed on the body; when they buy Poison, by Christian Dior, they sense that they are buying a dangerous, but alluring, love potion; when they buy Moondrops, Natural Wonder, Rainflower, Sunsilk, or Skin Dew cosmetics they feel that they are acquiring some of Nature's beauty resources; and when they buy Eterna 27, Clinique, Endocil, or Equalia beauty products they sense that they are getting products imbued with scientific validity. 'No-name' products do not engender such systems of connotations.

Incidentally, branding was, originally, the searing of flesh with a hot iron to produce a scar or mark with an easily recognizable pattern for identification or other purposes. Livestock were branded by the Egyptians as early as 2000 BC. In the late medieval period, trades people and guild members posted characteristic marks outside their shops, leading to the notion of trademark. Medieval swords and ancient Chinese pottery, for instance, were also marked with identifiable symbols so buyers could trace their origin and determine their quality. Among the best-known trademarks surviving from early modern times are the striped pole of the barbershop and the three-ball sign of the pawnbroker shop.

Names were first used towards the end of the nineteenth century when many American firms began to market packaged goods under such names. Previously, everyday household products were sold in neighbourhood stores from large bulk containers. Around 1880, soap manufacturers started naming their products so that they could be identified – e.g. Ivory, Pears', Sapolio, Colgate, etc. The first modern-day brand names were thus invented. As

Naomi Klein (2000: 6) aptly observes, branding became the general practice among manufacturers of products because the market was starting to be flooded by uniform mass-produced and, thus, indistinguishable products: 'Competitive branding became a necessity of the machine age'. By the early 1950s, it became obvious that branding was not just a simple strategy for product differentiation, but the very semiotic fuel that propelled corporate identity and product recognizability. Even the advent of no-name products, designed to cut down the cost of buying them to the consumer, has had little effect on the signifying power that branding has on the consciousness of people. Names such as Nike, Apple, Body Shop, Calvin Klein, Levi's, etc. have become signs recognized by virtually anyone living in a modern consumerist society. As Klein (2000: 16) goes on to remark, for such firms the brand name constitutes 'the very fabric of their companies'.

Iconic brand names are particularly effective, because they are memorable. A name such as Ritz Crackers, for example, assigns a sonority to the product that is simulative of sounds that crackers make as they are being eaten. Another example is the name Drakkar noir, chosen by Guy Laroche for one of its cologne products. The dark bottle conveys an imagery of 'fear', the 'forbidden', and the 'unknown'. Forbidden things take place under the cloak of the night; hence the name *noir* (French for 'black'). The sepulchral name of the cologne is clearly iconic with the bottle's design at a connotative level, reinforcing the idea that something desirous in the 'dark' will happen by splashing on the cologne. The guttural sound of 'Drakkar' is also suggestive of Dracula, the deadly vampire who mesmerized his sexual prey with a mere glance.

Logos

Logos (an abbreviation of logographs) are the pictorial counterparts of brand names. They are designed to generate the same kinds of connotative signification systems for a product through the visual modality.

Consider the apple logo adopted by the Apple Computer Company. It is, clearly, an iconic sign suffused with latent religious connotations suggesting, above all else, the story of Adam and Eve in the Western Bible, which revolves around the eating of an apple that was supposed to contain forbidden knowledge. In actual fact, the Hebrew account of the Genesis story tells of a 'forbidden' fruit, not specifically of an apple. The representation of this fruit as an apple came about in medieval depictions of the Eden scene, when painters became interested in the Genesis story artistically. Now, the Biblical symbolism of the apple as 'forbidden knowledge' continues to resonate in our culture, since at least medieval times; and that is the reason why the Apple computer company has not only named itself 'Apple', but has also chosen the icon of this fruit as its logo, symbolizing the fact that it, too, provides access to 'forbidden' knowledge to those who buy and use its products. Incidentally, the logo shows an apple that has had a bite taken from it, thus reinforcing the link between the company icon and the Genesis story by associating the use of Apple computers and products with Eve, the mother of humanity.

Logos can sometimes harbour more than one signification system. Consider the Playboy logo of a bunny wearing a bow tie. Its ambiguous design opens up at least two 'connotative chains' of meaning:

1 rabbit = 'female' = 'highly fertile' = 'sexually active' = 'promiscuous' = etc.
2 bow tie = 'elegance' = 'night club scene' = 'finesse' = etc.

The appeal and staying power of this logo is due, arguably, to its inbuilt ambiguity. As we shall see below, ambiguity is a fundamental characteristic of advertising textuality. It is the reason, in fact, why advertising is so 'semiotically powerful'.

Logos are now displayed on products for all to see. Until the 1970s, logos on clothes, for instance, were concealed discretely inside a collar or on a pocket. But since then, they can be seen conspicuously. Ralph Lauren's polo horseman and Lacoste's alligator, to mention but two, are now shown prominently on clothing items, evoking images of heraldry and, thus, nobility. They constitute symbols of 'cool' (Klein 2000: 69) that legions of people are seemingly eager to put on view in order to convey an aura of high class 'blue-blooded' fashionableness.

Advertising textuality

The signification systems that are built into brand names and logos are transferred creatively to ad texts. 'Advertising textuality' can be defined simply as the construction of advertisements and commercials on the basis of the specific signification systems built intentionally into products. Among the many textual strategies used to bring out such systems, the following five are the most common:

- the use of jingles which typically bring out some aspect of the product in a memorable way;
- the use of certain music genres to emphasize lifestyle: e.g. the use of jazz or classical music to convey a sense of superiority and high-class aspirations;
- the creation of fictitious characters so as to assign a visual portraiture to the product: e.g. *Speedy, Ronald McDonald, Tony the Tiger, Mr Clean*, etc.;

- using famous personages – actors, sports figures, etc. – to endorse the product;
- creating ads and commercials to represent the product's signification system in some specific way (e.g. through some visual depiction, through some narrative, etc.).

As an example of the last strategy, a popular television commercial for Miller beer that was shown during Sunday afternoon football games on American television in the early 1990s can be recalled here. The action of the commercial can be broken down into a sequence of actions as follows:

- As the commercial began, we saw a young handsome man who was seated at a bar counter in a crowded, smoke-filled room, with a beer glass nearby.
- He was surrounded by a group of male companions chatting and confabulating in ways young men are purported to do in such situations.
- At the other end of the bar, a matched group of males had congregated around another young handsome 'leader of the pack'.
- Suddenly, an attractive female entered the scene. Instantaneously, the 'leaders' of both male cliques made their way towards her.
- To block the second leader from getting to her, the first male clique cut off his path to the female in a strategic manner, leaving the first leader to 'get his prize'.
- The whole 'action' was described by the voice of a football announcer in a 'play-by-play' fashion.
- The commercial ended with the phrase 'Love is a game' appearing on the screen.

Given that the commercial was shown – i.e. positioned – during football game telecasts, and given that the actions took place in the context of a football game, a straightforward interpretation can easily be formulated. In a phrase, the action of the two cliques simulated an action play between two football teams. 'Winning' the game in this case is 'getting to' the female first. In order to accomplish this, the first male leader, or 'quarterback', needed the support of his 'team' to be successful in carrying out the crucial play, which of course he was able to do. By successfully blocking the path of the other team's quarterback, the first team won the 'game'. As a reward, the heroic quarterback 'scored' sexually, as the expression goes.

This interpretation was reinforced by the play-by-play description of an announcer whose voice simulated that of a television football announcer, as well as by the concluding metaphorical statement that appeared on the screen: 'Love is a game'. In sum, the commercial constituted a specific representation of the beer's signification system:

> *beer* = 'male bonding', 'interest in sports', 'interest in females', etc.

This system was easily recognizable in the commercial's narrative. The signification systems of many ads, however, are not so easily detected. Take, as a case-in-point, a truly ingenious ad for Versus cologne by Versace, which was found in lifestyle magazines in the mid-1990s. The actual surface text showed four rugged handsome young men who presumably wore Versus to smell as good as they looked. At this denotative level, the ad seemed to be merely saying: 'To look as *cool* as these men, all you have to do is splash on Versus'. But the subtext told another story, since it was imbued with many subtle innuendoes and allusions that transformed it into a highly suggestive ad.

To start off, let us consider the ad's most conspicuous iconic cues in terms of its layout:

- The name of the cologne starts with the letter 'V'.
- The bottle displayed a V-shaped intaglio in its shape.
- The men in the ad wore a shirt or jacket whose open collar made a V-shape outline.
- The men were dressed in black.
- Two of the men wore leather items.
- The bottle was centred at the bottom.
- A V-shape cut across the page.

The perfusion of Vs strengthens the syntagmatic association between the cologne's name, Versus, and its manufacturer, Versace. But Versus is also a word that connotes 'opposition' and 'violation', and the V-shape can also be interpreted as a symbol that connotes 'indentation', 'cleft', or 'fissure'. This chain of connotations is reinforced by the fact that the word 'Versus' crossed the entire ad, as if it were a line of separation between the men in the ad and the viewers of the ad.

The ad was clearly aimed at young affluent males who could afford to buy an expensive bottle of cologne. The men are, presumably, prototypes of what young urban professional males aspire to look like during leisure hours – hours devoted to mate selection and sexual fulfilment generally. During the day, the men probably wear business suits; during recreational hours they wear 'V-neck' apparel and dash on Versus. So, one possible interpretation of the ad's subtext is that Versus can be used by men propitiously for their 'sex-seeking' leisure activities. It is cologne designed to help them cross over, symbolically, from the work world to the leisure world – worlds that are in constant opposition. Reasoning mythically, the former world can be compared to the realm of Apollo – the god of male beauty, the fine arts, and order – and the latter to the realm of Dionysus – the male god of wine, the irrational, and the orgiastic. One interpretation of the Versus subtext, therefore, is the following one:

> Versus = 'the olfactory means by which a modern-day Apollo can cross over into the erotically enticing Dionysian realm'.

Several other features of the ad strengthen this interpretation:

- The V-shape of the men's collars and of the bottle design pointed downwards, i.e. down to the Dionysian underworld of carnality and sexual pleasure.
- The dark tones of the clothing and the bottle, which reinforce this indexical signified, suggested that something dark and dangerous, but nevertheless desirous, was about to happen.
- The word 'Versus' crossed the entire ad, seemingly inviting the male viewer to 'cross over' into the dark underworld of sex where he could satisfy his 'carnal nature'.
- There is no 'spark' in the men's eyes, which is suggestive of the fact that the underworld casts dark shadows which cover the eyes, the mirrors of the soul, because in the underworld, there is no soul, just carnality and ravenous cupidity.
- One of the men in the ad wore a leather hat and another a leather motorcycle jacket, both of which are synesthetically suggestive of sadomasochistic eroticism.
- The shape of the bottle, of the letter 'V' itself, and of the neckline configurations, are suggestive of female sexuality.

Such an interpretation is, of course, consistent with a signification system that is based on heterosexuality. The power of the ad, however, lies in its ability to summon up another signification system. One can ask, in fact, whether the object of the men's desire is not the 'opposite' of female sexuality, as the name Versus suggests at another subtextual level. In other words, does the cologne allow the men to descend even further into deeply-hidden homosexual desires? The good looks of the men, with their darkened eyes looking directly into the camera, muscular bodies and sensuously-protruding lips, leather apparel, together with the absence of women in the ad are features that are strongly suggestive of this other subtext.

Whether or not the two interpretations put forward here are 'correct', the point is that both are seemingly possible. The way the ad is laid out and designed creates an entangled web of ambiguous sexual connotations. Barthes (1977) referred to the ambiguity of such ads as *anchorage*, defining it as the ability of certain ads to evoke various equally probable subtexts, each of which is 'anchored' in a specific signification system.

Clearly, the design of the bottle with a V intaglio is a crucial part of the signification system(s) created for the above product. As Hine (1995) has amply shown, such things as bottles are, in effect, to be viewed as art objects. This is the reason why some products have been represented as true art objects by exponents of the *pop art* movement. Andy Warhol, for instance, made silk-screen prints of commonplace objects, people, events, etc., such as soup cans and photographs of celebrities. His painting of a Campbell's soup can (1964) made it obvious how intrinsic product imagery had become in communal consciousness.

Connotative chaining

The suggestive power of the Versus ad lies primarily in its inbuilt ambiguity, i.e. in its ability to generate various kinds of subtexts. The more subtexts, or *connotative chains*, that are built into the ad, the more likely will be its appeal. Such chains are created by the utilization of techniques such as the following ones used in the Versus ad:

1 *similarity* (a V-shape and a cleft);
2 *difference* (the same V-shape and its opposite meaning);
3 *contiguity* (the location of the V-shape below the men in the ad);
4 *intensity* (using dark colours in the ad);
5 *association* (V-shapes are associated with various signifieds, including 'clefts', 'fissures', and 'crossings'.

From a psychological standpoint, the human mind seems predisposed to link meanings together in such ways. And advertisers obviously know this. As Goldman and Papson (1996: 24) aptly put it, advertising is, in effect, an activity 'in which the raw material worked into commodities is *meaning*'.

There are various types of connotative chains that characterize subtexts. A common type is forged from narrative sources. As such, it constitutes a chain of meanings linked together by themes, plot-lines, characters, and settings suggested from the implicit storylines built into the surface presentations. The surface text of the Versus ad unfolds, in fact, as a storyline about male camaraderie and the lifestyle associated with being an upwardly mobile male in today's society; but one possible subtext is, as we saw, a mythic narrative text.

Another type of subtext is the one based on metaphor. Consider, as a case-in-point, a magazine ad for the perfume Volupté, a perfume designed to appeal to women in their 20s and 30s. The ad was found in lifestyle magazines of the mid-1990s. The perfume's name means 'voluptuousness' in French. The bottle was placed in the centre of the text. It had a dark, round cap. The phrase 'Trust your senses' was placed just below it, implying, at a denotative level, that the buyer would be able to smell the high quality of the perfume. However, the shape of the perfume bottle evoked a connotative subtext. The bottle cap was highly suggestive of an aroused nipple – a sign of successful sexual foreplay. In tandem with this image, the phrase 'Trust your senses' can now be interpreted as being suggestive of sexual 'sensing', since a breast involves most of the senses in foreplay – sight, smell, taste, and touch. The background scene in the ad reinforced this interpretation, since it showed a secluded, dark place where the bottle (= female breast?) could be looked at voyeuristically through the beam of light that fell upon it.

The signification systems built into the Versus and Volupté ads were relatively 'silent' ones, in the sense that the only meaningful words in them were the brand names themselves and, in the case of the Volupté ad, a metaphorical statement. But language is, more often than not, an important contributor to establishing the connotative structure of the product's signification system.

Many brand names, for instance, are metaphors. The perfume named Poison, for example, has an immediate impact because of the metaphorical association between danger (poison) and attraction. In addition to metaphor, there are a host of verbal techniques that advertisers use effectively in generating connotative chains and product textuality generally. Some of these are as follows (Dyer 1982: 151–82):

- *Jingles and slogans.* These have the effect of reinforcing the recognizability of a brand name: *Plop, plop, fizz, fizz, oh what a relief it is!*
- *Use of the imperative form.* This creates the effect of advice coming from an unseen authoritative source: *Pump some iron, Trust your senses,* etc.
- *Formulas.* These create the effect of making meaningless statements sound truthful: *Triumph has a bra for the way you are; A Volkswagen is a Volkswagen;* etc.
- *Alliteration.* This increases the likelihood that a brand name will be remembered: *The Superfree sensation* (alliteration of *s*); *Guinness is good for you* (alliteration of *g*); etc.
- *Absence of language.* Some ads strategically avoid the use of any language whatsoever suggesting, by implication, that the product speaks for itself. As Dyer (1982: 170) puts it, the absence of language in certain ad texts 'has the effect of making us think that meaningful reality lies directly behind the signs once we have succeeded in deciphering them'.
- *Intentional omission.* This technique is based on the fact that secrets grab our attention: *Don't tell your friends about . . .; Do you know what she's wearing?*; etc.
- *Parallelism.* This is the repetition of linguistic patterns (sentences,

phrases, etc.) which impart a poetic quality to the text: *It's longer/It's slimmer/It's surprisingly mild* (advertisement for *More* cigarettes).

In television and radio commercials the tone of voice, the sentence structure, and the use of various verbal ploys (jingles, slogans, etc.) are used as well to deliver product signification systems. The tone of voice can be seductive, friendly, cheery, insistent, foreboding, etc. as required by the signification system in question. The sentence structure of ads and commercials is usually informal and colloquial, unless the ad is about some 'high-class' product (e.g. a BMW automobile, a Parker pen, etc.), in which case it is normally more elegant and refined. Advertising also borrows discourse styles to suit its purposes: a commercial can take the form of an interview; a testimonial on the part of a celebrity; an official format (*Name:* Mary; *Age:* 15; *Problem:* acne); and so on.

The use of multiple media

The repetition of advertising messages in different media of the same system is a primary strategy used to strengthen product recognizability. Print ads reach people through newspapers, magazines, direct mail, and outdoor signs. Newspapers, on average, devote almost half of their space to advertising. These offer advertisers several advantages over other media. Most adults read a daily newspaper; and many specifically check the ads for information about products, services, or special sales. Newspaper advertising can also quickly incorporate a sudden demand for certain merchandise. Magazines, on the other hand, are usually read in a leisurely manner and may be kept for weeks or months before being discarded. They also offer better printing and colour reproduction. Direct mail advertising includes the use of leaflets, brochures, catalogues, and other printed advertisements that are delivered by a postal service. Outdoor signs are used because people pass by the signs repeatedly. In addition, large, colourful signs attract attention.

Print media now use computer and telecommunications technologies to create, produce, and print different versions of the same ad text. Called 'selective binding', this enables advertisers to stylize versions of their texts for selected groups of readers.

As we saw in chapter 4, radio advertising has the advantage that people can listen to programmes while doing other things, such as driving a car or working at home. Another advantage is that radio audiences, in general, are more highly selectable by the type of programming than are, say, television audiences. For example, stations that feature country music attract different kinds of listeners than do those that play rock. By selecting the station, advertisers can reach the people most likely to buy their products.

Television is probably the most effective contemporary medium for delivering product imagery. Advertisers can explain and demonstrate their products to viewers who are watching a specific genre of TV programme. Network television reaches a vast, nationwide audience at a very low cost per viewer. The majority of TV commercials consist of short spot announcements, most of which last 30 seconds to a minute. The commercials are usually run in groups of three to six.

Lastly, the Internet has made it possible for advertisers to reach vast audiences all over the world inexpensively. The Internet has, moreover, the advantage that it is simultaneously an impulse, a directional, and an interactive medium. The first refers to the fact that it induces large numbers of browsers to respond to commercial messages on a whim. The second refers to the fact that consumers can decide to buy a particular product at a company's website. And the third refers to the fact that the product makers and consumers can interact. The website for Hallmark cards exemplifies this. A 'reminder service' is available whereby customers are asked for prominent names and birthdays and are later contacted through e-mail when it is time to send that person a greeting card.

Ad campaigns

Advertising textuality is also built into ad campaigns. An ad campaign can be defined as the systematic creation of a series of slightly different ads and commercials based on the same theme, characters, jingles, etc. An ad campaign is comparable to the theme and variations form of music – where there is one theme with many variations.

Here are just a handful of examples of famous ad campaigns through the years:

- In 1892, the Coca-Cola logo appeared across the country, painted as a mural on walls, displayed on posters and soda fountains where the drink was served, imprinted on widely marketed, common household items (calendars, drinking glasses, etc.).
- In 1904, the Campbell's Soup company began its highly successful advertising campaign featuring the rosy-cheeked Campbell Kids and the slogan 'M'm! M'm! Good!' The campaign is still ongoing as I write.
- In 1970, McDonald's launched its highly successful 'You deserve a break today' advertising campaign.
- In 1985, Nike signed basketball player Michael Jordan as a spokesman, marking the beginning of a dramatic growth for the company. Nike marketed the Air Jordan line of basketball shoes and clothes with a series of striking advertising creations (ads and commercials). Those creations,

along with the company's 'Just Do It' campaign featuring football and baseball star Bo Jackson and motion-picture director Spike Lee, boosted Nike's profits considerably. In 1997, Nike entered a new period of high-profile product image when company spokesman Tiger Woods became the first African American to win the Professional Golf Association's Masters golfing tournament.

- In the early 1990s Joe Camel ads became highly successful in promoting an image of smoking as something 'refined'. In 1991, the American Medical Association criticized RJR Nabisco for using a cartoon character named Joe Camel in its Camel advertising campaign, claiming that the campaign was targeted at children. In 1992, the US Surgeon General asked the company to withdraw its ad and this request was followed by more government appeals in 1993 and 1994. The company responded to public concerns by promoting a campaign that encouraged store merchants and customers to obey the law prohibiting the sale of tobacco products to minors. In 1997, under increasing criticism, the company ended its Joe Camel ad campaign.

- The growth of the Gateway 2000 computer company in the 1990s was helped, in large part, by an unusual advertising campaign featuring employees standing in cow pastures. The company also shipped its computers in boxes splattered with black spots like those of Holstein cows, reflecting its Midwestern roots.

One of the primary functions of campaigns is to guarantee that the product's image keeps in step with the changing times. Thus, for example, the Budweiser commercials and ads of the 1980s and early 1990s emphasized rural, country-and-western ruggedness, and sexuality seen from a male viewpoint. The actors in the commercials were types who embodied a rural country-style ruggedness, *à la* Marlboro man. In the early 2000s, the same Company changed its imagery with its 'Whassup!' series of commercials, which showed young urban males who loved sport and who expressed their form of 'buddyism' humorously with the expression 'Whassup?' So widespread and appealing was the 'Whassup?' campaign that its 'verbal style' became a part of pop culture. Its signature catch phrase was joked about on talk shows, parodied on websites, mimicked in other media, and used by people commonly in their daily conversations. The makers of Budweiser had clearly coopted the essence of the language, styles, and attitudes of 20- and 30-year-old males in their clever ad campaign.

Cooption

Indeed, the most effective strategy of advertising is not only to keep up with the times but also to coopt them, so to speak. In the 1960s, for example, the image created by the media of self-proclaimed 'rebels' and 'revolutionaries', referred to generally as 'hippies', who genuinely thought they were posing a radical challenge to the ideological values and lifestyle mores of the mainstream consumerist culture, ended up becoming the incognizant trend-setters of the very culture they deplored, providing it with features of lifestyle and discourse that advertisers have, since the 1960s, been able to adapt and recycle into society at large. Counterculture clothing fashion was thus quickly converted into mainstream fashion, counterculture music style into mainstream music style, counterculture symbolism and talk into society-wide symbolism and discourse – hence the crystallization of a social mindset whereby every individual, of every political and ideological persuasion, could feel that he or she was a symbolic participant in the 'youth revolution'.

The use of the 'hippie image' in ads and commercials of the era occurred at a point in time when a dynamic advertising community decided it was in its best interest not to fight the images of youth insurgency, but rather to embrace them outright. One highly effective early strategy of this 'if-you-can't-beat-them-join-them' approach was the development of an advertising style that mocked consumerism and advertising itself! The strategy worked beyond expectations. Being young and rebellious came to mean having a 'cool look'; being anti-establishment and subversive came to mean wearing 'hip clothes'. The corporate leaders had cleverly 'joined the revolution', so to speak, by deploying the slogans and media images of youthful rebellion to market their goods and services. 'New' and 'different' became the two key words of the new advertising and marketing lexicon, coaxing people into buying goods, not because they necessarily needed them, but simply because they were new, cool, hip. The underlying system of signification of this ingenious marketing strategy allowed consumers to believe that what they bought transformed them into ersatz revolutionaries without having to pay the social price of true non-conformity and dissent.

Campaigns, such as the 'Pepsi Generation' and the Coke universal brotherhood ones, directly incorporated the images, rhetoric, and symbolism of the hippie counterculture, thus creating the illusion that the goals of the hippies and of the soft drink manufacturers were one and the same. Rebellion through purchasing became the subliminal thread woven into the pop culture mindset that the marketing strategists were starting to manipulate and control effectively. The 'Dodge Rebellion' and 'Oldsmobile Youngmobile' campaigns followed the soft drink ones, etching into the nomenclature of products themselves the powerful connotations of hippie rebellion and defiance. Even a sewing company, alas, came forward to urge people on to join its own type of surrogate revolution, hence its slogan 'You don't let the establishment make your world; don't let it make your clothes'. In effect, by claiming to 'join the revolution', advertising created the real revolution. This is why, since the late 1960s, the worlds of advertising, marketing, and entertainment have become totally intertwined with youth lifestyle movements, both responding and contributing to the rapid fluctuations in social trends and values that such movements entail.

Today, the advertising industry has appropriated 'cool images' completely. Sociologically, the end result has been a further obliteration of the crucial emotional difference that traditional cultures have maintained between the social categories of 'young' and 'old'. This is why nowadays the rhetoric of youth is quickly transformed by advertising textuality into the rhetoric of all; why the fashion trends of the young are recycled and marketed shortly after their invention as the fashion styles of all; and why the fluctuating aesthetics of the youth culture are quickly incorporated into the aesthetics of society at large. Cultural cool has, in effect, become the social norm.

Other strategies

Ad campaigns are not only designed to coopt trends and turn them to advantage for the product, they are often intended to create a 'history' for a product, thus linking it to a sense of cultural continuity and communal tradition. This is done, in part, by simply getting the product 'out there', so to speak, into social consciousness. The Coke campaigns, for example, have always been designed to appeal to everyone. This is why nearly everyone alive today will recognize Coke and have some understanding of its signification systems. This works especially well for products and services that appeal to everyone – automobiles, cosmetics, insurance, food, beverages, pain tablets, etc. It cannot be used for 'controversial' products, such as cigarettes and alcohol, and for things that do not have a broad appeal (e.g. certain music styles, certain types of books, etc.).

But perhaps the most effective strategy for getting the product into the social mindset is to create, simply, appealing ads for it, as the 'Whassup?' campaign demonstrated. These catch the attention of everyone through the aesthetic channel and, thus, quickly become integrated into communal consciousness. In a fascinating book, titled *Twenty Ads that Shook the World* (2000), James Twitchell identifies 20 ads and ad campaigns that have, in fact, become part of this consciousness, simply because they were designed cleverly and had mass appeal. As Twitchell (2000: 8) puts it, 'They got into our bloodstream.' Among the ads are De Beers' 'A Diamond Is Forever' campaign (1948), Hathaway's 'Hathaway Man' campaign (1951), Miss Clairol's 'Does She, or Doesn't She?' campaign (1955), Marlboro cigarette's 'Marlboro Man' campaign (1950s), Volkswagen's 'Think Small' campaign (1962), Coca Cola's 'Things Go Better with Coke' campaign (1964), Revlon's 'Charlie' campaign (1970s–1980s), Absolut Vodka's 'Larceny' campaign (1980s), and Nike's 'Air Jordan' campaign (1990s).

The power of the ad to affect people as if it were a 'work of art' became obvious with Apple Computer's brilliant '1984' commercial, which was shown on 22 January 1984, during the third quarter of Super Bowl XVIII on American television. Obviously evocative of George Orwell's *1984*, and directed by Ridley Scott, whose 1982 movie *Blade Runner* was discussed in chapter 5, the commercial won countless advertising awards and was characterized by advertising moguls as 'the commercial that outplayed the game'. Orwellian and other '1984-ish' themes have found their way into a host of commercial campaigns, including one by Zenith in early 2000, which showed automatonic, depersonalized human robots walking all in tandem, without eyes, and a little girl who, with bright eyes, sees a new Zenith television set sitting on a column in the midst of this arid, spiritless, totalitarian world. The apparition and her childlike discovery of it instantly humanize the mindless throng, as people's eyes emerge as if by metamorphosis from a cocoon. The social connotations that this ad evoked are self-evident.

Other strategies that now constitute an advertising meta-code for embedding product textuality into social consciousness are as follows:

- the something-for-nothing lure ('Buy one and get a second one free!', 'Send for free sample!', 'Trial offer at half price!', 'No money down!' etc.);
- the use of humour to generate a feeling of pleasantness towards a product;
- endorsement by celebrities to make a product appear reliable;
- inducing parents to believe that giving their children certain products will secure them a better life and future;
- appealing to children to 'ask mummy or daddy' to buy certain products, thus increasing the likelihood that parents will 'give in' to their children's requests;
- using 'scare copy' techniques designed to promote such goods and services as insurance, fire alarms, cosmetics, and vitamin capsules by evoking the fear of poverty, sickness, loss of social standing, and/or impending disaster;
- creating brand names, logos, packaging designs, magazine ads and radio and television commercials that are highly suggestive of erotic, sensual, mythic, and other kinds of psychologically powerful themes.

These techniques have become so common that they are no longer recognized consciously as stratagems. Advertising has become the fuel for an entertainment-driven society that seeks artifice as part of its routine of escapism from the deeper philosophical questions that would otherwise beset it.

Interestingly, in 2001 BMW hired several famous directors to make short 'digital films' featuring its cars. The movies were, in effect, extended commercials and were viewable only on the Web, but were promoted through TV spots. Each film was about six minutes long; each featured a prominent actor; and each portrayed BMWs used in a reckless, adventure-oriented fashion.

Advertising is powerful because it offers recognizable 'objects' and 'solutions' providing the hope of more money and better jobs, security against the hazards of old age and illness, popularity and personal prestige, praise from others, more comfort, increased enjoyment or pleasure, social advancement, improved appearance, better health, erotic stimulation, popularity, emotional security, and so on. The effectiveness of the techniques used to engender such meanings is limited only by the ingenuity of the advertiser, by the limits of the various channels of communication used to disseminate the product's textuality, by certain legal restrictions in place where the advertising messages are delivered, and by standards self-imposed by the advertising industry.

It is no exaggeration to say that the history of modern pop culture is intrinsically interwoven with the history of advertising. In looking back over the last century, it is obvious that the messages of advertisers, their styles of presentation, and the ways in which they have used language have become the very fabric of modern modes of representation and communication. As McLuhan (1964: 24) aptly put it, advertising has become the 'art' of the modern world.

9 Social impacts of the media

We live in a world ruled by fictions of every kind – mass merchandising, advertising, politics conducted as a branch of advertising, the instant translation of science and technology into popular imagery, the increasing blurring and intermingling of identities within the realm of consumer goods, the preempting of any free or original imaginative response to experience by the television screen. We live inside an enormous novel. For the writer in particular it is less and less necessary for him to invent the fictional content of his novel. The fiction is already there. The writer's task is to invent the reality.

J.G. Ballard (1930–)

It is ironic that a common theme in contemporary media representations is the one warning people about the nefarious control that media moguls – the 'Elliott Carvers' of the world (Introduction) – now exercise over vast numbers of people across the globe. Movies, popular book exposés, TV documentaries, and websites about the 'dangers of the media' are common. Therein lies the paradox of modern culture – it is a world in which media have become not only the means for controlling public thinking, but also for critiquing mediation itself in all its dimensions. The media are now perceived as a force for good and a source for bad at the same time. The mediated world has allowed vast numbers of people access to the kinds of representations to which only the élite had privilege in the past; but it has also created a society-wide 'distraction mindset', whereby entertainment is pursued relentlessly by hordes of people, as is 'newness', 'faddishness', and 'coolness'. The paradox of mediation has been the underlying theme of this book. The same culture that is capable of producing a work of inestimable cinematic art, such as *Amadeus*, is also capable of producing American TV wrestling matches, which are little more than mind-numbing, inane spectacles.

The goal of this book has been, in effect, to discuss this theme from the particular standpoint of semiotic analysis, whose aim it is, basically, to interpret media representations in terms of how they are put together textually, i.e. in terms of how a specific representation, X, is capable of generating a system of meanings Y, in some specific way, $X = Y$. To a semiotician, the specific medium in question is irrelevant, since print, audio, film, television, computer, and advertising media and genres produce, essentially, the same array of meanings. They do so by using different kinds of signifiers. The semiotic study of media is, therefore, essentially a study in signifier difference and in how this difference changes the delivery and impact of texts and their messages.

This final chapter has three objectives: (1) to go over schematically the main features of semiotic analysis; (2) to look a little more closely at the kinds of impacts that the media purportedly have on people; and (3) to offer concluding reflections on the relation between the media and contemporary culture.

Overview

The recording of ideas in a pictographic way made it possible to store and pass on knowledge and, thus, to establish a continuity to human ideas. With the advent of alphabetic writing, print became the first medium paving the way toward the establishment of a worldwide civilization. The Gutenberg Galaxy, as we saw, subsequently extended the availability of print and diversified its functions. One of these was distraction. When the book became widely available and affordable through printing press technology, it also became a medium through which people could pass their leisure hours enjoyably. The distraction function became even more prominent in representational activities with the advent of electronic and digital media in the twentieth century.

One of the subsidiary themes of this book has been that new media are not substitutive, but extensional: e.g. print extended orality, radio extended print, television extended radio, and so on. Many people assume that print literacy is the most elevated mode for encoding and communicating knowledge, and that all other kinds of media are somehow 'inferior' to print. But this assumption is not correct; nor is the one which claims that new media are disruptive of 'true' cultural development – whatever that may be. The many kinds of media used today may have indeed become vital cogs in the global consumerist-driven economic machine, as social critics descry, but they have in no way impugned the basic imaginative nature of human representation. On the contrary, they have provided even more fuel for the imagination to reign supreme in human affairs. Moreover, movies, pop music, and even TV programmes have made it possible for more people than at any other time in history to put their imaginations on display.

Today's Digital Galaxy is really an extension of the Gutenberg Galaxy. When Gutenberg invented movable type to print the Bible, he made possible a veritable revolution in human mental evolution and culture by making ideas readily available to a larger population. But rather than homogenizing the world, his revolution led to greater diversity and variety in representation, as we saw in chapter 3.

The semiotic perspective revisited

As argued mainly by illustration throughout this book, the globalization of pop culture has occurred at the level of the signifier, since all media are basically specific kinds of signifiers – i.e. physical systems with properties that allow people to encode or represent the same kinds of signifieds in particular ways. Differences among the media are, therefore, more often than not differences in the 'physics' of representation, rather than differences in content. Indeed, as the genres of one medium are adapted by another, their content is recycled, not discarded – e.g. when print genres were adopted by electronic media they were not changed as to their meanings; rather, they were converted into parallel genres delivered through new physical channels. Most movies, TV programmes, and other media representations do little more, therefore, than recycle the same kinds of signifieds in new ways. Figuring out how this is accomplished is one of the primary goals of media semiotics, as we have seen throughout this book.

Semiotic analyses of media texts will vary, first and foremost, according to type of text. In the case of a text, X, whose meaning, Y, is transparently obvious, the process of figuring out its $X = Y$ structure is rather straightforward. This type of analysis can be shown as a straight line, whereby X is imputed to mean Y directly (see Figure 9.1).

$X \longrightarrow Y$

Figure 9.1 Linear analysis

An example is a news report in a newspaper, whereby the text aims to report the content of some newsworthy event directly (e.g. the results of a political election, the scores of a series of hockey games, and so on). Obviously, the ways in which the $X = Y$ relation is represented will vary according to the newspaper, according to the writer, and so on. But, under normal circumstances, the overall structure of the story is linear, and thus generally entails a straightforward analysis.

A second main kind of text, *X*, is one in which its meaning, *Y*, is determinable in a roundabout, spiral fashion: i.e. by taking into account historical factors, intertextuality, etc. This type of analysis can be shown graphically as a spiral (see Figure 9.2).

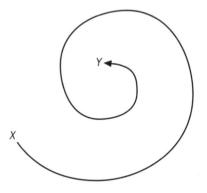

Figure 9.2   Spiral analysis

As an example consider, once again, the Airoldi watch ad discussed in the opening chapter. The interpretation of its subtext was determined to be that of the 'female-as-huntress'. Now, such an interpretation was made possible not in isolation, but by virtue of the fact that its mythic signified has appeared over and over, and across time, in such representations as ancient stories (e.g. the myth of Diana), contemporary movies (e.g. *Fatal Attraction*), and so on and so forth. It is understandable, therefore, not linearly, but in terms of its historical interconnectedness to other texts encoding the same kind of signified.

A third main kind of text, *X*, is one in which its meaning, *Y*, is accessed in a back and forth, zig-zag fashion: i.e. by comparing its features with the features of other texts. This type of analysis can be shown graphically as in Figure 9.3.

As an example, take, once again, a media character, such as the Lone Ranger. The serial of the same name originated in radio in 1930 on Detroit's WXYZ. It began with the fourth movement of the overture from the 1829 Rossini opera *William Tell* and an announcer saying, 'A fiery horse with the speed of light, a cloud of dust and a hearty "Hi-yo Silver", the Lone Ranger rides again'. With his aboriginal partner, Tonto, the masked hero became a media personality when the show moved to CBS in 1941 and then became a regular on Saturday morning television in the 1950s. Why was the Lone Ranger so popular? First of all, the programme constituted a weekly morality play, pitting the forces of Good against the forces of Evil. The mysterious lawman, whose identity was hidden behind his signature mask, was a

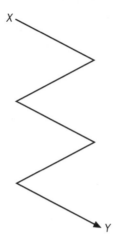

Figure 9.3   Zig-zag analysis

modern-day mythic hero. His white horse was symbolic of purity and honesty. His trusty companion was a symbol of equality among the races. The simple plots, in which potential victims were saved from the claws of ruthless gangsters, struck a basic chord among viewers. Now, the comic book, radio, TV, and movie versions of the Lone Ranger all delivered this very same set of 'meaning elements', i.e. of elements that can be compared, contrasted, and related to each other and to the elements present in other representations about heroes.

It is unlikely to find radically different semiotic interpretations of the above texts. For example, in the Airoldi ad, one may arrive at a different subtext that involves feral women. But the process of getting to the subtext is the same. It is 'spiral', as it has been characterized above. Similarly, one may wish to emphasize some mythological aspect of the basic storyline over another in the Lone Ranger text, or else flesh out some other feature of the serial. But the process of establishing the overall meaning of the text through a zig-zag process of comparison tends to remain fairly constant.

What is interesting, therefore, is not always what something means, but rather how it is represented. Different TV programmes today represent the same type of morality play as the Lone Ranger in diverse ways to suit changing social realities. The many science fiction and lawyer programmes on TV, for instance, deliver essentially the same content as the Lone Ranger serial, but in an 'updated way', incorporating into it a complex array of subtexts referring to contemporary psychological, social, and cultural issues.

Needless to say, many TV programmes, movies, radio dramas, etc. break with such patterns, treating philosophical, spiritual, and aesthetic themes in truly innovative ways. As mentioned above, and throughout this book, the paradox of contemporary media-based representation is that it is both distractive and creative, conformist and innovative.

The media syntext

Obviously, the whole line of inquiry that semiotics presupposes leads to conclusions and findings that cannot be proved. They can only be argued and debated. But this produces, in itself, critical understanding and self-reflection – both of which are crucial 'filters' for screening mediated messages.

A large chunk of contemporary semiotic analysis of media is influenced by Barthes' view of pop culture as a huge distraction factory, aimed at uprooting the traditional forms of art and meaning-making. Many today blame technology as the cause of this uprooting. But this is not true, as has been argued throughout this book. Media technology has led to a democratization of art. Today, anyone can buy a CD of any piece of classical music, a DVD of a classic movie, or acquire any novel he or she desires. Moreover, even television, with its focus on distraction, has a good side to it. It provides comfort and companionship for many people, especially elderly ones, during long solitary evenings.

In chapter 3, the notion of syntext was introduced to describe the way in which newspapers structured such disparate things as news reporting, movie reviews, comics, etc. into an overall text which, as a consequence, transmitted the feeling to readers that they were all interconnected, as if in, say, a novel. The same term can be used to characterize the entire mediated world in which we live. It is one huge syntext that imparts coherence within, and continuity among, the multifarious representations to which we are exposed on a daily basis. As a consequence, the media have converged semiotically to become an overarching *social text*. People utilize the media social text to evaluate their lives, to emulate various components of its content (e.g. lifestyle), and so on.

The ultimate goal of media semiotics is to describe and analyse this syntext through a step-by-step analysis of the separate media forms (print, audio, etc.) that constitute it. This implies the study of how specific signifiers are interconnected to each other. The interconnectedness of signifiers in a culture is the reason why, from tribes to advanced technological societies, signifying orders impart a sense of wholeness and, thus, of purpose to the activities that people carry out. In effect, the extraction of meaning from specific media products is dependent upon knowledge of how they are linked within a specific culture.

The main implication for the study of media that crystallizes from semiotic analysis is that the meaning of a specific representation (a TV programme, a music genre, etc.) is determinable largely in terms of its interconnectedness to other representations. As an example of how a specific text 'works semiotically' as a component of a larger syntext, let us turn to the domain of advertising. Consider the ads used to promote a man's cologne, named resonantly *Drakkar noir*, which filled the pages of magazines all over the world a few years ago. In general, the ads spotlighted a cologne bottle, with a ghastly, frightful black colour and a strange shape. Darkness, as we saw, connotes fear, evil, and the unknown. Forbidden things take place under the cloak of night. The sepulchral name, *Drakkar noir*, reinforces the feeling that something dark and scary, but nevertheless sexually desirous, will materialize by dousing oneself with the cologne.

The theme of vampirism can be extracted from this text for the simple reason that it is part of folklore. The Dracula legend was introduced to the modern world through the pen of Bram Stoker (1847–1912), whose novel *Dracula* was first published in 1897 and has remained in print ever since. His treatment became the yardstick by which all future vampires in literature and film would be measured. The figure of Dracula has, in effect, become a part of pop culture lore.

Clearly, the overall presentation of the cologne was not designed in a random fashion. Rather, it was structured to evoke a connotative chain of meanings that are interconnected textually and historically:

darkness = evil = something desirable = Dracula = sexuality = etc.

Needless to say, other connotative chains can also be envisioned, because the vampire figure also symbolizes other things, especially the breaking of taboos. The figure of Dracula challenges authority, putting forward a fine line between passion and power, and resuscitating the mythical search for eternal youth and immortality. Stoker's Dracula was the embodiment of evil, but the Dracula that finds its way into modern-day representations has evolved into a much more ambivalent creature – a clear reflection of the blurring of the boundaries between Good and Evil in pop culture.

Mediation

The above discussion and, in fact, the discussion throughout this book begs the question of the impact of mediation on people. Many influential thinkers today point the finger at mass communications technology and the mass media as 'perverting influences'. The German philosopher Jürgen Habermas, (1929–), for instance, claimed that Western industrial democracies had created a mediated culture solely in the service of economic efficiency. Barthes and Baudrillard, as we have seen, also blamed the economically-rooted media for inculcating the view that pleasure was the chief good in life and that the pursuit of consumption was the basic goal of life. Since the late 1950s, 'media bashing' has become prevalent from both the right and the left of the political and moral spectra. The media are blamed for causing everything from street violence and family break-ups to philosophical nihilism. Are the mass media the tools of moral destruction that Habermas, Barthes, Baudrillard and others descry?

There is no doubt that the media used in a culture to represent ideas have an impact on the way people living in that culture perceive the world. This is, actually, an old view. Already in the ancient world, the Greek historian Herodotus (c.484–425 BC) claimed that Egyptians thought differently from the Greeks because they wrote their books from right to left rather than from left to right, as did the Greeks. Herodotus thus put forward the notion that the physical characteristics of the medium used by a culture to carry out its representational activities determined how the members of that culture understood the world. A similar view was articulated by the fourteenth century Algerian scholar Ibn Khaldun (1332–1406), who wrote a truly fascinating treatise in which he noted that the subtle behavioural differences that existed between nomadic and city-dwelling Bedouins were due to their differences in language and in how they used such differences to represent reality. The same type of view was reiterated centuries later by the philosopher Johann Gottfried von Herder (1744–1803), the philologist Wilhelm von Humboldt (1767–1835), and the philosopher Georg Wilhelm Friedrich Hegel (1770–1831). A little later, Martin Heidegger (1889–1976) claimed, *tout court*, that technological society had deprived human life of meaning. He called the psychic state that such a society induced 'nihilism' – a term that has become widely used.

One impact that contemporary forms of mediation have undoubtedly had on society has been called juvenilization in this book. This refers, it may be recalled, to an unconscious perception that the lifestyles represented in the media are for all, not just the young, beautiful, and affluent. The roots of this phenomenon can be traced to the first decades of the twentieth century, when for the first time in history a single economic system – the one that took shape after the Industrial Revolution of the nineteenth century – was capable of guaranteeing a certain level of affluence to increasingly larger segments of society. With more wealth and leisure time at their disposal, common people became more inclined to live the good life. And with the economic capacity to improve their chances of staying healthier, and thus of living much longer than previous generations, a desire to preserve youth for a much longer period of life started to define the collective state of mind. This desire was nurtured by the messages that bombarded society from radio and print advertising in the early part of the century – messages that became more persuasive and widespread with the advent of television as a social text in the early 1950s. By the 1960s, the desire to be 'young' not only meant the desire to stay and look healthier for a longer period of life, but also to act and think young. By the end of the decade, the process of juvenilization had reached a critical mass, becoming the defining feature of the mindset of an entire society.

But even a notion such as juvenilization only tells a partial story, as I shall attempt to argue in the remainder of this chapter. It is easy to blame the products of 'media semiosis' for thwarting the more 'noble goals' of life that people would otherwise purportedly pursue. But then, this would mean that the 'blamers' have some secret knowledge of what those goals are and, more importantly, of why people should pursue them. As at any other period of human history, it is difficult, if not impossible, to pinpoint what is 'ennobling' and what is 'demeaning' from the current slate of media representations. History teaches, in fact, that representations that accomplish the former tend to persist on their own, while those that do the latter will disappear into oblivion very quickly, also on their own.

The hypodermic needle view

In recent years, various branches of mass communications and media studies have arisen specifically to study the impacts of media critically. These are based typically on content analysis, i.e. on a description of the kinds of content that media messages contain and the purported effects that such content has on people. The general impression one gets from reading the relevant research in this domain is that media content no longer just mirrors cultural values but, rather, that it now largely shapes them (see, for in-depth discussions, Meyrowitz 1985, Croteau and Hoynes 1997, Dutton 1997, Berman 1998, Ryan 1999, and McChesney 1999). If true, then it is clear that this situation has been brought about by the diffusion of media. The 'Big Brother' that George Orwell (1903–50) described in his 1949 novel 1984 has, seemingly, been reified in the form of one worldwide TV screen. However, many questions arise with regard to such research.

The theory that the mass media can directly influence behaviour is called hypodermic needle theory (HNT). It claims that media are capable of directly swaying minds with the same kind of impact a hypodermic needle has on the body. The phenomenon of 'junk food' is often cited in support of this theory. When fast food eateries first appeared in the 1950s – called burger and milkshake 'joints' – they were designed to be socializing sites for adolescents. The food served at such places was viewed, correctly, to be 'junk': injurious to one's health and only to be consumed by young people, because their metabolism could ostensibly break it down more quickly and because they could purportedly recover from its negative health effects more easily than older people. But in no time whatsoever junk food, promoted by effective advertising campaigns, became an indulgence sought by anyone of any age, from very young children to seniors. The compulsion to consume junk food has, consequently, become a fact of contemporary life, inducing dangerous eating habits. The inordinate consumption of junk food is, in fact, one of the main factors contributing to the rise in obesity (Schlosser 2000).

But the negative impact of promoting junk food through the media is hardly just physical, the researchers suggest. Obesity is at odds with the ultra-slim body images that the media perpetrate as the norm for attractiveness. This disjunction of fact and image has generated culture-based diseases, previously unknown. Anorexia nervosa, the fear of gaining weight leading to excessive weight loss from restricted food intake and excessive exercise, is one of these. Predictably, it occurs chiefly during adolescence, especially in young women, who tend to perceive body image as critical to their sociability among peers. Sufferers may also exhibit bulimia, the habit of eating large quantities of food followed by induced vomiting. No standard therapy for anorexia nervosa exists, nor can exist, given its cultural etiology. Psychotherapy is often used, but it is rarely effective.

But the 'hypodermic needle' view of media-induced eating disorders ignores history. The ravages of overeating or undereating are not just contemporary phenomena. They have always been symptomatic of the excesses of affluent lifestyles. A more moderate version of HNT is thus called for. One such version is multistep flow theory. This asserts that media impacts are indirect and are mediated by group leaders. This view is in fact partially verifiable, since people within different social classes come up with very different interpretations of media products. They tend to perceive them as interpretive communities, which are inclined to coincide with real communities such as families, unions, neighbourhoods, and churches.

In my view, the factor that makes HNT virtually futile is selective perception, or the tendency of people to select from a media text what they are predisposed to do. Anti-pornography individuals who watch a TV debate on freedom of expression have been shown to take away from the debate only the views that are consistent with their particular viewpoints; libertarian individuals, on the other hand, tend to take away from it a sense of triumph by virtue of the fact that the debate occurred in the first place (thus legitimizing the topic). This suggests that media may have limited impacts on most individuals, and that the communities in which they are reared have more of an influence on their worldview than do media messages and images.

The above critique of HNT in no way implies that a mediated culture has no impacts on individuals. As we saw in chapter 8, television has had mythological, compression, and fabrication effects on society at large. But these are vastly different from those that HNT supporters claim are produced by media. There is, however, one effect that is undeniable. As more and more people listen to the same kinds of music the world over, see the same kinds of fashion styles, and watch the same kinds of movies and TV programmes, the tendency for a 'global media syntext' to emerge is strong.

All this raises the question of what content is 'kosher', so to speak and, more importantly, who has the right (if any) of deciding what goes into the syntext. The danger in pin-pointing certain representations as 'harmful' and others as 'acceptable' is akin to the dangers posed by such horrific movements as the Inquisition in Europe and McCarthyism in the United States. The former was a judicial institution, established by the papacy in the Middle Ages, charged with seeking out, trying, and sentencing persons guilty of heresy; the latter refers to the public investigations over which the infamous US Senator Joseph McCarthy presided, in which he accused army officials, members of the media, and public figures of being Communists.

In actual fact, most people can easily distinguish between what is art and what is not. Great works of art foster engagement; many popular media artefacts, on the other hand, are designed solely to provide distraction, even though often the dividing line between engagement and distraction is blurry indeed. Many of the forms intended originally for distraction have themselves evolved into works of highly engaging art. Some pieces of jazz and rock music, as we saw in the fourth chapter, are worthy of being listed alongside the works of the great classical composers; many movies, as we saw in the fifth chapter, are among the greatest works of visual art ever created; and even some TV programmes, past and present, have significant artistic merit. Some types of advertising, too, are artistically interesting in and of themselves. Although we may be inclined to condemn the overall objectives of advertising, as an aesthetic-inducing experience we invariably enjoy it. Advertisements sway, please, and seduce.

It is useless, in my view, to propose drastic measures to censor or repress media expressions of any kind, in order to counteract any purported hypodermic needle effect. For one thing, media messages produce such an effect only if individuals are already predisposed towards their content; and for another, media moguls will find ways around such measures. In early 1998, the US Congress banned the Joe Camel and Marlboro Man figures from cigarette advertising. In response, ad creators came up with even more 'hypodermically-effective' alternatives, so to speak. In a subsequent 1998 ad for Salem cigarettes, for instance, there is a pair of peppers curled together to look like a pair of lips, with a cigarette dangling from them. Benson and Hedges ads in the same year portrayed cigarettes acting like people – floating in swimming pools, lounging in armchairs, etc. As it turned out, this new 'government-permissible' form of advertising was even more persuasive in suggesting the glamour and pleasure of smoking than was the figure of Joe Camel, as witnessed by the fact that smoking among teenagers went up significantly from 1999 to 2000 (according to national surveys published in newspapers and magazines).

More and more groups in America and Britain have started to suggest censorship as a means of gaining control over the levers of the media. But the answer to the dilemma of the media is not to be found in censorship or in any form of state control. Even if it were possible in a consumerist culture to control the contents of media, this would invariably prove to be counterproductive. The answer is, in my view, to become aware of the meanings that are generated by the media. When the human mind is aware of the hidden meanings in texts, it will be better able to fend off any undesirable effects that such texts may cause.

This is in fact what more enlightened individuals and groups are now doing. In *Culture Jam* (2000), for instance, the Canadian activist Kalle Lasn makes a persuasive case against the globalization of consumerist culture. As a leading voice in the so-called 'culture jamming' movement, Lasn (who is also the founder of *Adbusters* magazine, which satirizes ads and commercials) is at the vanguard of a new movement that decries the mindless consumerism of modern society. Culture jammers are a loose global network of media activists aiming to change the way media and corporate institutions wield power. Lasn believes that corporate America is no longer a country, but one overarching 'brand' shaped by the cult of celebrity and the spectacles that generate it. Culture and marketing are, according to Lasn, one and the same.

Lasn's fears are not unfounded. There are 10 colossal media conglomerates that literally operate the global distraction factory today. These are: Disney, Time Warner, Bertelsmann, Viacom, News Corporation, PolyGram (owned by Phillips), NBC (owned by General Electric), MCA (owned by Seagram), Sony, and TCI (McChesney 1997: 12). Global advertising is now under the control of, basically, a handful of global advertising agencies based in New York, London, Paris, and Tokyo.

Aware of the social dangers that such a state of affairs poses, Lasn has issued a 'Media Manifesto', in obvious parallelism with the many other manifestos that have been issued and that have 'changed the world' (of which Karl Marx's is probably the most famous). The manifesto has five main resolutions that culture jammers are determined to maintain (cited in Hazen and Winokur 1997: 49):

- 'We will take on the archetypal mind polluters – Marlboro, Budweiser, Benetton, Coke, McDonald's, Calvin Klein – and beat them at their own game'.
- 'We will uncool their billion dollar images with uncommercials on TV,

subvertisements in magazines and anti-ads right next to theirs in the urban landscape'.

- 'We will take control of the role that the tobacco, alcohol, fashion, cosmetics, food and automobile corporations play in our lives. We will hold their marketing strategies up to public scrutiny and set new agendas in their industries'.
- 'We will culture jam the pop culture marketeers – MTV, Time Warner, Sony – and bring their image factories to a sudden, shuddering halt'.
- 'On the rubble of the old media culture, we will build a new one with a non-commercial heart and soul'.

The counterpart to culture jamming in the domain of television is Paper Tiger Television which, since 1981, has been putting on programmes throughout the US criticizing our mediated pop culture world. Similarly, Globalvision, which was launched in 1987, and Independent Television Service, which provides programmes for various public channels, provide news information and challenging programming that is not tied to any vested interest whatsoever.

However, even with such concerned groups there are problems. For one thing, the leaders of the culture jamming movement do not have any follow-up alternatives to the corporate homogenization of global culture. It was the very capitalist system that they critique which brought democracy to Europe in the first place by competing with the hegemony of the religious order of medieval times, eventually replacing it. Although it has become itself a 'new world' religion, strangely blending puritanical religious values with pop culture mores, it has never taken the drastic measures that the religious order did in attempting to preserve its control of society. There are no capitalist Inquisitions. After all, it is up to the individual in a consumerist culture to simply say 'No'. There is nothing more effective, in my view, than personal choice. This is one of the main reasons why I wrote this book in the first place. Even something as seemingly banal as the widespread use of cosmetics has been useful socially, as Kathy Peiss (1998) has recently intimated, because it liberated women to express their sexuality – something that religious cultures have always tended to strictly forbid. The founders and early leaders of the 'cosmetic movement' were simple women – Elizabeth Arden (1884–1966), a Canadian, was the daughter of poor tenant farmers, Helena Rubinstein (1870–1965), was born of poor Jewish parents in Poland, and Madam C.J. Walker (1867–1919) was born to former slaves in Louisiana. While it is true that advertising has preyed on social fears associated with 'bad complexions', 'ageing', etc. it has at the same time allowed women to assert their right to emphasize their sexuality, not conceal it.

Moreover, it is somewhat ironic to note that those who most condemn the media are the ones most inclined to use it for their own purposes. Take, for example, the vociferous 'religious right' groups in the US, who are wont to blame the media for all that ails the country. Yet, the leaders of that movement use television to great advantage themselves. Through the despised 'tube' they purvey their ideas and their own products (videos, CDs, etc.) promising salvation and comfort to all their viewers. Televangelism is a perfect example of how the very people who condemn the media use it for their own ends. The scary part is that many of these characters have the full support of some media moguls. Indeed, in the 1988 election one such televangelist, Pat Robertson, ran for president of the US with the full support of various media moguls, including Rupert Murdoch. Robertson's religious fanaticism was well known, since he claimed to speak in tongues and have direct access to God. The media culture in which we live is a strange one indeed!

A more rational approach to the advertising–pop culture world of today is the one taken by a San Francisco-based group that calls itself the Public Media Center (Hazen and Winokur 1997: 50–1), which is lobbying to make advertising more 'honest'. And, of course, the many 'media literacy' organizations that are springing up all over the world can help enlighten the discussion on the impact of the media.

For the sake of concreteness the idea of distraction versus engagement can be formulated in terms of a 'continuum'. At one end of this continuum, one can easily locate music that is intended solely for distraction, and remains as nothing more than that over time. At the other, one can easily locate music intended solely for engagement, even though it may have been intended originally for entertainment. For instance, the operas of Giuseppe Verdi (1813–1901), as great as they are, had an initial distraction function – people went to them to be entertained, plain and simple. The fact that such music rose above its entertainment function is a consequence of various factors, not the least of which is the musical genius of the composer. Everyone in our mediated world can easily locate a jingle such as the Alka Seltzer one ('Plop, plop, fizz, fizz, oh what a relief it is') at the distraction end, and a musical work such as Mozart's powerful Requiem at the other. As apparent as this line of reasoning is, it nonetheless brings out concretely that people, by and large, can discern quality in the smorgasbord of options that our media culture makes available. The problem lies in media products that fall on other parts of the continuum, creating cultural confusion.

Needless to say, the interpretant is a major factor in determining where someone will locate a specific text on the continuum. Recall from chapter 2 (and elsewhere in this book) that this term refers to the specific type of meaning that an individual, as a member of a social group, will derive from a text. Human beings are not automaton-like consumers of cultural meanings; they are creative users of these meanings.

The problem with our mediated culture is that the critics and defenders of media are *both* right. The goal of the distraction industries is to promote a consumerist lifestyle, as Barthes, McLuhan, Baudrillard, and others mentioned in this book have suggested in their writings. Day in and day out the fragmented images of life coming out of the media are bound to influence our overall view that reality is illusory and surreal, that human actions are a montage of disconnected images, desires, feelings, and that the only achievable goal of life is pleasure through consumption. It is also true, as such media critics argue, that the messages of consumerism are modern-day surrogates for traditional forms of religious discourse, whose goal has always been the promulgation of the 'good news'. Today, the gospel, as Bachand (1992: 6) quips, 'is being announced by advertisers'. But within the same world it is possible to expose the banality of consumerism and the dangers of technology. Therein lies the paradox of modern pop culture.

Pop art

Aware of the power of the media, some visual artists even formed an art movement based on the images perpetrated by pop culture itself. Known as pop art, it gained momentum in the 1950s and 1960s, principally in the United States and Britain. The idea of the early pop artists was to represent scenes and objects taken from mass culture, sometimes with actual objects incorporated into the artworks, including materials of modern technology, such as plastic. This movement began as a reaction against abstract expressionism, an abstruse style of the 1940s and 1950s. Pop artists wanted instead to depict everyday life and to provide an impersonal and immediate perception of reality.

Pop art expanded in the 1960s, as brand-name commercial products, fast-food items, and comic-strip frames were used in art displays and forms. Several pop artists produced 'happenings', or theatrical events staged as art objects. In the 1960s the American artist Andy Warhol (mentioned several times in this book) became a well-known leader of the pop art movement, stimulating much debate on the nature of art with his controversial paintings and silk-screen prints of commonplace images, such as soup cans and photographs of celebrities.

But there is something about pop art that is, in my view, not quite right. Although it is somewhat engaging, it seems to have a singular ironic purpose – to critique the distraction factory of pop culture by using its very signifiers. But, does pop art truly engage people in thinking about daily life in some profound or critical way? On the contrary, it seems to have had the opposite effect. Given their elevation to artistic status, today people probably tend to perceive shoes, cars, pieces of jewellery, and the like as *objets d'art*. Pop art has, in effect, helped to blur the distinction between engagement and distraction even further.

Concluding reflections

Semiotic inquiry is grounded on the assumption that there exists a 'need for meaning' in all human beings and that this is, arguably, the reason why media products of all types are so engaging, despite their distractive functions. They provide representations that feed our need for meaning. This need has, of course, not only led human beings to create inane pop culture forms, but also to invent myths, art, rituals, languages, mathematics, science, and other truly remarkable things that set it apart from all other species. The mediated culture in which we live today is, really, no more than a contemporary vehicle for satisfying this need, no matter how bizarre or trivial its representational products may appear to be. And, of course, let us not forget that those in the media themselves are often the ones who are determined to 'make the world better'. Hordes of TV reporters, newspaper journalists, and the like are constantly holding the 'system' accountable. Creative media makers also provide truly meaningful alternatives to the 'dumbed-down' fare that dominates the mainstream 'distraction factory'.

The problem, argues Umiker-Sebeok (1997), is that in the Digital Galaxy there is no transcendent narrative to provide moral underpinnings, nor are there strong social institutions that control the flood of information produced by technology. But then who should be given the levers of control? Should it be put in the hands of traditional religious institutions? As Plato complained, who should run the ideal republic?

There are no answers, no solutions. Cultures resolve their problems and set their future goals dynamically and synergistically from within. While it is true that the globalization of media has transformed the world into a consumer-frenzied 'factory' with mega-companies controlling its operation, it is also true that constant changes to this factory are coming from within, making it unstable at best. The only thing is to ensure that future generations understand the historical and signifying forces at work in the operation of this factory. Simply put, it behoves us to make sure that our children will be able to distinguish a meaningful news documentary from an ad for running shoes. Ironically, the best way to do this is through the media.

As the Digital Galaxy expands, the use of the media will become even more widespread. As emphasized in the James Bond movie cited in the introduction to this book, media moguls are the 'leaders' of the global village, as it is presently constituted. This is why computer companies have moved away from just making software and CD-ROMs, and are now investing in all aspects of the distraction factory. Microsoft, for instance, has invested in traditional entertainment companies, including DreamWorks and SKG. Yet, here's the rub – while the Internet may seem to be under the control of media moguls, it has also made it possible for virtually everyone to join into the fray and gain an audience for his or her 'voice'.

Deep down inside the public harbours an intuitive understanding that for all the flaws of the media, ultimately human beings will come down on the side of democracy and not be allowed to let themselves be controlled by a few. That is the lesson of the communist fiasco in Russia and of many other social experiments in 'mind control'. The 'Elliott Carvers' simply cannot confine and imprison the human imagination for very long. The ancient Israelites used the word *hychma* to describe this aspect of human nature, defining it as the 'science of the heart'. That science will not let the media steal the heart of humanity.

Glossary

abstract referent	concept formed in the mind and thus not directly demonstrable
actant	role, theme, etc. (a hero, an opponent) that recurs in all kinds of stories
addressee	receiver of a message; the individual(s) to whom a message is directed
addresser	the sender of a message; the creator of a message
advertising	any type or form of public announcement designed to promote the sale of specific commodities or services
aesthesia	the experience of sensation; in art appreciation it refers to the fact that our senses and feelings are stimulated holistically by art works
alliteration	the repetition of the initial consonant sounds or features of words
alphabet	the graphic code whereby individual characters stand for individual sounds (or sound combinations)
anchorage	Roland Barthes' notion that visual images in advertisements are polysemous (having many meanings) which are, however, anchored to particular meaning domains by specific interpreters
archetype	an original model or type after which other similar things are patterned
artefact	an object produced or shaped by human craft, especially a tool, a weapon, or an ornament of archaeological or historical interest; by extension, any media form (a TV programme, a recording, etc.)
artefactual medium	any human artefact (a book, a painting, etc.) that extends the natural modes of message creation and delivery

artificial intelligence	the branch of computer science concerned with the development of machines having the ability to carry out human mental functions
audience	specified groups of individuals towards whom media products are directed
birth and rebirth myth	a myth informing people about how life can be renewed or about the coming of an ideal society or saviour
brand image	the creation of a personality for a product: i.e. the intentional creation of a product's name, packaging, price, and advertising style in order to create a recognizable personality for the product that is meant to appeal to specific consumers
brand name	name given to a product
CD-ROM	(Compact Disc Read-Only Memory) compact disc for reading digital data, allowing users to navigate to topics within a page of text by simply clicking on them
channel	the physical means by which a signal or message is transmitted
character	a person portrayed in an artistic piece, such as a drama or novel
closed text	text that elicits a singular, or a very limited, range of interpretations
code	the system in which signs are organized and which determines how they relate to each other and can thus be used for representation and communication
codex	type of proto-book used in the Middle Ages, used specially to write about classic works or the Scriptures
cognitive compression effect	the term used in this book to refer to the fact that TV presents personages, events, and information globally and instantly leaving little time for reflection on the topics, implications, words, etc. contained in a message, thus leading to a state by which information is desired and understood mainly in a 'compressed' form
comics	narratives told by means of a series of drawings arranged in horizontal lines, strips, or rectangles, called panels, and read like a verbal text from left to right

communication	social interaction through messages; the production and exchange of messages and meanings; the use of specific modes and media to transmit messages
compact disc (CD)	small optical disk on which matter such as data or music is encoded
conative	the effect of a message on the addressee
concept	a connection made by the human mind (within cultural contexts)
conceptual metaphor	a generalized metaphorical formula that defines a specific abstraction ('love' = 'sweet')
conceptual metonym	a generalized metonymical formula that defines a specific abstraction ('the face' = 'the person')
concrete referent	something existing in reality or in real experience and is, normally, perceptible by the senses
connotation	the extended or secondary meaning of a sign; the symbolic or mythic meaning of a certain signifier (word, image, etc.)
connotative chain	a chain of connotations associated with a product as generated by ads and commercials about the product, by the brand name used, etc.
connotative index	the degree of connotation associated with a product; a measure of the number of connotations generated by an ad, commercial, brand name, etc.
consumer advertising	advertising directed toward the promotion of some product
contact	the physical channel employed in communication and the psychological connections between addresser and addressee
context	the situation – physical, psychological, and/or social – in which a sign or text is used or occurs, or to which it refers
conventional sign	a sign that has no apparent connection to any perceivable feature of its referent; a sign created by human beings in specific social contexts
cosmogonic myth	myth explaining how the world came into being
cultural modelling	the association of various concrete ideas with an abstract one, producing an overall, or culture-specific, model of the abstract idea

culture hero myth	myth describing beings who discover a cultural artefact or technological process that radically changes the course of history
cuneiform writing	system of writing whereby characters are formed by the arrangement of small wedge-shaped elements; used in ancient Sumerian, Akkadian, Assyrian, Babylonian, and Persian cultures
decoding	the process of deciphering a text on the basis of the code or codes and the media used
denotation	the primary, intensional meaning of a sign, text, etc.
diachronic	the historical dimension of signs
Digital audio broadcasting (DAB)	radio broadcasting system that consists of transmitters and receivers using digital formats
Digital Galaxy	term coined in imitation of Marshall McLuhan's Gutenberg Galaxy to characterize the new social order ushered in by the invention of computer media
digital media	computer-based systems of transmission
Digital subscriber line (DSL)	telephone service that transmits audio, video, and computer data over conventional phone lines and via satellite
digital television	television that is transmitted in a digital (computer-based) format
Digital versatile disc (DVD)	digital disk that allows for the reproduction of audio, video, graphics, etc.
Direct-broadcast satellite (DBS)	television service that allows individual households to receive hundreds of channels carried by satellites directly into their homes
displacement	the ability of the human mind to conjure up the things to which signs refer even though these might not be physically present for the senses to perceive
e-book	digital book (published on the Internet)
Electronic Galaxy	term coined in imitation of Marshall McLuhan's Gutenberg Galaxy to characterize the social order ushered in by the invention of electronic media
electronic media	devices such as records and radios that allow for the sending and reception of electromagnetic signals

e-mail	(electronic mail) online service that permits people to send messages to each other via the Internet or some other computer network system
emotive	the addresser's emotional intent in communicating something
encoding	the use of a code or codes to select or create a sign or text according to a medium through which the sign will be transmitted
eschatological myth	a myth that describes the end of the world
e-toon	digital comic or cartoon (published on the Internet)
e-zine	digital magazine (published on the Internet)
feedback	reaction to transmitted messages that informs the sender as to the nature of its reception
fiction	a literary work whose content is produced by the imagination and is not necessarily based on fact
ground	the part of a metaphor that generates meaning
Gutenberg Galaxy	term coined by Marshall McLuhan to characterize the radical new social order ushered in by the invention of the printing press
hardware	actual physical computer and the associated physical equipment directly involved in the performance of its data-processing or communications functions
hermeneutics	the science or art of interpretation of texts
hieroglyphic writing	ancient Egyptian system of writing, in which pictorial symbols were used to represent meaning or sounds or a combination of both
high-definition television (HDTV)	television broadcasting system that consists of transmitters and receivers using digital formats
history fabrication effect	the term used in this book to refer to the fact that TV both shapes and documents historical events
hypertextuality	system for linking different texts and images within a computer document or over a network

icon	a sign that has a direct (non-arbitrary) connection to a referent
iconicity	the process of representing referents with iconic signs
ideograph	writing symbol that represents abstract ideas pictorially
image	representation of a product or service in order to enhance its value aesthetically, socially, etc.
image schema	mental impression of locations, movements, shapes, etc.
index	a sign that has an existential connection to a referent (indicating that something or someone is located somewhere)
indexicality	the process of representing referents with indexical signs
information	measure of data that can be stored and retrieved by humans or machines
Internet	matrix of networks that connects computers around the world
interpretant	the process of adapting a sign's meaning to personal and social experience
interpretation	the process of figuring out what some sign (word, text, programme, etc.) means
intertextuality	the allusion within a text to some other text
irony	the use of words to express something different from and often opposite to their literal meaning
jingle	an easy rhythmic and simple repetition of sound, etc., as in poetry and music
juvenilization	social phenomenon by which people think of themselves as 'forever young' both physically and socially
literacy	ability to understand and use written language to transmit knowledge
logo	a distinctive company or brand signature, trademark, colophon, motto, newspaper nameplate, etc.
logograph	full symbol or character representing a word
magazine	paper-based publication consisting of a collection of articles or stories, or both, published at regular intervals

marketing	the business of positioning goods and services to the right audience
meaning	the concept that anything in existence has a design or purpose beyond its mere occurrence
mechanical medium	any device or technological system that extends both natural and artefactual media (a telephone, a radio, etc.)
media convergence	convergence of all media into digital formats and, thus, their integration into a single transmission system
media genre	category of media product that is used to create and deliver messages to audiences
mediation	intercession of a medium between a referent and its representation, and thus between what people perceive and the reality behind the perception
medium	the physical means or process required to encode a certain type of message and deliver it through some channel to a specific type of receiver
message	communication transmitted by words, signals, or other means from one person, station, or group to another
metalingual	the communicative function by which the code being used is identified
metaphor	the signifying process by which two signifying domains (A, B) are connected (A = B) explicitly or implicitly
metonymy	the signifying process by which an entity is used to refer to another that is related to it
multimedia	combined use of several media, such as movies, music, print, etc. producing a type of representation on a computer system that integrates printed text, graphics, video, and sound
myth	any story or narrative that aims to explain the origin of something
mythologizing effect	the term used in this book to refer to the fact that TV imbues its characters with a mythological aura
mythology	the set of mythic connotations associated with some media product
name	a sign that identifies a human being or, by connotative extension, an animal, an object (such as a commercial product), and event (such as a hurricane)

narrative mode	the use of narrative as the cognitive means by which something is conceptualized and then expressed – 'narrated' – in verbal and/or non-verbal ways
narrative structure	the presence of universal elements of plot, character, and setting in storytelling practices
narrative	something narrated, told or written, such as an account, story, tale, and even scientific theory
narrativity	the innate human capacity to produce and comprehend narratives
narratology	the branch of semiotics that studies narrativity
narrator	the teller of the narrative
narreme	a minimal unit of narrative structure
narrowcasting	broadcasting designed to reach specific types of audiences
natural medium	any biologically-inherited ability or capacity for encoding and decoding a message, including the voice (speech), the face (expressions), and the body (gesture, posture, etc.)
natural sign	a sign that is produced by Nature (such as a symptom)
newspaper	paper-based publication, usually issued on a daily or weekly basis, the main function of which is to report the news
noise	some interfering element (physical or psychological) in the channel that distorts or partially effaces a message
nominalists	late medieval scholars who maintained that all universal or abstract terms are mere necessities of thought or conveniences of language and therefore exist as names only and have no general realities corresponding to them
novel	a fictional prose narrative of considerable length, typically having a plot that is unfolded by the actions, speech, and thoughts of the characters
object	a synonym for referent or signified; what a sign refers to
objective/objectivity	perception of a known or perceived sign or text as existing on its own, and not existing only in the mind of the maker or perceiver of the sign or text
online services	computer services made available through commercial computer networks to which subscribers pay monthly or hourly fees

onomatopoeia	the feature of words by which they represent a referent through the simulation of one or several of its audio features ('drip', 'boom', etc.)
open text	text that entails a complex interpretive range
opposition	the process by which signs are differentiated through a minimal change in their forms (signifiers)
orality	the use of spoken language to transmit knowledge
Othello effect	lying in order to emphasize the truth
paradigm	a structural relation between signs that keeps them distinct and therefore recognizable
paradigmaticity	a differentiation property of signs
parallelism	the repetition of linguistic patterns (sentences, phrases, etc.)
persona	the Self that one presents in specific social situations
perspective	a specific point of view in understanding or judging things or events, which sees them in their relations to one another or other things and events
phatic	a communicative function by which contact between addresser and addressee is established
phonography	writing system in which characters stand for parts of words
pictography	writing using pictures
plot	the plan of events or main story in a narrative
poetic	a communicative function based on poetic language
pop art	artistic movement depicting objects or scenes from everyday life and employing techniques of commercial art and popular illustration
positioning	the placing or marketing of a product for the right people
postmodernism	the state of mind which believes that all knowledge is relative and human-made, and that there is no purpose to life beyond the immediate and the present
print media	media based on paper (or similar) technology
propaganda	any systematic dissemination of doctrines, views, etc. reflecting specific interests and ideologies (political, social, and so on)

public relations	the activities and techniques used by organizations and/or individuals to establish favourable attitudes and responses in their behalf on the part of the general public or of special groups
publicity	the craft of disseminating any information that concerns a person, group, event, or product through some form of public media
receiver	the one who decodes a message
redundancy	repetition of parts of a message built into codes for counteracting noise
referent	what is referred to by a sign (any object, being, idea, or event in the world)
referential	the communicative function by which a straightforward transmission is intended
representamen	Peirce's term for the physical part of a sign
representation	the process of giving a form to some referent with signs
rhetoric	the study of the techniques used in all kinds of discourses, from common conversation to poetry
sacred sign	a sign that is believed to be metaphysical (divine, religious, etc.) in origin
Scholasticism	the system of logic, philosophy, and theology of medieval university scholars, from the tenth to the fifteenth century, based upon Aristotelian logic
semantic differential	the technique used in semiotics for fleshing our connotations from a concept or representation
semantics	the study of meaning in language
semiology	Ferdinand de Saussure's term for the study of signs, now restricted, by and large, to the study of verbal signs
semiosis	the comprehension and production of signs
semiotics	the science or doctrine that studies signs and their uses in representation
sender	the transmitter of a message
sense ratio	the level at which one of the senses is activated during the encoding and decoding of forms

setting	the place and conditions where a narrative takes place
sign	something that stands for something (someone) else in some capacity
signal	any transmission, natural or mechanical
signification	the relation that holds between a sign and its referent
signification system	system of meanings evoked by something
signified	that part of a sign that is referred to (the referent); also called image, object, or concept
signifier	that part of a sign that does the referring/the physical part of a sign
signifying order	the interconnected system of signs, texts, codes, etc. that constitutes a culture
slogan	a catchword or phrase used to advertise a product
software	programs, routines, and symbolic languages that control the functioning of the hardware and direct its operation
source domain	the set of vehicles (concrete forms) that is used to deliver the meaning of an abstract concept
structure	any repeatable or predictable aspect of signs, codes, and texts
subtext	a concealed system of connotative meanings within a text
symbol	a sign that has an arbitrary (conventional) connection with a referent
symbolism	symbolic meaning in general
symptom	a bodily sign that stands for some ailment, physical condition, disease, etc.
synchronic	the study of signs as they are at a specific point in time (usually the present)
synecdoche	the signifying process by which a part stands for the whole
synesthesia	the evocation of one sense modality (e.g. vision) by means of some other (e.g. hearing); the juxtaposition of sense modalities (e.g. 'loud colours')
syntagm	the structural relation that combines signs in code-specific ways

syntagmatic	the structural relation by which signs are combined in code-dependent ways
syntext	term used in this book to refer to a text such as a newspaper that creates the illusion that there is connectivity among what would otherwise be perceived as fragmented random events
target domain	what a conceptual metaphor is about (the abstract concept that is metaphorized)
tautology	a statement that is a repetition of an idea in different words
technology	the system of objects made by humans
tenor	the subject of a metaphor
text	a complex sign put together in a specific way
textuality	the complex of meanings generated by texts
topic	the subject of a metaphor
trade advertising	advertising that is directed toward dealers and professionals through appropriate trade publications and media
transmission	the sending and reception of messages
trope	a figure of speech; figurative language generally
Turing machine	originally a sort of automatic typewriter that used symbols instead of letters; this 'universal machine' would be programmed to duplicate the function of any other machine
vehicle	the part of a metaphor that makes a concrete statement about the tenor
virtual reality (VR)	computer simulation of a real or imaginary system that enables a user to perform operations on the simulated system, which shows the effects in real time
World Wide Web	an information server on the Internet composed of interconnected sites and files, accessible with a browser program
writing	the process of representing speech with characters

Bibliography

The following bibliography includes both the works cited in the text and more generally the works that have constituted the bibliographical backbone to the exposition of the various topics treated in this book. It thus constitutes a source of reference and a general reading list.

Aaker, D.A. 1996. *Building strong brands*. New York: The Free Press.

Abercrombie, N. 1996. *Television and society*. Cambridge: Polity Press.

Abercrombie, N. and Longhurst, B. 1998. *Audiences*. London: Sage.

Ackerman, F. 1997. *The history of consumer society*. Washington, DC: Island Press.

Adatto, K. 1993. *Picture perfect: the art and artifice of public image making*. New York: Basic Books.

Albion, M. and Farris, P. 1981. *The advertising controversy*. Boston: Auburn House.

Alsted, C. and Larsen, H.H. 1991. Choosing complexity of signs in ads. *Marketing Signs* **10**, 1–14.

Anderson, M. 1984. *Madison Avenue in Asia: politics and transnational advertising*. Cranbury, NJ: Associated University Presses.

Anderson, W.T. 1992. *Reality isn't what it used to be*. San Francisco: HarperCollins.

Andren, G.L., Ericsson, L., Ohlsson, R. and Tännsjö, T. 1978. *Rhetoric and ideology in advertising*. Stockholm: AB Grafiska.

Argyle, M. 1988. *Bodily communication*. New York: Methuen.

Arnheim, R. 1969. *Visual thinking*. Berkeley: University of California Press.

Atwan, R. 1979. *Edsels, Luckies and Frigidaires: advertising the American way*. New York: Dell.

Avletta, K. 1991. *Three blind mice: how the TV networks lost their way*. New York: Random House.

Axtell, R.E. 1991. *Gestures*. New York: John Wiley.

Bachand, D. 1992. The art of (in) advertising: from poetry to prophecy. *Marketing Signs* **13**, 1–7.

Bal, M. 1985. *Narratology: introduction to the theory of the narrative*. Toronto: University of Toronto Press.

Baldwin, H. 1989. *How to create effective TV commercials*. Lincolnwood, Ill.: NTC Business Books.

Barker, C. 1999. *Television, globalization, and cultural identities*. Buckingham: Open University Press.

Barnouw, E. 1978. *The sponsor: notes on a modern potentate.* Oxford: Oxford University Press.

Barthel, D. 1988. *Putting on appearances: gender and advertising.* Philadelphia: Temple University Press.

Barthes, R. 1957. *Mythologies.* Paris: Seuil.

Barthes, R. 1967. *Système de la mode.* Paris: Seuil.

Barthes, R. 1968. *Elements of semiology.* London: Cape.

Barthes, R. 1970. *S/Z*, trans. by R. Miller. New York: Hill & Wang.

Barthes, R. 1977. *Image-music-text.* London: Fontana.

Baudrillard, J. 1973. *The implosion of meaning in the media.* New York: Semiotexte Press.

Baudrillard, J. 1978. *Toward a critique of the political economy of the sign.* St Louis: Telos Press.

Baudrillard, J. 1988. *The mirror of production.* St Louis: Telos Press.

Baudrillard, J. 1998. *The consumer society.* London: Sage Publications.

Bauman, Z. 1992. *Intimations of postmodernity.* London: Routledge.

Beasley, R., Danesi, M. and Perron, P. 2000. *Signs for sale: an outline of semiotic analysis for advertisers and marketers.* Ottawa: Legas Press.

Bell, S. 1990. Semiotics and advertising research: a case study. *Marketing Signs* 8, 1–6.

Berger, A.A. 1996. *Manufacturing desire: media, popular culture, and everyday life.* New Brunswick, NJ: Transaction Publishers.

Berger, A.A. 2000. *Ads, fads, and consumer culture: advertising's impact on American character and society.* Lanham: Rowman & Littlefield.

Berger, J. 1972. *Ways of seeing.* Harmondsworth: Penguin.

Berman, N. (ed.) 1998. *The mass media: opposing viewpoints.* San Diego: Greenhaven Press.

Bernardelli, A. (ed.) 1997. *The concept of intertextuality thirty years on: 1967–1997.* Special Issue of *Versus* **77/78.** Milano: Bompiani.

Bignell, J. 1997. *Media semiotics: an introduction.* Manchester: Manchester University Press.

Black, M. 1962. *Models and metaphors.* Ithaca: Cornell University Press.

Bolter, J.D. and Grusin, R. 1999. *Remediation: understanding new media.* Cambridge, Mass.: MIT Press.

Branston, G. and Stafford, R. 1999. *The media student's book.* London: Routledge.

Brierley, S. 1995. *The advertising handbook.* London: Routledge.

Briggs, A. and Cobley, P. (eds) 1998. *The media: an introduction.* Harlow: Longman.

Brown, R.W. 1986. *Social psychology.* New York: Free Press.

Bruce, V. and Young, A. 1998. *In the eye of the beholder: the science of face perception.* Oxford: Oxford University Press.

Bruner, J.S. 1986. *Actual minds, possible worlds.* Cambridge, Mass.: Harvard University Press.

Bühler, K. 1934. *Sprachtheorie: die Darstellungsfunktion der Sprache.* Jena: Fischer.

Burton, G. 2000. *Talking television: an introduction to the study of television.* London: Arnold.

Campbell, J. 1969. *Primitive mythology.* Harmondsworth: Penguin.

Cashmore, E. 1994. *And there was television*. London: Routledge.

Cassirer, E.A. 1944. *An essay on man*. New Haven: Yale University Press.

Cassirer, E.A. 1946. *Language and myth*. New York: Dover.

Cassirer, E.A. 1957. *The philosophy of symbolic forms*. New Haven: Yale University Press.

Cherry, C. 1966. *On human communication*. Cambridge, Mass.: MIT Press.

Cherwitz, R. and Hikins, J. 1986. *Communication and knowledge: an investigation in rhetorical epistemology*. Columbia: University of South Carolina Press.

Clarke, D.S. 1987. *Principles of semiotic*. London: Routledge and Kegan.

Classen, C. 1993. *Worlds of sense: exploring the senses in history and across cultures*. London: Routledge.

Classen, C., Howes, D. and Synnott, A. 1994. *Aroma: the cultural history of smell*. London: Routledge.

Cleveland, C.E. 1986. Semiotics: determining what the advertising message means to the audience. In J. Olson and K. Sentis (eds), *Advertising and consumer psychology*, Vol. 3. New York: Praeger, 227–41.

Cobley, P. (ed.) 1996. *The communication theory reader*. London: Routledge.

Cobley, P. 2000. *The American thriller*. London: Palgrave.

Cobley, P. (ed.) 2001. *The Routledge companion to semiotics and linguistics*. London: Routledge.

Colton, H. 1983. *The gift of touch*. New York: Putnam.

Connor, M.K. 1995. *Cool: understanding Black manhood in America*. New York: Crown.

Cooper, B.L. and Haney, W.S. 1995. *Rock music in American popular culture*. New York: Harrington Park Press.

Coupland, D. 1991. *Generation X*. New York: St Martin's.

Courtenoy, A.E. and Whipple, T.W. 1983. *Sex stereotyping in advertising*. Lexington, Mass.: Lexington Books.

Craik, J. 1993. *The face of fashion: cultural studies in fashion*. London: Routledge.

Craik, K. 1943. *The nature of explanation*. Cambridge: Cambridge University Press.

Crispin Miller, M. 1988. *Boxed in: the culture of TV*. Evanston: Northwestern University Press.

Croteau, D. and Hoynes, W. 1997. *Media/Society: industries, images, audiences*. Thousand Oaks: Pine Forge Press.

Crowley, D. and Heyer, P. (eds) 1999. *Communication in history, technology, culture, society*. New York: Longman.

Culler, J. 1983. *On deconstruction*. London: Routledge.

Czerniawski, R.D. and Maloney, M.W. 1999. *Creating brand loyalty*. New York: Amacom.

Dance, F. and Larson, C. 1976. *The functions of communication: a theoretical approach*. New York: Holt, Rinehart and Winston.

Danesi, M. 1994. *Cool: the signs and meanings of adolescence*. Toronto: University of Toronto Press.

Danesi, M. 1999. *Of cigarettes, high heels, and other interesting things: an introduction to semiotics*. New York: St Martin's.

Danesi, M. and Perron, P. 1999. *Analyzing cultures.* Bloomington: Indiana University Press.

Danna, S.R. 1992. *Advertising and popular culture: studies in variety and versatility.* Bowling Green, Ohio: Bowling Green State University Popular Press.

Darley, A. 2000. *Visual digital culture: surface play and spectacle in media genres.* London: Routledge.

Davis, F. 1992. *Fashion, culture, and identity.* Chicago: University of Chicago Press.

Davis, H. 1983. *Language, image, media.* Oxford: Blackwell.

Day, T. 2000. *A century of recorded music.* New Haven: Yale University Press.

Deely, J. 1990. *Basics of semiotics.* Bloomington: Indiana University Press.

Deely, J. 2001. *Four ages of understanding: the first postmodern survey of philosophy from ancient times to the turn of the twentieth century.* Toronto: University of Toronto Press.

Derrida, J. 1976. *Of grammatology,* trans. by G.C. Spivak. Baltimore: Johns Hopkins Press.

Dingena, M. 1994. *The creation of meaning in advertising interaction of figurative advertising and individual differences in processing styles.* Amsterdam: Thesis Publishers.

Dizard, W. 1997. *Old media, new media.* New York: Longman.

Docker, J. 1994. *Postmodernism and popular culture: a cultural history.* Cambridge: Cambridge University Press.

Douglas, S.J. 1994. *Where the girls are: growing up female with the mass media.* New York: Times.

Driver, J.C. and Foxall, G.R. 1984. *Advertising policy and practice.* New York: Holt, Rinehart and Winston.

Drummond, G. 1991. An irresistible force: semiotics in advertising practice. *Marketing Signs* 10, 1–7.

Dubois, P. 1988. *L'acte photographique.* Brussels: Labor.

Dutton, B. 1997. *The media.* Harlow: Longman.

Dyer, G. 1982. *Advertising as communication.* London: Routledge.

Eco, U. 1976. *A theory of semiotics.* Bloomington: Indiana University Press.

Eco, U. 1979. *The role of the reader: explorations in the semiotics of texts.* Bloomington: Indiana University Press.

Eco, U. 1984. *Semiotics and the philosophy of language.* Bloomington: Indiana University Press.

Eco, U. 1990. *The limits of interpretation.* Bloomington: Indiana University Press.

Elliot, B. 1962. *A history of English advertising.* London: Batsford.

Epstein, D. 1999. *Twentieth century pop culture.* New York: Quadrillion Publishing.

Epstein, J. 2000. *Book business: publishing past, present and future.* New York: Norton.

Erenberg, L.A. 1998. *Swingin' in the dream: big band jazz and the rebirth of American culture.* Chicago: University of Chicago Press.

Ewen, S. 1976. *Captains of consciousness.* New York: McGraw-Hill.

Ewen, S. 1988. *All consuming images.* New York: Basic Books.

Fiske, J. 1979. *Introduction to communication studies.* London: Methuen.

Fiske, J. 1987. *Television culture.* London: Methuen.

Fleming, D. 1996. *Powerplay: toys as popular culture.* Manchester: Manchester University Press.

Forceville, C. 1996. *Pictorial metaphor in advertising.* London: Routledge.

Forsdale, L. 1981. *Perspectives on communication.* Reading, Mass.: Addison-Wesley.

Foucault, M. 1972. *The archeology of knowledge,* trans. by A.M. Sheridan Smith. New York: Pantheon.

Foucault, M. 1976. *The history of sexuality.* London: Allen Lane.

Foules, J. 1996. *Advertising and popular culture.* Thousand Oaks: Sage.

Fowles, L. 1976. *Mass advertising as social forecast: a method for futures research.* Westport: Greenwood Press.

Fox, S. 1984. *The mirror makers.* New York: William Morrow.

Friedberg, A. 1993. *Window shopping: cinema and the postmodern.* Berkeley: University of California Press.

Frith, K.T. 1997. *Undressing the ad: reading culture in advertising.* New York: Peter Lang.

Frutiger, A. 1989. *Signs and symbols.* New York: Van Nostrand.

Frye, N. 1981. *The great code: the bible and literature.* Toronto: Academic Press.

Frye, N. 1990. *Words with power.* Harmondsworth: Penguin.

Gardner, H. 1985. *The mind's new science: a history of the cognitive revolution.* New York: Basic Books.

Gee, J.P. 1999. *An introduction to discourse analysis: theory and method.* London: Routledge.

Geiss, M.L. 1982. *The language of television advertising.* New York: Academic.

Genosko, G. 1999. *McLuhan and Baudrillard.* London: Routledge.

Gibbs, R.W. 1994. *The poetics of mind: figurative thought, language, and understanding.* Cambridge: Cambridge University Press.

Goatley, A. 1997. *The language of metaphors.* London: Routledge.

Goffman, E. 1959. *The presentation of self in everyday life.* New York: Anchor.

Goffman, E. 1979. *Gender advertisements.* New York: Harper & Row.

Goldman, R. 1994. *Reading ads socially.* London: Routledge.

Goldman, R. and Papson, R. 1996. *Sign wars: the cluttered landscape of advertising.* New York: Guilford.

Goodwin, A. 1992. *Dancing in the distraction factory: music television and popular culture.* Minneapolis: University of Minnesota Press.

Gordon, W.T. 1997. *Marshall McLuhan: escape into understanding: a biography.* New York: Basic.

Gottdiener, M. 1995. *Postmodern semiotics: material culture and the forms of postmodern life.* London: Blackwell.

Greimas, A.J. 1987. *On meaning: selected essays in semiotic theory,* trans. by P. Perron and F. Collins. Minneapolis: University of Minnesota Press.

Harris, A.C. 1995. Absolutely a semiome: visual and linguistic manipulation in print advertising. In C.W. Spinks and J. Deely (eds), *Semiotics 1994.* New York: Peter Lang, 360–9.

Harris, R. and Seldon, A. 1962. *Advertising and the public.* London: André Deutsch.

Hartley, J. 1992. *The politics of pictures: the creation of the public in the age of popular media*. London: Routledge.

Hausman, C.R. 1989. *Metaphor and art*. Cambridge: Cambridge University Press.

Hawkes, T. 1977. *Structuralism and semiotics*. Berkeley: University of California Press.

Hazen, D. and Winokur, J. (eds) 1997. *We the media: a citizen's guide to fighting for media democracy*. New York: The New Press.

Heighton, E. and Cunningham, D. 1976. *Advertising in the broadcast media*. Belmont: Wadsworth.

Herman, A. and Swiss, T. (eds) 2000. *The World Wide Web and contemporary cultural theory*. London: Routledge.

Hindley, D. and Hindley, G. 1972. *Advertising in Victorian England*. London: Wayland.

Hine, T. 1995. *The total package: the secret history and hidden meanings of boxes, bottles, cans, and other persuasive containers*. Boston: Little, Brown & Co.

Hjelmslev, L. 1963. *Prolegomena to a theory of language*. Madison: University of Wisconsin Press.

Hodge, R. and Kress, G. 1988. *Social semiotics*. Ithaca: Cornell University Press.

Holbrook, M.B. and Hirschman, E.C. 1993. *The semiotics of consumption: interpreting symbolic consumer behavior in popular culture and works of art*. Berlin: Mouton de Gruyter.

Holland, P. 2000. *The television handbook*. London: Routledge.

Horn, R.E. 1998. *Visual language: global communication for the 21st century*. Bainbridge Island: MacroVU.

Horrocks, C. 2000. *Marshall McLuhan and virtuality*. Duxford: Icon Books.

Howes, D. (ed.) 1991. *The varieties of sensory experience*. Toronto: University of Toronto Press.

Hudson, L. 1972. *The cult of the fact*. New York: Harper & Row.

Huizinga, J. 1924. *The waning of the medieval ages*. Garden City: Doubleday.

Ikuta, Y. 1988. *American romance: the world of advertising art*. Tokyo: Heibonsha.

Inglis, F. 1972. *The imagery of power: a critique of advertising*. London: Heinemann.

Irwin, W., Conard, M.T. and Skoble, A.J. 2001 (eds). *The Simpsons and philosophy*. Chicago: Open Court.

Jacobson, M.F. and Mazur, L.A. 1995. *Marketing madness*. Boulder: Westview.

Jager, E. 2000. Books, computers, and other metaphors of memory. *The Chronicle of Higher Education*, 22 September 2000, Section B, 14–15.

Jakobson, R. 1960. Linguistics and poetics. In T.A., Sebeok (ed.), *Style and language*. Cambridge, Mass.: MIT Press, 34–45.

Jakobson, R. 1985. *Selected writings VII*, Rudy, S. (ed.). Berlin: Mouton.

Jameson, F. 1991. *Postmodernism or the cultural logic of late capitalism*. Durham: Duke University Press.

Jawitz, W. 1996. *Understanding mass media*. Lincolnwood: National Textbook Company.

Jaworski, A. and Coupland, N. (eds) 2000. *The discourse reader*. London: Routledge.

Jean, G. 1966. *La poésie*. Paris: Seuil.

Jensen, K.B. 1995. *The social semiotics of mass communication.* London: Sage Publications.

Jhally, S. 1987. *The codes of advertising.* New York: St Martin's Press.

Johnson, M. 1987. *The body in the mind: the bodily basis of meaning, imagination and reason.* Chicago: University of Chicago Press.

Johnson-Laird, P.N. 1983. *Mental models.* Cambridge, Mass.: Harvard University Press.

Johnson-Laird, P.N. 1988. *The computer and the mind.* Cambridge: Harvard University Press.

Jones, J.P. (ed.) 1999. *How to use advertising to build strong brands.* London: Sage.

Judge, M.G. 2000. *If it ain't got that swing: the rebirth of grown-up culture.* New York: Spence.

Jung, C.G. 1956. *Analytical psychology.* New York: Meridian.

Jung, C.G. 1957. *The undiscovered self.* New York: Mentor.

Karmen, S. 1989. *Through the jungle: the art and business of making music for commercials.* New York: Billboard Books.

Kearney, R. 1991. *Poetics of imagining: from Husserl to Lyotard.* New York: HarperCollins.

Kellner, D. 1995. *Media culture.* London: Routledge.

Key, W.B. 1972. *Subliminal seduction.* New York: Signet.

Key, W.B. 1976. *Media sexploitation.* New York: Signet.

Key, W.B. 1980. *The clam-plate orgy.* New York: Signet.

Key, W.B. 1989. *The age of manipulation.* New York: Holt.

Kilbourne, J. 1999. *Can't buy my love: how advertising changes the way I feel.* New York: Simon & Schuster.

Kinzle, D. 1982. *Fashion and fetishism: a social history of the corset, tight-lacing and other forms of body-sculpture in the West.* Totowa: Rowman & Littlefield.

Klein, N. 2000. *No logo: taking aim at the brand bullies.* Toronto: Alfred A. Knopf.

Konner, M. 1991. Human nature and culture: biology and the residue of uniqueness. In J.J. Sheehan and M. Sosna (eds), *The Boundaries of Humanity.* Berkeley: University of California Press, 103–24.

Kubey, R. and Csikszentmihalyi, M. 1990. *Television and the quality of life.* Hillsdale, NJ: Lawrence Erlbaum Associates.

Kuhn, T.S. 1970. *The structure of scientific revolutions.* Chicago: University of Chicago Press.

Lakoff, G. 1987. *Women, fire and dangerous things: what categories reveal about the mind.* Chicago: University of Chicago Press.

Lakoff, G. and Johnson, L. 1980. *Metaphors we live by.* Chicago: Chicago University Press.

Lakoff, G. and Johnson, M. 1999. *Philosophy in flesh: the embodied mind and its challenge to Western thought.* New York: Basic.

Lakoff, G. and Turner, M. 1989. *More than cool reason: a field guide to poetic metaphor.* Chicago: University of Chicago Press.

Langacker, R.W. 1987. *Foundations of cognitive grammar.* Stanford: Stanford University Press.

Langacker, R.W. 1990. *Concept, image, and symbol: the cognitive basis of grammar.* Berlin: Mouton de Gruyter.

Langer, S. 1948. *Philosophy in a new key.* Cambridge: Harvard University Press.

Langer, S. 1957. *Problems of art.* New York: Scribner's.

Lasn, K. 2000. *Culture jam: the uncooling of America.* New York: Morrow.

Leach, E. 1976. *Culture and communication.* Cambridge: Cambridge University Press.

Lefebvre, H. 1968. *La vie quotidienne dans le monde moderne.* Paris: Gallimard.

Leiss, W., Kline, S., and Jhally, S. 1990. *Social communication in advertising,* 2nd edn. Toronto: Nelson.

Leitch, T.M. 1986. *What stories are: narrative theory and interpretation.* University Park: Pennsylvania State University Press.

Lévi-Strauss, C. 1958. *Structural anthropology.* New York: Basic Books.

Lévi-Strauss, C. 1962. *La pensée sauvage.* Paris: Plon.

Lévi-Strauss, C. 1962. *Le totémisme aujourd'hui.* Paris: Presses Universitaires de France.

Lévi-Strauss, C. 1964. *The raw and the cook(ed).* London: Cape.

Lévi-Strauss, C. 1978. *Myth and meaning: cracking the code of culture.* Toronto: University of Toronto Press.

Levin, S.R. 1988. *Metaphoric worlds.* New Haven: Yale University Press.

Leymore, V. 1975. *Hidden myth: structure and symbolism in advertising.* London: Heinemann.

Liebert, R.M. and Sprafkin, J.M. 1988. *The early window: effects of television on children and youth.* New York: Pergamon.

Liszka, J.J. 1989. *The semiotic study of myth: a critical study of the symbol.* Bloomington: Indiana University Press.

Locke, J. 1690 [1975]. *An essay concerning human understanding,* P.H. Nidditch (ed.). Oxford: Clarendon Press.

Logan, R.K. 1987. *The alphabet effect.* New York: St Martin's Press.

Lotman, Y. 1990. *The universe of the mind: a semiotic theory of culture.* Bloomington: Indiana University Press.

Luciano, L. 2000. *Looking good: male body image in modern America.* New York: Hill & Wang.

Lyotard, J.-F. 1984. *The postmodern condition: a report on knowledge.* Minneapolis: University of Minnesota Press.

MacCannell, D. and MacCannell, J.F. 1982. *The time of the sign: a semiotic interpretation of modern culture.* Bloomington: Indiana University Press.

Maetin, R. and Miller, T. (eds) 1999. *SportCult.* Minneapolis: University of Minnesota Press.

Marchand, P. 1989. *Marshall McLuhan: the medium and the messenger.* New York: Ticknor & Fields.

Marchand, R. 1985. *Advertising the American dream: making the way for modernity, 1920–1940.* Berkeley: University of California Press.

Markham, A. 1998. *Life online.* London: Altamira Press.

May, R. 1991. *The cry for myth.* New York: Norton.

McChesney, R.W. 1997. The media goes global. In D. Hazen and J. Winokur (eds), *We the media: a citizen's guide to fighting for media democracy*. New York: The New Press, pp. 12–13.

McChesney, R.W. 1999. *Rich media, poor democracy*. Chicago: University of Illinois Press.

McCracken, G. 1988. *Culture and consumption*. Bloomington: Indiana University Press.

McCracken, G. 1995. *Big hair: a journey into the transformation of self*. Toronto: Penguin.

McDannell, C. 1995. *Material christianity: religion and popular culture in America*. New Haven: Yale University Press.

McLuhan, M. 1951. *The mechanical bride: folklore of industrial man*. New York: Vanguard.

McLuhan, M. 1962. *The Gutenberg galaxy*. Toronto: University of Toronto Press.

McLuhan, M. 1964. *Understanding media*. London: Routledge & Kegan Paul.

McLuhan, M. and McLuhan, E. 1988. *Laws of media: the new science*. Toronto: University of Toronto Press.

McNair, B. 1999. *News and journalism in the UK*. London: Routledge.

McQueen, D. 1998. *Television: a media student's guide*. London: Arnold.

Merrell, F. 1997. *Peirce, signs, and meaning*. Toronto: University of Toronto Press.

Metz, C. 1974. *Film language: a semiotics of the cinema*. Chicago: University of Chicago Press.

Meyrowitz, J. 1985. *No sense of place: the impact of electronic media on social behavior*. New York: Oxford University Press.

Miller, M.C. 1988. *Boxed in: the culture of TV*. Evanston: Northwestern University Press.

Minsky, M. 1986. *Society of mind*. New York: Simon & Schuster.

Mirzoef, N. (ed.) 1998. *The visual culture reader*. London: Routledge.

Mittelart, A. 1991. *Advertising international*. London: Routledge.

Moog, C. 1990. *Are they selling her lips? Advertising and identity*. New York: Morrow.

Morris, C.W. 1938. *Foundations of the theory of signs*. Chicago: Chicago University Press.

Morris, C.W. 1946. *Signs, language and behavior*. Englewood Cliffs, NJ: Prentice-Hall.

Morse, M. 1998. *Virtualities: television, media art, and cyberculture*. Bloomington: Indiana University Press.

Myers, G. 1994. *Words in ads*. London: Arnold.

Nash, C. 1994. *Narrative in culture*. London: Routledge.

Newcomb, H. (ed.) 1996. *Encyclopedia of television*. Chicago: Fitzroy Dearborn.

Nochimson, M. 1992. *No end to her: soap opera and the female subject*. Berkeley: University of California Press.

Norris, C. 1991. *Deconstruction: theory and practice*. London: Routledge.

Nöth, W. 1990. *Handbook of semiotics*. Bloomington: Indiana University Press.

O'Barr, W.M. 1994. *Culture and the ad*. Boulder: Westview Press.

O'Sullivan, T., Dutton, B. and Rayner, P. 1998. *Studying the media*. London: Arnold.

O'Toole, M. 1994. *The language of displayed art*. London: Leicester University Press.

Ogden, C.K. and Richards, I.A. 1923. *The meaning of meaning*. London: Routledge & Kegan Paul.

Ortony, A. (ed.) 1979. *Metaphor and thought*. Cambridge: Cambridge University Press.

Osgood, C.E., Suci, G.J. and Tannenbaum, P.H. 1957. *The measurement of meaning*. Urbana: University of Illinois Press.

Packard, V. 1957. *The hidden persuaders*. New York: McKay.

Panati, C. 1984. *Browser's book of beginnings*. Boston: Houghton Mifflin.

Panati, C. 1996. *Sacred origins of profound things*. New York: Penguin.

Parmentier, R.J. 1994. *Signs in society: studies in semiotic anthropology*. Bloomington: Indiana University Press.

Peirce, C.S. 1931–58. *Collected papers of Charles Sanders Peirce*, Vols 1–8, C. Hartshorne and P. Weiss (eds). Cambridge, Mass.: Harvard University Press.

Peiss, K. 1998. *Hope in a jar: the making of America's beauty culture*. New York: Metropolitan Books.

Polanyi, L. 1989. *Telling the American story: a structural and cultural analysis of conversational storytelling*. Cambridge, Mass.: MIT Press.

Pollay, R.W. 1979. *Information sources in advertising history*. Westport: Greenwood.

Pollio, H., Barlow, J., Fine, H. and Pollio, M. 1977. *The poetics of growth: figurative language in psychology, psychotherapy, and education*. Hillsdale, NJ: Lawrence Erlbaum Associates.

Pope, D. 1983. *The making of modern advertising*. New York: Basic.

Popper, K. 1972. *Objective knowledge: an evolutionary approach*. Oxford: Clarendon.

Popper, K. and Eccles, J. 1977. *The self and the brain*. Berlin: Springer.

Posner, R., Robering, K. and Sebeok, T.A. 1997–98. *Semiotics: a handbook on the sign-theoretic foundations of nature and culture*, 2 volumes. Berlin: Walter de Gruyter.

Presbrey, F. 1968. *The history and development of advertising*. Westport: Greenwood.

Price, S. 1998. *Media studies*. Harlow: Longman.

Prince, G. 1982. *Narratology: the form and functioning of narrative*. Berlin: Mouton.

Propp, V.J. 1928. *Morphology of the folktale*. Austin: University of Texas Press.

Randazzo, S. 1995. *The myth makers*. Chicago: Probus.

Real, M. 1996. *Exploring media culture: a guide*. Thousands Oaks: Sage.

Reiss, A. and Trout, J. 1981. *Positioning: the battle for your mind*. New York: McGraw-Hill.

Reynolds, R. 1992. *Super heroes: a modern mythology*. Jackson: University of Mississippi Press.

Richards, B. 1994. *Disciplines of delight: the psychoanalysis of popular culture*. London: Free Association Books.

Richards, I.A. 1936. *The philosophy of rhetoric*. Oxford: Oxford University Press.

Ricouer, P. 1983. *Time and narrative*. Chicago: University of Chicago Press.

Ross, S.J. 1998. *Working-class Hollywood: silent film and the shaping of class in America*. Princeton: Princeton University Press.

Rossi, W. 1976. *The sex lives of the foot and shoe*. New York: Dutton.

Rotzoll, K., Haefner, J. and Sandage, C. 1976. *Advertising and society: perspectives towards understanding*. Columbus: Copywright Grid.

Rowe, D. 1995. *Popular cultures: rock music, sport and the politics of pleasure*. London: Sage.

Rowe, D. 1999. *Sport, culture and the media*. Buckingham: Open University Press.

Royce, A.P. 1977. *The anthropology of dance*. Bloomington: Indiana University Press.

Rubinstein, R.P. 1995. *Dress codes: meanings and messages in American culture*. Boulder: Westview.

Ruesch, J. 1972. *Semiotic approaches to human relations*. The Hague: Mouton.

Ryan, J. 1999. *Media and society*. Boston: Allyn and Bacon.

Saint-Martin, F. 1990. *Semiotics of visual language*. Bloomington: Indiana University Press.

Sapir, E. 1921. *Language*. New York: Harcourt Brace.

Sardar, Z. and Cubitt, S. (eds) 2000. *Aliens R Us: cinema, science fiction and the other*. London: Pluto Press.

Sassienie, P. 1994. *The comic book*. Toronto: Smithbooks.

Saussure, F. de. 1916. *Cours de linguistique générale*. Paris: Payot.

Schifrin, A. 2000. *The business of books*. New York: Verso.

Schiller, H. 1989. *The corporate takeover of public expression*. New York: Oxford University Press.

Schlosser, E. 2000. *Fast food nation*. Boston: Houghton Mifflin.

Schmandt-Besserat, D. 1978. The earliest precursor of writing. *Scientific American* **238**, 50–9.

Schmandt-Besserat, D. 1989. Two precursors of writing: plain and complex tokens. In W.M. Senner (ed.), *The Origins of Writing*. Lincoln: University of Nebraska Press, 27–40.

Schmandt-Besserat, D. 1992. *Before writing*, 2 vols. Austin: University of Texas Press.

Schogt, H. 1988. *Linguistics, literary analysis, and literary translation*. Toronto: University of Toronto Press.

Scholes, R. 1982. *Semiotics and interpretation*. New Haven: Yale University Press.

Schrag, R. 1990. *Taming the wild tube*. Chapel Hill: University of North Carolina Press.

Schramm, W. 1982. *Men, women, messages and media*. New York: Harper & Row.

Schudson, M. 1984. *Advertising: the uneasy persuasion*. New York: Basic.

Sculatti, G. 1982. *Cool: a hipster's directory*. London: Vermilion.

Seabrook, J. 2000. *Nobrow: the culture of marketing – the marketing of culture*. New York: Knopf.

Searle, J.R. 1969. *Speech acts: an essay in the philosophy of language*. Cambridge: Cambridge University Press.

Searle, J.R. 1984. *Minds, brain, and science*. Cambridge, Mass.: Harvard University Press.

Searle, J.R. 1992. *The rediscovery of the mind*. Cambridge, Mass.: MIT Press.

Sebeok, T.A. 1976. *Contributions to the doctrine of signs*. Lanham: University Press of America.

Sebeok, T.A. 1979. *The sign and its masters*. Austin: University of Texas Press.

Sebeok, T.A. 1986. *I think I am a verb: more contributions to the doctrine of signs*. New York: Plenum.

Sebeok, T.A. 1991. *A sign is just a sign.* Bloomington: Indiana University Press.

Sebeok, T.A. 1994. *Signs: an introduction to semiotics.* Toronto: University of Toronto Press.

Sebeok, T.A. and Danesi, M. 2000. *The forms of meaning: modeling systems theory and semiotics.* Berlin: Mouton de Gruyter.

Sebeok, T.A. and Umiker-Sebeok, J. (eds.) 1994. *Advances in visual semiotics.* Berlin: Mouton de Gruyter.

Seiter, E. 1987. Semiotics and Television. In Allen Robert Clyde (ed.), *Channels of discourse: television and contemporary criticism.* Chapel Hill: University of North Carolina Press, 17–41.

Seiter, E. 1995. *Sold separately: parents and children in consumer culture.* New Brunswick, NJ: Rutgers University Press.

Shaffer, P. 1973. *Equus.* London: Penguin.

Shaffer, P. 1993, orig. 1980. *Amadeus.* London: Penguin.

Shannon, C.E. 1948. A mathematical theory of communication. *Bell Systems Technical Journal* 27: 379–423.

Shuker, R. 1994. *Understanding popular culture.* London: Routledge.

Silverman, K. 1983. *The subject of semiotics.* Oxford: Oxford University Press.

Sinclair, J. 1987. *Images incorporated: advertising as industry and ideology.* Beckenham: Croom Helm.

Singer, B. 1986. *Advertising and society.* Toronto: Addison-Wesley.

Solomon, J. 1988. *The signs of our time.* Los Angeles: J. P. Tarcher.

Sontag, S. 1978. *Illness as metaphor.* New York: Farrar, Straus & Giroux.

Sontag, S. 1989. *AIDS and its metaphors.* New York: Farrar, Straus & Giroux.

Sorgem, Y.K. 1991. Ad games: postmodern conditions of advertising. *Marketing Signs* 11, 1–15.

Sparshott, F. 1995. *A measured pace: toward a philosophical understanding of the arts of dance.* Toronto: University of Toronto Press.

Spigel, L. and Mann, D. (eds) 1992. *Private screenings: television and the female consumer.* Minneapolis: University of Minnesota Press.

Spitzer, L. 1978. La publicité américaine comme art populaire. *Critique* 35, 152–71.

Stahl, S. 1989. *Literary folkloristics and the personal narrative.* Bloomington: Indiana University Press.

Stark, S. 1997. *Glued to the set.* New York: Free Press.

Steele, V. 1995. *Fetish: fashion, sex, and power.* Oxford: Oxford University Press.

Stern, J. and Stern, M. 1992. *Encyclopedia of pop culture.* New York: Harper.

Straubhaar, J. and Larose, R. 2000. *Media now: communications media in the information age.* Belmont: Wadsworth.

Strinati, D. 2000. *An introduction to studying popular culture.* London: Routledge.

Sutton-Smith, B. 1986. *Toys as culture.* New York: Gardner.

Swann, P. 2000. *TVdotCom: the future of interactive television.* New York: TV Books.

Synnott, A. 1993. *The body social: symbolism, self and society.* London: Routledge.

Tannen, D. 1994. *Gender and discourse.* Oxford: Oxford University Press.

Thomas, F. 1997. *The conquest of cool.* Chicago: University of Chicago Press.

Todenhagen, C. 1999. Advertising in word and image: textual style and semiotics of English language print advertising. *Zanglist Am* **47**, 169–70.

Todorov, T. 1977. *Theories of the symbol.* Ithaca: Cornell University Press.

Toolan, M.J. 1988. *Narrative: a critical linguistic introduction.* London: Routledge.

Tuckwell, K. 1995. *Advertising in action.* Englewood Cliffs: Prentice-Hall.

Tufte, E.R. 1997. *Visual explanations: images and quantities, evidence and narrative.* Cheshire: Graphics Press.

Twitchell, J.B. 2000. *Twenty ads that shook the world.* New York: Crown.

Uexküll, J. von 1909. *Umwelt und Innenwelt der Tierre.* Berlin: Springer.

Umiker-Sebeok, J. (ed.) 1987. *Marketing signs: new directions in the study of signs for sale.* Berlin: Mouton.

Umiker-Sebeok, J. 1997. The semiotic swarm of cyberspace: cybergluttony and Internet addiction in the Global Village. *Semiotica* **117**, 239–97.

Valentine, T., Brennen, T. and Brédart, S. 1996. *The cognitive psychology of proper names.* London: Routledge.

Vardar, N. 1992. *Global advertising: rhyme or reason?* London: Chapman.

Verene, D.P. 1981. *Vico's science of imagination.* Ithaca: Cornell University Press.

Vestergaard, T. and Schrøder, K. 1985. *The language of advertising.* London: Blackwell.

Vroon, P. and Amerongen, A. van 1996. *Smell: the secret seducer.* New York: Farrar, Straus and Giroux.

Warren, D. 1997. Advertising analysis: Cold War versus big thaw vodka advertising. In Irmengard Rauch and Gerald F. Carr (eds), *Semiotics around the world: synthesis in diversity.* Berlin: Mouton de Gruyter, 1251–4.

Watts, S. 1997. *The magic kingdom: Walt Disney and the American way of life.* Boston: Houghton Mifflin.

Wenner, L. (ed.) 1998. *MediaSport.* London: Routledge.

Wernick, A. 1991. *Promotional culture: advertising, ideology, and symbolic expression.* London: Sage.

White, R. 1988. *Advertising: what it is and how to do it.* London: McGraw-Hill.

Whorf, B.L. 1956. *Language, thought, and reality,* J.B. Carroll (ed.). Cambridge, Mass.: MIT Press.

Wiener, N. 1949. *Cybernetics, or control and communication in the animal and the machine.* Cambridge, Mass.: MIT Press.

Williamson, J. 1978/1985. *Decoding advertisements: ideology and meaning in advertising.* London: Marion Boyars.

Williamson, J. 1985. *Consuming passions.* London: Marion Boyars.

Williamson, J. 1996. But I know what I like: the function of art in advertising. In Paul Cobley (ed.), *The Communication Reader.* London: Routledge, 396–402.

Wilson, B. 1998. *Media technology and society: from telegraph to Internet.* London: Routledge.

Winner, E. 1982. *Invented worlds: the psychology of the arts.* Cambridge, Mass.: Harvard University Press.

Winner, E. 1988. *The point of words: children's understanding of metaphor and irony.* Cambridge, Mass.: Harvard University Press.

Wise, R. 2000. *Multimedia: a critical introduction.* London: Routledge.

Wolfe, O. 1989. Sociosemiology and cross-cultural branding strategies. *Marketing Signs* 3, 3–10.

Woodward, G.C. and Denton, R.E. 1988. *Persuasion and influence in American life.* Prospect Heights, Ill.: Waveland.

Wright, B.W. 2000. *Comic book nation.* Baltimore: Johns Hopkins.

Index